TEXT BOOK OF DRUG DELIVERY SYSTEM

[According to latest syllabus of M. Pharm (MPH102T) semester – 1 of Pharmacy Council of India]

Prof. (Dr.) Vijay Sharma

Professor & Head of Department

Department of Pharmaceutics,

SGT University,

Gurugram (Haryana)

Dr. Kamaldeep Singh

Associate Professor

Lala Lajpat Rai College of Pharmacy,

Moga (Punjab)

Notion Press

TEXT BOOK OF

DRUG DELIVERY SYSTEM

First Edition 2024

Published by:

NOTION PRESS

Publisher and distributor

Head office: Notion press Media Pvt. Ltd.

7, Red cross Road,

Egmore, Chennai,Tamil Nadu 60008

Website: www.notionpress.com

TEXT BOOK OF DRUG DELIVERY SYSTEM
NOTION PRESS
PREFACE

The authors feel great pleasure in presenting the first edition of the book **"Text Book of Drug Delivery System"** for graduate and post graduate students. The present book on **Text Book of Drug Delivery System** has been written according to the latest syllabus of M. Pharm (MPH102T) semester – 1 of Pharmacy Council of India and covers full course of the subject.

THE SALIENT FEATURES OF THE BOOK ARE: -

- *Easy to understand style of writing* which makes the book a self-study material.

- *Each new concept has been introduced through day-today problem of interest* to the students which makes the subject matter interesting.

- *The language of the book, on the whole, is lucid and easy to understand.*

- Wherever needed *neatly labeled figures have been drawn.*

The authors hope that the students, teachers and other readers will find the book interesting and to the point covering the course. We hope that the students will receive the book warmly.

I express a sincere thank you to the Management of Department of Pharmaceutics, SGT University and Lala Lajpat Rai College of Pharmacy for their support during the writing of this book.

Every effort is made to keep the book error free. The author will gratefully acknowledge the suggestions to improve the book to make it more useful.

Wishing our readers success in examination and life ahead. The authors feel that their efforts will be fully rewarded if the book serves the purpose for which it is written.

TEXT BOOK OF DRUG DELIVERY SYSTEM
CONTENTS

- Principles of Rate Controlled Drug Delivery Systems
- Fundamentals of Rate Controlled Drug Delivery Systems
- Types of Rate Controlled Drug Delivery Systems
- Activation of Rate Controlled Drug Delivery Systems
- Modulated Drug Delivery Systems
- Mechanically activated
- pH activated
- Enzyme activated,
- Osmotic activated Drug Delivery Systems Feedback
- Regulated Drug Delivery Systems; Principles & Fundamentals

- Principle of Gastro-Retentive Drug Delivery Systems
- concepts of Gastro-Retentive Drug Delivery Systems
- advantages of Gastro-Retentive Drug Delivery Systems
- Disadvantages of Gastro-Retentive Drug Delivery Systems
- Modulation of GI transit time approaches to extend GI transit.
- Buccal Drug Delivery Systems
  - Principle of muco adhesion
  - Advantages of Buccal Drug Delivery Systems
  - Disadvantages of Buccal Drug Delivery Systems
  - Mechanism of drug permeation
  - Methods of formulation of Buccal Drug Delivery Systems
  - Evaluations of Buccal Drug Delivery Systems

- Introduction of Ocular Drug Delivery Systems

CHAPTER – 1

SUSTAINED RELEASE (SR) AND CONTROLLED RELEASE (CR) FORMULATIONS

INTRODUCTION:

Sustained Release (SR) and Controlled Release (CR) formulations are advanced drug delivery systems designed to release medication at a predetermined rate, achieving a consistent and prolonged therapeutic effect. These formulations improve patient compliance, optimize drug efficacy, and reduce side effects compared to conventional immediate-release formulations.

Sustained Release (SR) Formulations

Definition: Sustained release formulations are designed to release a drug slowly over an extended period, maintaining a consistent drug concentration in the bloodstream.

Mechanism:

1. **Matrix Systems**: Drug is embedded in a matrix that dissolves or erodes over time, releasing the drug slowly.
2. **Reservoir Systems**: Drug is encapsulated within a rate-controlling membrane that regulates the drug release.

Advantages:

1. Reduces the frequency of dosing.
2. Maintains a more consistent blood concentration.
3. Minimizes peaks and troughs in drug levels, reducing side effects.

Examples:

1. Oral tablets with a polymer matrix.
2. Injectables with biodegradable polymers.
3. Transdermal patches with rate-controlling membranes.

Controlled Release (CR) Formulations

Definition: Controlled release formulations precisely control the rate and duration of drug release, maintaining optimal therapeutic levels over an extended period.

Mechanism:

1. **Polymer-based systems**: Use of polymers to control the diffusion of the drug.
2. **Osmotic pumps**: Utilize osmotic pressure to deliver the drug at a controlled rate.
3. **Ion exchange resins**: Drug is bound to a resin, releasing in response to ionic exchange in the gastrointestinal tract.

Advantages:

1. Offers precise control over drug release rates.
2. Can target drug release to specific sites within the body.
3. Improves therapeutic outcomes by maintaining drug levels within a narrow therapeutic window.

Examples:

1. Oral tablets with enteric coatings that dissolve at specific pH levels.
2. Implantable devices that release medication over months or years.
3. Nanoparticle systems designed to deliver drugs to specific cells or tissues.

Key Differences between SR and CR

1. **Release Pattern:**
   a. **SR**: Provides a gradual release of the drug over time.
   b. **CR:** Provides a precise and controlled release of the drug over time, often including mechanisms to start and stop release based on environmental triggers.
2. **Complexity:**
   a. **SR:** Generally simpler formulations, focusing on extending the release period.

b. **CR:** More complex systems, often incorporating advanced technologies for precise control.

3. **Applications:**

a. **SR**: Used for drugs requiring less frequent dosing and consistent blood levels.

b. **CR:** Used for drugs requiring precise dosing schedules and targeted delivery.

Technologies in SR and CR Formulations

1. **Microencapsulation:** Encapsulating drugs in micro-sized particles to control the release rate.

2. **Liposome**s: Spherical vesicles used to deliver drugs, with the release controlled by the lipid bilayer.

3. **Hydrogels**: Network of polymer chains that can hold water and release drugs in response to environmental conditions.

4. **Nanoparticles:** Extremely small particles designed for targeted drug delivery and controlled release.

5. **Biodegradable Polymers**: Polymers that degrade over time, providing a sustained release of the drug as they break down.

Benefits and Challenges

Benefits:

1. Enhanced patient adherence to medication regimens.

2. Improved therapeutic efficacy and safety.

3. Reduced dosing frequency, leading to better patient convenience.

Challenges:

1. Complex manufacturing processes.

2. Higher cost compared to conventional formulations.

3. Regulatory hurdles for approval due to the complexity of the systems.

BASIC CONCEPTS OF SUSTAINED RELEASE (SR) AND CONTROLLED RELEASE (CR) FORMULATIONS

Sustained Release (SR) and Controlled Release (CR) formulations are innovative drug delivery systems designed to improve the therapeutic effectiveness and patient compliance of medications. They achieve this by releasing the drug at a controlled and predictable rate, maintaining optimal drug levels in the bloodstream over extended periods. Below are the detailed basic concepts of both SR and CR formulations.

Sustained Release (SR) Formulations

Definition: Sustained Release (SR) formulations are designed to release a drug slowly and continuously over an extended period. The goal is to maintain a consistent therapeutic drug concentration in the blood, minimizing fluctuations and extending the duration of action.

Mechanisms of SR Formulations:

1. **Diffusion-Controlled Systems:**
   a. **Matrix Diffusion Systems**: The drug is dispersed within a polymer matrix, and as the matrix slowly dissolves or swells, the drug diffuses out at a controlled rate.
   b. **Reservoir Diffusion Systems**: The drug is enclosed in a core surrounded by a polymeric membrane. The drug diffuses through the membrane at a predictable rate.
2. **Dissolution-Controlled Systems:**
   a. **Matrix Dissolution Systems**: The drug is dispersed in a matrix that slowly dissolves in the gastrointestinal fluids, releasing the drug over time.
   b. **Encapsulated Dissolution Systems**: The drug is coated with a material that dissolves at a slower rate, controlling the release.
3. **Osmotic Systems:**

a. Utilize osmotic pressure to drive the release of the drug through a semi-permeable membrane.

4. Erosion-Controlled Systems:

a. The drug is embedded in a matrix that erodes over time, gradually releasing the drug.

Advantages of SR Formulations:

1. **Reduced dosing frequency**: Enhances patient compliance by decreasing the number of doses required.

2. **Stable drug levels**: Maintains a more consistent plasma concentration, avoiding peaks and troughs.

3. **Minimized side effects**: Reduces the likelihood of side effects associated with high drug concentrations.

Examples of SR Formulations:

1. **Oral SR tablets and capsules**: Containing polymers that control drug release.

2. **Injectable SR formulations**: Using biodegradable polymers for long-term release.

3. **Transdermal patches**: Providing continuous drug delivery through the skin.

Controlled Release (CR) Formulations

Definition: Controlled Release (CR) formulations are advanced drug delivery systems designed to deliver drugs at a predetermined, controlled rate and often at specific times or locations in the body. These formulations offer precise control over drug release kinetics.

Mechanisms of CR Formulations:

1. Polymer-Based Systems:

a. **Reservoir Systems**: The drug is encased in a polymer shell, with release controlled by the diffusion of the drug through the polymer.

b. **Matrix Systems**: The drug is uniformly dispersed in a polymer matrix, with release occurring as the polymer matrix swells or degrades.

2. **Osmotic Systems:**

   a. These systems use osmotic pressure to push the drug out of a small orifice at a controlled rate. The rate can be finely tuned based on the osmotic agent and membrane properties.

3. **Ion Exchange Resins:**

   a. Drugs are bound to resins and released in response to ionic changes in the gastrointestinal environment.

4. **Multi-Compartment Systems:**

   a. **Multiparticulate Systems**: Include pellets, beads, or microspheres that release the drug at different rates.

   b. **Pulsatile Release Systems**: Designed to release the drug in a pulsatile manner, mimicking the body's natural rhythms or targeting specific times.

Advantages of CR Formulations:

1. **Precise control**: Offers fine-tuned control over drug release profiles.

2. **Targeted delivery**: Can be designed to release drugs at specific sites within the body, enhancing efficacy and reducing side effects.

3. **Improved therapeutic outcomes**: Maintains drug levels within a narrow therapeutic window, optimizing treatment effectiveness.

Examples of CR Formulations:

1. **Oral CR tablets and capsules**: Designed with complex layers or coatings that control drug release.

2. **Implantable CR devices**: Such as implants that release drugs over several months or years.

3. **CR injectable formulations**: Using advanced polymer technologies for long-term drug release.

Key Differences between SR and CR Formulations

1. **Release Pattern:**

    a. **SR:** Gradual, extended release of the drug to maintain consistent levels.

    b. **CR:** Precisely controlled release, which can be constant, variable, or targeted to specific times or locations.

2. **Complexity:**

    a. **SR:** Generally simpler, focusing on extending the release period.

    b. **CR**: More complex, involving advanced technologies for precise and targeted control.

3. **Applications:**

    a. **SR:** Suitable for drugs requiring less frequent dosing and stable blood levels.

    b. **CR:** Ideal for drugs requiring precise dosing schedules, targeted delivery, or specific release profiles.

ADVANTAGES OF SUSTAINED RELEASE (SR) AND CONTROLLED RELEASE (CR) FORMULATIONS

Sustained Release (SR) and Controlled Release (CR) formulations offer numerous benefits over conventional immediate-release formulations. These advantages contribute to improved therapeutic outcomes, enhanced patient compliance, and overall better management of various medical conditions. Below are the detailed advantages of both SR and CR formulations.

Advantages of Sustained Release (SR) Formulations

1. **Reduced Dosing Frequency:**

    a. SR formulations release the drug slowly over an extended period, reducing the need for frequent dosing. This is particularly beneficial for medications that require multiple doses per day, making it easier for patients to adhere to their treatment regimen.

2. **Improved Patient Compliance:**

a. With fewer doses required, patients are more likely to stick to their prescribed medication schedule, reducing the risk of missed doses and improving overall treatment adherence.

3. **Stable Drug Levels:**

   a. SR formulations maintain a more consistent drug concentration in the bloodstream, avoiding the peaks and troughs associated with immediate-release formulations. This leads to better therapeutic control and more predictable pharmacological effects.

4. **Minimized Side Effects:**

   a. By avoiding high peaks in drug concentration, SR formulations can reduce the incidence and severity of side effects that may occur with higher doses. This can enhance the overall safety profile of the medication.

5. **Prolonged Therapeutic Effect:**

   a. The extended release of the drug ensures a longer duration of action, which can be particularly beneficial for managing chronic conditions that require stable medication levels over time.

6. **Enhanced Bioavailability:**

   a. Some SR formulations can improve the bioavailability of drugs that are otherwise rapidly metabolized or excreted, ensuring more of the drug reaches the systemic circulation and exerts its therapeutic effect.

Examples:

1. **Oral SR tablets and capsules**: Providing a steady release of medication for conditions like hypertension, diabetes, and chronic pain.

2. **Injectable SR formulations**: Offering long-term management options for conditions such as schizophrenia and hormone deficiencies.

3. **Transdermal patches**: Ensuring continuous drug delivery for medications like nicotine for smoking cessation or hormones for birth control.

Advantages of Controlled Release (CR) Formulations

1. **Precise Control Over Drug Release:**
   a. CR formulations allow for precise control over the rate and timing of drug release, enabling tailored dosing schedules that can optimize therapeutic outcomes.

2. **Targeted Delivery:**
   a. CR systems can be designed to release the drug at specific sites within the body, enhancing the efficacy of the medication and reducing systemic side effects. This is particularly useful for treatments targeting specific organs or tissues.

3. **Reduced Frequency of Administration:**
   a. Similar to SR formulations, CR formulations reduce the frequency of dosing, but with added precision in controlling when and how the drug is released. This is beneficial for medications requiring very specific timing to align with physiological processes or circadian rhythms.

4. **Maintenance of Therapeutic Levels:**
   a. CR formulations help maintain drug levels within a narrow therapeutic window, ensuring that the drug remains effective without reaching toxic concentrations. This can be crucial for medications with a small therapeutic index.

5. **Improved Patient Convenience:**
   a. The reduced need for frequent dosing and the potential for single-dose treatments (such as implants or long-acting injectables) significantly improve patient convenience and adherence to the prescribed treatment.

6. **Potential for Pulsatile Release:**

   a. Some CR systems are designed for pulsatile release, delivering the drug in bursts at specific times. This mimics the natural release patterns of certain hormones or targets the timing of symptom exacerbation in diseases like asthma or arthritis.

Examples:

1. **Oral CR tablets and capsules**: Designed with complex coatings or multi-layer structures to control the release rate of drugs for conditions like ADHD, cardiovascular diseases, and gastrointestinal disorders.

2. **Implantable CR devices**: Providing long-term drug release for conditions like chronic pain, cancer, and hormonal therapies.

3. **Injectable CR formulations**: Utilizing advanced polymer technologies to deliver medications over weeks or months for chronic conditions such as diabetes and schizophrenia.

DISADVANTAGES OF SUSTAINED RELEASE (SR) AND CONTROLLED RELEASE (CR) FORMULATIONS

While Sustained Release (SR) and Controlled Release (CR) formulations offer numerous advantages, they also present certain challenges and limitations. Understanding these disadvantages is crucial for optimizing drug delivery systems and ensuring appropriate therapeutic outcomes.

Disadvantages of Sustained Release (SR) Formulations

1. **Complex Manufacturing Processes:**

   a. SR formulations often require sophisticated manufacturing techniques and specialized equipment. This can increase production costs and complicate the manufacturing process, potentially leading to higher prices for consumers.

2. **Dose Dumping Risk:**

   a. If the controlled-release mechanism fails (e.g., due to damage to the formulation), there is a risk of dose dumping, where a large amount of the drug is released at once. This can lead to toxic levels of the drug in the bloodstream and cause adverse effects.

3. **Limited Flexibility in Dosage Adjustment:**

   a. SR formulations are designed to release a specific dose over a certain period. Adjusting the dosage or timing can be challenging, which may not be suitable for patients requiring frequent dose adjustments.

4. **Reduced Absorption in Certain Conditions:**

   a. Some SR formulations may not release the drug effectively in certain physiological conditions, such as altered gastrointestinal pH or motility. This can impact the drug's efficacy in patients with gastrointestinal disorders.

5. **Potential for Incomplete Drug Release:**

   a. In some cases, SR formulations may not release the entire dose of the drug, leading to reduced therapeutic efficacy. Factors such as incomplete matrix dissolution or inadequate erosion can contribute to this issue.

6. **Size and Swallowing Difficulties:**

   a. SR tablets or capsules are often larger than immediate-release forms, which can be problematic for patients with difficulty swallowing or for pediatric and geriatric populations.

Examples:

1. **Oral SR tablets**: Complex layering or matrix systems may be prone to dose dumping if the tablet is broken or chewed.

2. **Injectable SR formulations**: Biodegradable polymer systems may not fully degrade or release the drug uniformly.

Disadvantages of Controlled Release (CR) Formulations

1. **High Development and Production Costs:**

a. CR formulations involve advanced technologies and materials, making their development and production more expensive compared to conventional formulations. This can limit their availability and increase the cost for patients.

2. **Complex Regulatory Approval:**

   a. Due to their sophisticated nature, CR formulations often face stringent regulatory scrutiny. Obtaining approval can be time-consuming and expensive, delaying the availability of new CR medications.

3. **Risk of Over- or Under-Release:**

   a. If the controlled-release mechanism is not perfectly tuned, there is a risk of either too much or too little drug being released. This can lead to suboptimal therapeutic outcomes or increased risk of side effects.

4. **Limited Use for Drugs with Short Half-Lives:**

   a. Drugs with very short half-lives may not be suitable for CR formulations, as maintaining consistent blood levels over extended periods can be challenging.

5. **Patient Variability:**

   a. Individual differences in physiology, such as variations in gastrointestinal transit time or enzymatic activity, can affect the performance of CR formulations, leading to variable therapeutic outcomes among different patients.

6. **Potential for Incomplete Drug Release:**

   a. Similar to SR formulations, CR systems may not always release the entire dose of the drug, particularly in systems relying on complex mechanisms like osmosis or ion exchange.

Examples:

1. **Oral CR tablets and capsules**: May fail to release the drug uniformly if the gastrointestinal conditions are not ideal.

2. **Implantable CR devices**: Issues with biocompatibility or mechanical failure can lead to suboptimal drug release.

FACTORS INFLUENCING, OF SUSTAINED RELEASE (SR) AND CONTROLLED RELEASE (CR) FORMULATIONS

The performance and effectiveness of Sustained Release (SR) and Controlled Release (CR) formulations depend on a variety of factors. These factors can be broadly classified into drug-related factors, formulation-related factors, and physiological factors. Understanding these factors is crucial for designing effective SR and CR drug delivery systems.

Drug-Related Factors

1. **Solubility:**
   a. Drugs with poor solubility may require special techniques, such as the use of solubilizing agents or altering the drug's crystalline form, to ensure consistent release over time.

2. **Stability:**
   a. The chemical stability of the drug must be maintained throughout the release period. Drugs prone to degradation may require protective coatings or encapsulation within stable matrices.

3. **Partition Coefficient:**
   a. The drug's lipophilicity or hydrophilicity influences its ability to diffuse through polymer matrices or membranes, affecting the release rate.

4. **Molecular Weight:**
   a. Higher molecular weight drugs typically have slower diffusion rates, which can be advantageous for sustained or controlled release.

5. **Dose:**

a. The drug dose plays a critical role in the design of SR and CR formulations. High doses may require larger dosage forms or multiple units to achieve the desired release profile.

Formulation-Related Factors

1. **Polymer Type:**

   a. The choice of polymer (e.g., hydrophilic, hydrophobic, biodegradable) affects the release mechanism and rate. Hydrophilic polymers swell in contact with body fluids, controlling release by diffusion and erosion, while hydrophobic polymers provide a barrier to drug release.

2. **Matrix Systems:**

   a. In matrix systems, the drug is dispersed within a polymer matrix. The matrix composition, porosity, and degradation rate influence drug release.

3. **Coating Materials:**

   a. Coatings control the release rate by acting as a barrier. The thickness, composition, and permeability of the coating material are critical factors.

4. **Particle Size:**

   a. Smaller particle sizes increase the surface area, enhancing the dissolution rate. For SR and CR formulations, controlling particle size is important to achieve the desired release profile.

5. **Release Mechanism:**

   a. The release mechanism (e.g., diffusion, erosion, osmosis) must be carefully selected based on the drug's properties and the therapeutic goal.

6. **Manufacturing Process:**

    a. The method of manufacturing (e.g., granulation, extrusion, coating) impacts the consistency and reliability of the release profile. Precise control over the process is essential for reproducibility.

Physiological Factors

1. **Gastrointestinal Transit Time:**

   a. The time a dosage form spends in the gastrointestinal (GI) tract affects drug release. Variations in transit time can lead to variability in drug absorption and therapeutic effect.

2. **pH Variations:**

   a. The pH of different segments of the GI tract influences the solubility and stability of the drug. Enteric coatings or pH-sensitive polymers can be used to target specific release sites.

3. **Enzymatic Activity:**

   a. Enzymatic degradation in the GI tract can impact drug release. Protecting the drug from enzymatic activity through encapsulation or coating can improve stability and release control.

4. **Food Effects:**

   a. Food intake can alter GI pH, transit time, and enzyme activity, influencing drug release and absorption. Formulations must be designed to minimize food-related variability.

5. **Patient-Specific Factors:**

   a. Individual variations such as age, gender, disease state, and genetic factors can affect drug metabolism and GI physiology, leading to differences in drug release and absorption.

Specific Factors for SR and CR Formulations

Specific Factors for SR Formulations

1. **Polymer Degradation Rate:**

a. The rate at which the polymer matrix degrades affects the release rate. Biodegradable polymers must be selected to match the desired release duration.

2. **Diffusion Pathway:**

   a. The length and tortuosity of the diffusion pathway within the matrix or coating material influence the release kinetics. Optimizing the diffusion pathway is crucial for consistent drug release.

3. **Swelling Behavior:**

   a. Hydrophilic polymers that swell upon contact with bodily fluids can control drug release through a combination of swelling and diffusion. The extent and rate of swelling must be controlled.

Specific Factors for CR Formulations

1. **Osmotic Pressure:**

   a. In osmotic systems, the osmotic pressure gradient drives drug release. The formulation must ensure a consistent osmotic gradient throughout the release period.

2. **Membrane Permeability:**

   a. The permeability of the rate-controlling membrane in reservoir systems is critical. It must allow a consistent rate of drug diffusion while protecting the drug from degradation.

3. **Trigger Mechanisms:**

   a. CR formulations designed for triggered release (e.g., pH-sensitive, enzyme-sensitive) must ensure the trigger mechanism functions reliably in the intended physiological environment.

PHYSICOCHEMICAL & BIOLOGICAL APPROACHES FOR SR/CR FORMULATION

Developing effective Sustained Release (SR) and Controlled Release (CR) formulations involves both physicochemical and biological strategies.

These approaches are tailored to optimize drug release rates, enhance bioavailability, and improve therapeutic outcomes. Below are the detailed approaches used in SR and CR formulations.

Physicochemical Approaches

1. **Matrix Systems:**
   a. **Diffusion Matrix**: The drug is uniformly dispersed in a polymer matrix. Release occurs as the drug diffuses through the matrix material. Common polymers include hydroxypropyl methylcellulose (HPMC), ethyl cellulose, and carbopol.
   b. **Erosion Matrix**: The drug is embedded in a matrix that gradually erodes in bodily fluids, releasing the drug over time. Polymers like polylactic acid (PLA) and polyglycolic acid (PGA) are often used.

2. **Reservoir Systems:**
   a. **Coated Reservoir**: The drug core is surrounded by a rate-controlling membrane that regulates drug diffusion. Materials like ethyl cellulose or polyvinyl acetate are used for the coating.
   b. **Osmotic Pumps**: Utilize osmotic pressure to drive the drug through a semi-permeable membrane at a controlled rate. Components typically include an osmotic agent and a semi-permeable membrane made of cellulose acetate.

3. **Microencapsulation:**
   a. The drug is encapsulated in a micro-sized polymer shell, allowing for controlled release. Techniques include spray drying, coacervation, and solvent evaporation. Common encapsulating materials are gelatin, poly(lactic-co-glycolic acid) (PLGA), and alginate.

4. **Ion Exchange Resins:**

a. Drugs are bound to ion exchange resins and released in response to changes in ionic concentration in the gastrointestinal tract. This approach is useful for drugs with narrow absorption windows.

5. **Hydrogels:**
   a. Hydrogels are polymeric networks that swell in the presence of water, controlling drug release through diffusion and erosion. They are made from polymers like polyvinyl alcohol (PVA), polyethylene glycol (PEG), and polyacrylic acid (PAA).

6. **Liposomes and Nanospheres:**
   a. Liposomes are spherical vesicles with a lipid bilayer, while nanospheres are solid, spherical particles. Both can encapsulate drugs, providing controlled release through diffusion and degradation. Materials include phospholipids for liposomes and PLGA for nanospheres.

7. **Biodegradable Polymers:**
   a. Biodegradable polymers, such as PLA, PGA, and their copolymers, are used to fabricate drug delivery systems that degrade in the body, releasing the drug over time.

Biological Approaches

1. **Enzyme-Triggered Release:**
   a. Formulations designed to release the drug in response to specific enzymes present in the target tissue or organ. For example, protease-sensitive hydrogels can release drugs in response to protease activity in tumors.

2. **pH-Sensitive Systems:**
   a. Utilize polymers that swell or degrade at specific pH levels, targeting drug release to particular regions of the gastrointestinal tract (e.g., stomach vs. intestines). Polymers like Eudragit are commonly used.

3. **Targeted Delivery Systems:**
   a. Employ ligands such as antibodies, peptides, or aptamers attached to drug carriers (e.g., liposomes, nanoparticles) to target specific cell receptors. This ensures the drug is delivered precisely to the diseased tissue, reducing systemic side effects.

4. **Bioadhesive Systems:**
   a. Utilize bioadhesive polymers to adhere to mucosal tissues, prolonging the residence time of the drug at the absorption site. Polymers like chitosan and carbopol are used to enhance mucoadhesion.

5. **Gene Therapy Vectors:**
   a. Viral or non-viral vectors are used to deliver therapeutic genes that can regulate drug release in response to specific cellular signals. This approach is still largely experimental but holds potential for highly targeted and controlled drug release.

6. **Stimuli-Responsive Systems:**
   a. Formulations that respond to external stimuli such as temperature, magnetic fields, or light to control drug release. For example, thermosensitive hydrogels release drugs when they reach a certain temperature.

Integrating Physicochemical and Biological Approaches

To achieve optimal SR and CR formulations, it is often beneficial to integrate physicochemical and biological strategies. This integration can enhance the precision, efficacy, and safety of the drug delivery system.

Examples:

1. **Combination of pH-Sensitive Polymers and Enzyme-Triggered Systems:**
   a. A drug could be encapsulated in a pH-sensitive polymer that dissolves in the intestines, releasing an enzyme-sensitive

microcapsule that further controls the release rate based on enzyme activity.

2. **Targeted Nanoparticles with Controlled Release Coatings:**
   a. Nanoparticles can be designed to target specific cells and be coated with a polymer that provides controlled release, ensuring the drug is released at the desired site and rate.

3. **Bioadhesive Matrix Systems:**
   a. Incorporating bioadhesive polymers in matrix systems can prolong the residence time at the absorption site, providing sustained release in targeted regions like the buccal cavity or gastrointestinal tract.

MECHANISM OF DRUG DELIVERY FROM SR/CR FORMULATION

The mechanism of drug delivery from Sustained Release (SR) and Controlled Release (CR) formulations is designed to control the rate and duration of drug release to achieve a therapeutic effect. The primary goal is to maintain drug concentrations within the therapeutic window for an extended period while minimizing side effects. Below are the detailed mechanisms involved in SR and CR formulations:

1. Diffusion-Controlled Systems

Matrix Diffusion Systems:
   a. **Description**: The drug is dispersed within a polymer matrix. The release occurs as the drug diffuses through the pores or the polymer network of the matrix.
   b. **Mechanism**: The drug molecules migrate from the regions of higher concentration within the matrix to the outer surface, where they are released into the surrounding medium.
   c. **Examples**: Hydrophilic matrices (e.g., hydroxypropyl methylcellulose) and hydrophobic matrices (e.g., ethyl cellulose).

Reservoir Diffusion Systems:

a. **Description**: The drug core is enclosed by a rate-controlling polymer membrane.

b. **Mechanism:** The drug diffuses through the polymer membrane at a controlled rate. The thickness and permeability of the membrane are critical in determining the release rate.

c. **Examples:** Transdermal patches, coated tablets.

2. Dissolution-Controlled Systems

Matrix Dissolution Systems:

a. **Description:** The drug is uniformly distributed in a matrix made of a dissolvable polymer.

b. **Mechanism**: As the polymer matrix dissolves in the bodily fluids, the drug is gradually released. The rate of dissolution of the polymer controls the release rate of the drug.

c. **Examples:** Formulations using polymers like polyvinyl alcohol (PVA).

Reservoir Dissolution Systems:

a. **Description**: The drug is contained within a dissolvable coating or capsule.

b. **Mechanism:** The release rate is controlled by the dissolution of the outer coating, which governs the exposure of the drug to the dissolution medium.

c. **Examples**: Enteric-coated tablets that dissolve in the intestines.

3. Osmotic Pressure-Activated Systems

Osmotic Pumps:

a. **Description**: These systems contain a core with the drug and an osmotic agent, enclosed in a semi-permeable membrane with a laser-drilled orifice.

b. **Mechanism**: Water enters the core through the semi-permeable membrane, creating osmotic pressure that pushes the drug solution out through the orifice at a controlled rate.

c. **Examples**: Osmotic-controlled release oral delivery systems (OROS).

4. Erosion-Controlled Systems

Bulk Erosion:

a. **Description**: The drug is embedded in a biodegradable polymer matrix.

b. **Mechanism**: The entire matrix undergoes degradation, leading to the release of the drug. The degradation rate of the polymer determines the drug release rate.

c. **Examples**: Polylactic acid (PLA) and polyglycolic acid (PGA) systems.

Surface Erosion:

a. **Description**: The drug is contained within a polymer matrix that erodes layer by layer.

b. **Mechanism:** The outer layers of the polymer matrix erode over time, gradually releasing the drug. This type of erosion is more predictable and can provide a constant release rate.

c. **Examples**: Polyanhydrides and polyorthoesters.

5. Ion Exchange Systems

Ion Exchange Resins:

a. **Description**: Drugs are bound to ion exchange resins.

b. **Mechanism:** The drug is released in exchange for ions (e.g., Na+, K+) in the gastrointestinal fluids. The rate of ion exchange controls the release rate of the drug.

c. **Examples**: Chlorpheniramine and phenylephrine ion exchange formulations.

6. Swelling-Controlled Systems

Hydrogels:

a. **Description:** These are polymeric systems that swell upon contact with water.

b. **Mechanism:** The swelling of the polymer network allows the drug to diffuse out. The rate and extent of swelling control the drug release.

c. **Examples:** Hydrogels made from polyvinyl alcohol (PVA) or polyethylene glycol (PEG).

7. Stimuli-Responsive Systems

pH-Sensitive Systems:

a. **Description**: These systems are designed to release the drug in response to changes in pH.

b. **Mechanism**: The polymer swells, dissolves, or undergoes a structural change in response to the pH of the surrounding medium, controlling the release of the drug.

c. **Examples**: Enteric-coated tablets that release the drug in the more basic environment of the intestines.

Enzyme-Sensitive Systems:

a. **Description**: These systems release the drug in response to specific enzymatic activity.

b. **Mechanism**: The presence of specific enzymes in the target site triggers the degradation of the polymer, releasing the drug.

c. **Examples**: Protease-sensitive hydrogels for cancer therapy.

Temperature-Sensitive Systems:

a. **Description**: These systems respond to changes in temperature.

b. **Mechanism:** The polymer undergoes a phase transition at a specific temperature, controlling the release of the drug.

c. **Examples**: Thermosensitive hydrogels that release drugs at body temperature.

POLYMERS

Polymers play a crucial role in the design and functionality of Sustained Release (SR) and Controlled Release (CR) formulations. They are used to control the release rate of the drug, protect the drug from degradation, and target the delivery to specific sites in the body. Below is a detailed discussion of the types of polymers used in SR and CR formulations, their properties, and their applications.

Types of Polymers in SR and CR Formulations

1. Hydrophilic Polymers

Characteristics:

a. Hydrophilic polymers swell in the presence of water, forming a gel-like structure that controls the release of the drug through diffusion and erosion.

Common Hydrophilic Polymers:

a. **Hydroxypropyl Methylcellulose (HPMC):** Used in matrix tablets to control the release rate by swelling and forming a gel barrier.

b. **Polyethylene Glycol (PEG):** Acts as a plasticizer and can be used to modify the release characteristics of other polymers.

c. **Polyvinyl Alcohol (PVA):** Forms hydrogels that control drug release through swelling and erosion.

d. **Carbopol:** Used in gel formulations and as a matrix former for controlled release tablets.

Applications:

a. Oral sustained release tablets

b. Hydrogels for topical applications

c. Injectable controlled release systems

2. Hydrophobic Polymers

Characteristics:

Hydrophobic polymers do not swell significantly in water and control drug release by forming a barrier that the drug must diffuse through.

Common Hydrophobic Polymers:

a. **Ethyl Cellulose:** Used as a coating material for controlled release tablets and pellets.

b. **Polymethacrylates (Eudragit):** A range of polymers with different properties used for enteric coatings and controlled release matrices.

c. **Polyvinyl Acetate (PVA):** Forms non-soluble matrices that control the release rate by diffusion.

d. **Polydimethylsiloxane (Silicone**): Used in implants and transdermal patches for controlled release.

Applications:

a. Coated tablets and pellets

b. Transdermal patches

c. Implants

3. Biodegradable Polymers

Characteristics:

a. Biodegradable polymers degrade into non-toxic by-products that are absorbed or excreted by the body, making them ideal for long-term drug delivery systems.

Common Biodegradable Polymers:

a. **Polylactic Acid (PLA):** Used in microspheres and implants for sustained release.

b. **Polyglycolic Acid (PGA):** Often combined with PLA to form PLGA, which has adjustable degradation rates.

c. **Poly(lactic-co-glycolic acid) (PLGA):** Used in injectable microspheres and implants for controlled release.

d. **Polycaprolactone (PCL):** Degrades slowly, making it suitable for long-term drug delivery systems.

Applications:

a. Injectable microspheres

b. Implantable devices

c. Biodegradable stents

4. Natural Polymers

Characteristics:

Natural polymers are biocompatible and often biodegradable, making them suitable for various drug delivery applications.

Common Natural Polymers:

a. **Chitosan:** Derived from chitin, used in matrix tablets, and films for controlled release.

b. **Alginate:** Extracted from seaweed, used in gel formulations and beads for controlled release.

c. **Gelatin**: Used in microencapsulation and as a matrix for controlled release.

d. **Starch:** Used as a binder and disintegrant in tablets, and can be modified for controlled release applications.

Applications:

a. Matrix tablets

b. Microencapsulation

c. Injectable gels

5. Smart Polymers

Characteristics:

Smart polymers respond to external stimuli such as pH, temperature, and enzymes, enabling targeted and controlled drug release.

Common Smart Polymers:

a. **pH-sensitive Polymers**: Such as Eudragit L and S, which dissolve at specific pH values for targeted release in the gastrointestinal tract.

b. **Temperature-sensitive Polymers**: Such as poly(N-isopropylacrylamide) (PNIPAAm), which undergo phase transitions at certain temperatures.

c. **Enzyme-sensitive Polymers**: Designed to degrade in the presence of specific enzymes, enabling targeted release in diseased tissues.

Applications:

a. Targeted drug delivery

b. Injectable responsive gels

c. Oral formulations with site-specific release

Functions and Applications of Polymers in SR and CR Formulations

Matrix Systems

Hydrophilic Matrix Systems:

a. Drugs are dispersed within a hydrophilic polymer matrix. Upon contact with bodily fluids, the polymer swells, and the drug is released through the swollen matrix.

b. Examples: HPMC-based tablets for oral sustained release.

Hydrophobic Matrix Systems:

a. Drugs are embedded in a hydrophobic polymer matrix. The release occurs primarily through diffusion.

b. **Example**s: Ethyl cellulose matrix tablets for controlled release.

Reservoir Systems

Polymer Coated Systems:

a. The drug core is surrounded by a polymer coating that controls the release rate by diffusion through the coating.

b. **Examples**: Enteric-coated tablets using Eudragit for delayed release in the intestines.

Osmotic Systems:

a. Utilize osmotic pressure to drive the drug out through a semi-permeable membrane at a controlled rate.

b. **Examples:** Osmotic-controlled release oral delivery systems (OROS) using cellulose acetate membranes.

Bioadhesive Systems

Mucoadhesive Polymers:

a. Polymers that adhere to mucosal surfaces, prolonging the residence time and enhancing drug absorption.

b. **Examples**: Chitosan-based buccal tablets.

Injectable and Implantable Systems

Biodegradable Polymers:

a. Polymers that degrade in the body, providing controlled release of the drug over time.

b. **Examples:** PLGA microspheres for injectable sustained release.

Smart Drug Delivery Systems

pH-Sensitive Systems:

a. Polymers that dissolve or swell in response to pH changes, enabling targeted drug release.

b. **Example**s: Eudragit-coated tablets for colonic delivery.

Temperature-Sensitive Systems:

a. Polymers that undergo a phase change at specific temperatures, controlling drug release.

b. **Examples**: Thermosensitive hydrogels for injectable drug delivery.

Definition of polymers:

Polymers are large molecules composed of repeating structural units (monomers) bonded together through covalent chemical bonds. In the context of pharmaceutical formulations, polymers are used to control the release rate of drugs, protect active ingredients, and target drug delivery to specific sites within the body.

In Sustained Release (SR) and Controlled Release (CR) formulations, polymers serve as the matrix or barrier through which the drug is released. These polymers can be either natural or synthetic and are chosen based on their physical and chemical properties, which influence the drug release mechanism.

Types of Polymers Used in SR and CR Formulations

1. Hydrophilic Polymers

Hydrophilic polymers are water-attracting and swell upon contact with bodily fluids. This swelling forms a gel-like structure that controls the drug release through diffusion and erosion.

Common Hydrophilic Polymers:

a. **Hydroxypropyl Methylcellulose (HPMC):** A semi-synthetic, hydrophilic polymer widely used in oral sustained release tablets.

b. **Polyethylene Glycol (PEG):** Used to modify the release characteristics and act as a plasticizer.

c. **Polyvinyl Alcohol (PVA):** Forms hydrogels that control drug release through swelling and erosion.

d. **Carbopol:** Used in gel formulations and as a matrix former for controlled release tablets.

Applications:

a. Oral sustained release tablets

b. Hydrogels for topical applications

c. Injectable controlled release systems

2. Hydrophobic Polymers

Hydrophobic polymers do not swell significantly in water and control drug release by forming a barrier through which the drug must diffuse.

Common Hydrophobic Polymers:

a. **Ethyl Cellulose**: Used as a coating material for controlled release tablets and pellets.

b. **Polymethacrylates (Eudragit)**: A range of polymers with different properties used for enteric coatings and controlled release matrices.

c. **Polyvinyl Acetate (PVA):** Forms non-soluble matrices that control the release rate by diffusion.

d. **Polydimethylsiloxane (Silicone):** Used in implants and transdermal patches for controlled release.

Applications:

a. Coated tablets and pellets

b. Transdermal patches

c. Implants

3. Biodegradable Polymers

Biodegradable polymers degrade into non-toxic by-products that are absorbed or excreted by the body, making them ideal for long-term drug delivery systems.

Common Biodegradable Polymers:

a. **Polylactic Acid (PLA):** Used in microspheres and implants for sustained release.

b. **Polyglycolic Acid (PGA):** Often combined with PLA to form PLGA, which has adjustable degradation rates.

c. **Poly(lactic-co-glycolic acid) (PLGA):** Used in injectable microspheres and implants for controlled release.

d. **Polycaprolactone (PCL):** Degrades slowly, making it suitable for long-term drug delivery systems.

Applications:

a. Injectable microspheres

b. Implantable devices

c. Biodegradable stents

4. Natural Polymers

Natural polymers are biocompatible and often biodegradable, making them suitable for various drug delivery applications.

Common Natural Polymers:

a. **Chitosan:** Derived from chitin, used in matrix tablets, and films for controlled release.

b. **Alginate**: Extracted from seaweed, used in gel formulations and beads for controlled release.

c. **Gelatin:** Used in microencapsulation and as a matrix for controlled release.

d. **Starch: Used** as a binder and disintegrant in tablets, and can be modified for controlled release applications.

Applications:

a. Matrix tablets

b. Microencapsulation

c. Injectable gels

5. Smart Polymers

Smart polymers respond to external stimuli such as pH, temperature, and enzymes, enabling targeted and controlled drug release.

Common Smart Polymers:

a. **pH-sensitive Polymers**: Such as Eudragit L and S, which dissolve at specific pH values for targeted release in the gastrointestinal tract.

b. **Temperature-sensitive Polymers**: Such as poly(N-isopropylacrylamide) (PNIPAAm), which undergo phase transitions at certain temperatures.

c. **Enzyme-sensitive Polymers**: Designed to degrade in the presence of specific enzymes, enabling targeted release in diseased tissues.

Applications:

a. Targeted drug delivery

b. Injectable responsive gels

c. Oral formulations with site-specific release

Role of Polymers in SR and CR Formulations

1. Matrix Systems

Hydrophilic Matrix Systems:

a. Drugs are dispersed within a hydrophilic polymer matrix. Upon contact with bodily fluids, the polymer swells, and the drug is released through the swollen matrix.

b. Examples: HPMC-based tablets for oral sustained release.

Hydrophobic Matrix Systems:

a. Drugs are embedded in a hydrophobic polymer matrix. The release occurs primarily through diffusion.

b. **Examples:** Ethyl cellulose matrix tablets for controlled release.

2. Reservoir Systems

Polymer Coated Systems:

 a. The drug core is surrounded by a polymer coating that controls the release rate by diffusion through the coating.

 b. **Examples:** Enteric-coated tablets using Eudragit for delayed release in the intestines.

Osmotic Systems:

 a. Utilize osmotic pressure to drive the drug out through a semi-permeable membrane at a controlled rate.

 b. **Examples:** Osmotic-controlled release oral delivery systems (OROS) using cellulose acetate membranes.

3. Bioadhesive Systems

Mucoadhesive Polymers:

 a. Polymers that adhere to mucosal surfaces, prolonging the residence time and enhancing drug absorption.

 b. **Example**s: Chitosan-based buccal tablets.

4. Injectable and Implantable Systems

Biodegradable Polymers:

 a. Polymers that degrade in the body, providing controlled release of the drug over time.

 b. Examples: PLGA microspheres for injectable sustained release.

5. Smart Drug Delivery Systems

pH-Sensitive Systems:

 a. Polymers that dissolve or swell in response to pH changes, enabling targeted drug release.

 b. **Examples:** Eudragit-coated tablets for colonic delivery.

Temperature-Sensitive Systems:

 a. Polymers that undergo a phase change at specific temperatures, controlling drug release.

b. **Examples:** Thermosensitive hydrogels for injectable drug delivery.

Classification of polymers:

The classification of polymers in Sustained Release (SR) and Controlled Release (CR) formulations is based on various factors such as their chemical composition, physical properties, biodegradability, and responsiveness to environmental stimuli. These polymers are classified into different categories, each with its distinct characteristics and applications in drug delivery systems. Below is a detailed classification of polymers used in SR and CR formulations:

1. Based on Chemical Composition

a. Synthetic Polymers:

    1. Hydrophilic Polymers:

        i. **Examples**: Hydroxypropyl Methylcellulose (HPMC), Polyethylene Glycol (PEG), Polyvinyl Alcohol (PVA), Carbopol.

        ii. **Characteristics**: These polymers swell in water and form gel-like structures, controlling drug release through diffusion and erosion.

        iii. **Applications:** Oral sustained release tablets, topical gels, injectable controlled release systems.

    2. Hydrophobic Polymers:

        i. **Examples:** Ethyl Cellulose, Polymethacrylates (Eudragit), Polyvinyl Acetate (PVA), Polydimethylsiloxane (Silicone).

        ii. **Characteristics**: These polymers do not swell significantly in water and control drug release by forming diffusion barriers.

        iii. **Applications**: Coated tablets, transdermal patches, implants.

    3. Biodegradable Polymers:

        i. **Examples:** Polylactic Acid (PLA), Polyglycolic Acid (PGA), Poly(lactic-co-glycolic acid) (PLGA), Polycaprolactone (PCL).

        ii. **Characteristics**: These polymers degrade into non-toxic by-products, making them suitable for long-term drug delivery.

iii. **Application**s: Injectable microspheres, implantable devices, biodegradable stents.

b. Natural Polymers:

1. Polysaccharides:

i. **Examples**: Chitosan, Alginate, Starch.

ii. **Characteristic**s: Biocompatible and often biodegradable, these polymers are derived from natural sources.

iii. **Application**s: Matrix tablets, microencapsulation, injectable gels.

2. Proteins:

i. **Examples:** Gelatin, Albumin, Collagen.

ii. **Characteristic**s: These polymers offer excellent biocompatibility and can be modified for controlled release applications.

iii. **Applications:** Microencapsulation, sustained release formulations.

2. Based on Release Mechanism

a. Diffusion-Controlled Polymers:

1. Matrix Systems:

i. Polymers form a matrix in which drug molecules are dispersed. Drug release occurs through diffusion.

ii. **Examples:** HPMC, Ethyl Cellulose.

2. Reservoir Systems:

i. Drug is contained within a core surrounded by a polymer coating that controls release through diffusion.

ii. **Example**s: Eudragit-coated tablets, OROS systems.

b. Erosion-Controlled Polymers:

1. Bulk Erosion Systems:

i. The entire polymer matrix degrades, releasing the drug.

ii. **Examples**: PLA, PGA, PLGA.

2. Surface Erosion Systems:

i. Outer layers of the polymer erode gradually, controlling drug release.

ii. **Examples:** Polyanhydrides, Polyorthoesters.

c. Osmosis-Controlled Polymers:

1. Osmotic Pumps:

i. Utilize osmotic pressure to drive drug release through a semi-permeable membrane.

ii. **Examples**: Osmotic-controlled release oral delivery systems (OROS).

3. Based on Responsiveness to Environmental Stimuli

a. pH-Sensitive Polymers:

1. pH-Responsive Systems:

i. Polymers dissolve or swell in response to pH changes, enabling targeted drug release.

ii. **Examples:** Eudragit, Pectin.

b. Temperature-Sensitive Polymers:

1. Thermoresponsive Systems:

i. Polymers undergo phase transitions at specific temperatures, controlling drug release.

ii. **Examples**: Poly(N-isopropylacrylamide) (PNIPAAm).

c. Enzyme-Sensitive Polymers:

1. Enzyme-Responsive Systems:

i. Polymers degrade in the presence of specific enzymes, enabling targeted release in diseased tissues.

ii. **Examples**: Protease-sensitive hydrogels.

Properties of polymers:

The properties of polymers used in Sustained Release (SR) and Controlled Release (CR) formulations play a crucial role in determining the efficacy, safety, and performance of the drug delivery system. These properties influence factors such as drug release kinetics, stability, biocompatibility, and manufacturability. Below are the detailed properties of polymers relevant to SR and CR formulations:

1. Biocompatibility:

Polymers used in SR and CR formulations must be biocompatible to ensure they do not cause adverse reactions or tissue damage when administered to patients. Biocompatibility refers to the ability of the polymer to interact safely with biological systems without eliciting toxic or immunogenic responses.

2. Degradation Rate:

For biodegradable polymers, the degradation rate is a critical property. It determines the duration of drug release and the eventual breakdown of the polymer into biocompatible by-products. The degradation rate can be tailored based on the chemical structure of the polymer, allowing for controlled release over specific time periods.

3. Mechanical Strength:

Polymers should possess adequate mechanical strength to withstand processing techniques such as compression (for tablet formation), injection molding (for implants), or coating (for modified-release formulations). Mechanical strength ensures the integrity of the drug delivery system during manufacturing, storage, and administration.

4. Solubility:

The solubility of polymers affects their dissolution behavior, which, in turn, influences drug release kinetics. Hydrophilic polymers swell upon contact with water, forming a gel-like matrix that controls drug diffusion. Hydrophobic polymers, on the other hand, do not readily dissolve in water and control drug release through diffusion or erosion mechanisms.

5. Swelling Capacity:

Hydrophilic polymers exhibit swelling behavior when exposed to aqueous environments. The swelling capacity of a polymer determines its ability to absorb water and form a gel matrix, which affects drug diffusion and release kinetics. Polymers with higher swelling capacities typically result in more sustained drug release profiles.

6. Adhesion:

In mucoadhesive formulations or transdermal patches, polymers should have sufficient adhesive properties to adhere to mucosal surfaces or skin. Adhesive polymers prolong the residence time of the drug delivery system at the application site, enhancing drug absorption and bioavailability.

7. Thermal Stability:

Polymers used in SR and CR formulations should be thermally stable to withstand processing temperatures during manufacturing and storage conditions. Thermal stability ensures that the polymer maintains its physical and chemical integrity, preventing degradation or alteration of drug release properties.

8. pH Sensitivity:

pH-sensitive polymers respond to changes in pH, enabling targeted drug delivery to specific regions of the gastrointestinal tract. These polymers dissolve, swell, or undergo conformational changes in response to pH variations, controlling drug release in acidic or alkaline environments.

9. Compatibility with Active Ingredients:

Polymers should be compatible with the active pharmaceutical ingredients (APIs) to ensure stability and efficacy. Compatibility studies assess the interactions between polymers and APIs, including chemical reactivity, physical compatibility, and preservation of drug potency.

10. Processability:

Polymers should be easily processable into various dosage forms such as tablets, capsules, microspheres, or implants. Processability encompasses factors such as melt viscosity, powder flowability, compressibility, and ease of formulation.

Application of polymers:

Polymers play a significant role in the development of Sustained Release (SR) and Controlled Release (CR) formulations, offering precise control over drug release kinetics, enhancing therapeutic efficacy, and improving patient compliance. Their diverse properties and functionalities make them versatile materials for various drug delivery applications. Below are detailed applications of polymers in SR and CR formulations:

1. Matrix Systems:

a. Hydrophilic Matrix Systems:

i. **Application**: Hydrophilic polymers like Hydroxypropyl Methylcellulose (HPMC) are widely used to form matrix tablets for sustained drug release.

ii. **Mechanism:** The drug is dispersed uniformly within the polymer matrix, and upon contact with bodily fluids, the polymer swells, forming a gel-like structure that controls drug release through diffusion.

iii. **Benefits:** Provides prolonged drug release, maintains drug concentration within the therapeutic range, and improves patient compliance due to reduced dosing frequency.

b. Hydrophobic Matrix Systems:

i. **Application**: Hydrophobic polymers like Ethyl Cellulose are used as matrix formers in controlled release tablets.

ii. **Mechanism**: The drug is embedded in a hydrophobic polymer matrix, and drug release occurs primarily through diffusion.

iii. **Benefits:** Offers sustained drug release, protects the drug from environmental factors, and provides flexibility in modifying release kinetics by altering polymer characteristics.

2. Reservoir Systems:

a. Polymer-Coated Systems:

i. **Application**: Polymers like Eudragit are used as coating materials for tablets and pellets in delayed or extended-release formulations.

ii. **Mechanism:** The drug core is surrounded by a polymer coating that controls drug release by diffusion through the coating.

iii. **Benefit**s: Enables targeted release, protects the drug from degradation, and allows for the modulation of release rates by adjusting coating thickness or composition.

b. Osmotic Systems:

i. **Application**: Osmotic-controlled release oral delivery systems (OROS) utilize semi-permeable membranes made of polymers such as cellulose acetate for controlled drug release.

ii. **Mechanism:** Osmotic pressure drives the drug out through a laser-drilled orifice in the membrane, providing controlled release over an extended period.

iii. **Benefits:** Offers precise control over drug release kinetics, minimizes dose dumping, and enhances therapeutic efficacy.

3. Injectable and Implantable Systems:

a. Biodegradable Polymers:

i. **Application**: Biodegradable polymers such as Poly(lactic-co-glycolic acid) (PLGA) are used to formulate injectable microspheres and implants for sustained drug release.

ii. **Mechanism:** The polymer degrades over time, releasing the encapsulated drug in a controlled manner.

iii. **Benefits:** Provides long-lasting drug delivery, eliminates the need for frequent dosing, and allows for localized drug delivery to specific tissues or organs.

4. Targeted Drug Delivery Systems:

a. pH-Sensitive Polymers:

i. **Application**: Polymers like Eudragit are used to formulate pH-sensitive coatings for tablets, enabling targeted drug release in specific regions of the gastrointestinal tract.

ii. **Mechanism**: The polymer coating dissolves or swells in response to changes in pH, releasing the drug at the desired site.

iii. **Benefits:** Enables site-specific drug delivery, improves drug bioavailability, and reduces systemic side effects.

b. Mucoadhesive Polymers:

i. **Application**: Mucoadhesive polymers such as Chitosan are used in buccal tablets or nasal sprays for sustained drug release.

ii. **Mechanis**m: The polymer adheres to mucosal surfaces, prolonging drug residence time and enhancing drug absorption.

iii. **Benefits**: Provides localized drug delivery, improves drug bioavailability, and enhances patient comfort and compliance.

5. Transdermal Drug Delivery Systems:

a. Polymer-Based Patches:

i. **Application**: Polymers like Polyvinyl Alcohol (PVA) are used to formulate transdermal patches for controlled drug release.

ii. **Mechanism:** The drug is incorporated into a polymer matrix, which controls drug diffusion through the skin over time.

iii. **Benefits**: Offers sustained drug release, avoids first-pass metabolism, and provides convenient and non-invasive drug administration.

Multiple Choice Questions (MCQs) from the Chapter

1. What is the primary goal of Sustained Release (SR) formulations?

    A) To reduce the therapeutic effect

    B) To maintain a consistent drug concentration over time

    C) To increase the frequency of dosing

D) None of the above

2. Which system is used in SR formulations where the drug is embedded in a matrix?

   A) Diffusion-Controlled Systems

   B) Dissolution-Controlled Systems

   C) Osmotic Systems

   D) Erosion-Controlled Systems

3. What is the mechanism of drug release in a reservoir diffusion system?

   A) The drug diffuses through a membrane at a controlled rate

   B) The drug is released at random intervals

   C) The drug is released by a mechanical pump

   D) None of the above

4. What advantage does Controlled Release (CR) formulations offer over SR formulations?

   A) Faster drug release

   B) Reduced control over drug release

   C) Precise control over drug release rates

   D) Higher peaks in drug levels

5. Which type of system utilizes osmotic pressure to deliver drugs in CR formulations?

   A) Matrix systems

   B) Reservoir systems

   C) Osmotic systems

   D) Microencapsulation systems

6. What is a common use of ion exchange resins in drug formulations?

   A) To decrease the drug's solubility

   B) To release drugs in response to ionic changes

   C) To block the drug's action

   D) To color the drug tablets

7. Which of the following is NOT an advantage of SR formulations?

A) Reduced dosing frequency

B) Stable drug levels

C) Increased side effects

D) Minimized side effects

8. Controlled Release (CR) formulations are particularly useful for drugs that require:

A) Frequent dosing schedules

B) Immediate release

C) Less precise dosing

D) Targeted delivery

9. Which polymer is commonly used for making hydrogel drug delivery systems?

A) Polyvinyl Alcohol (PVA)

B) Polylactic Acid (PLA)

C) Polyethylene Glycol (PEG)

D) Polydimethylsiloxane (Silicone)

10. What is the function of biodegradable polymers in drug delivery systems?

A) To provide immediate drug release

B) To enhance the flavor of the drug

C) To degrade over time, releasing the drug gradually

D) To make the drug waterproof

11. What is a potential disadvantage of using SR formulations?

A) Increased patient compliance

B) Complex manufacturing processes

C) Faster drug release

D) Lower production costs

12. Which approach is NOT used to enhance the control of drug release in SR/CR formulations?

A) Enzyme-triggered release

B) pH-sensitive systems

C) Temperature-insensitive systems

D) Bioadhesive systems

13. Microencapsulation in drug formulations is primarily used for:

A) Coloring the drugs

B) Enhancing the smell of drugs

C) Controlling the release of drugs

D) Increasing the weight of the tablet

14. The use of liposomes in drug delivery systems is primarily to:

A) Decrease the effectiveness of the drug

B) Control the release of the drug through the lipid bilayer

C) Prevent the drug from reaching the target site

D) Increase the cost of drug production

15. Hydrophilic polymers are used in drug formulations because they:

A) Do not swell in water

B) Reduce the drug's effectiveness

C) Swell in water, forming a gel-like structure that controls drug release

D) Break down immediately upon contact with water

16. Which is a characteristic of hydrophobic polymers in drug formulations?

A) They swell extensively in water

B) They control drug release by forming a diffusion barrier

C) They are primarily used to decrease drug stability

D) They are less effective than hydrophilic polymers

17. A major challenge in the development of CR formulations is:

A) Decreased regulatory scrutiny

B) High development and production costs

C) Simplified manufacturing processes

D) Reduced need for precision in drug release

18. Pulsatile release systems are designed to:

    A) Release drugs at a constant rate

    B) Mimic the body's natural rhythms

    C) Release drugs only in response to a mechanical trigger

    D) Provide immediate drug release

19. Which type of polymer is typically used for enteric coatings in drug tablets?

    A) Enzyme-sensitive polymers

    B) Temperature-sensitive polymers

    C) pH-sensitive polymers

    D) Light-sensitive polymers

20. The primary function of mucoadhesive polymers in drug formulations is to:

    A) Decrease the drug's absorption

    B) Prolong the residence time of the drug at the absorption site

    C) Immediately dissolve the drug

    D) Act as a flavoring agent

Short Answer Type Questions (Subjective)

1. Explain how sustained release (SR) formulations enhance patient compliance.

2. Describe the mechanism of matrix diffusion systems in SR formulations.

3. What are the advantages of using reservoir systems in drug formulations?

4. How do controlled release (CR) formulations maintain therapeutic drug levels?

5. List some examples of drugs that are suitable for controlled release formulations.

6. What role do polymers play in the design of SR and CR formulations?

7. Discuss the benefits of microencapsulation in drug delivery.

8. How do hydrogels contribute to drug release in SR formulations?

9. Explain the concept of targeted drug delivery in CR formulations.

10. What are the challenges faced in the manufacturing of SR and CR formulations?

11. How do osmotic systems control drug release in CR formulations?

12. What is dose dumping and what risks does it pose in SR formulations?

13. Discuss the impact of physiological factors on the effectiveness of SR and CR formulations.

14. How does the gastrointestinal transit time affect drug release and absorption?

15. Explain the use of biodegradable polymers in drug delivery systems.

16. What are the main differences between hydrophilic and hydrophobic polymers used in drug formulations?

17. Describe how pH-sensitive polymers are used in targeted drug delivery.

18. What are the advantages of using mucoadhesive polymers in drug formulations?

19. How can enzyme-sensitive systems be used for targeted drug release?

20. Explain the role of temperature-sensitive polymers in controlled drug delivery.

Long Answer Type Questions (Subjective)

1. Describe the principles and mechanisms involved in the formulation of sustained release (SR) drug delivery systems and how they differ from traditional drug delivery methods.

2. Discuss the advantages and disadvantages of using controlled release (CR) formulations for chronic disease management.

3. Explain the role of ion exchange resins in CR formulations and their impact on drug release kinetics.

4. Provide a detailed analysis of how osmotic pressure is utilized in CR systems to control the rate of drug delivery.

5. Discuss the importance of polymer selection in the design of SR and CR formulations, focusing on the impact of polymer properties on drug release profiles.

6. Explain how nanoparticle systems are used in CR formulations to target drug delivery to specific cells or tissues.

7. Provide an in-depth discussion of the regulatory challenges faced by SR and CR formulations and strategies to overcome these hurdles.

8. Describe the integration of physicochemical and biological approaches in the development of SR/CR formulations and how they contribute to enhanced drug delivery.

9. Discuss the impact of patient-specific factors on the performance of SR and CR drug delivery systems and strategies to personalize drug delivery.

10. Explain the development and application of stimuli-responsive systems in drug delivery, focusing on how they respond to changes in the external environment to control drug release.

Answer Key

1. (B) To maintain a consistent drug concentration over time
2. (A) Diffusion-Controlled Systems
3. (A) The drug diffuses through a membrane at a controlled rate
4. (C) Precise control over drug release rates
5. (C) Osmotic systems
6. (B) To release drugs in response to ionic changes
7. (C) Increased side effects
8. (D) Targeted delivery
9. (A) Polyvinyl Alcohol (PVA)
10. (C) To degrade over time, releasing the drug gradually
11. (B) Complex manufacturing processes
12. (C) Temperature-insensitive systems

13.(C) Controlling the release of drugs

14.(B) Control the release of the drug through the lipid bilayer

15.(C) Swell in water, forming a gel-like structure that controls drug release

16.(B) They control drug release by forming a diffusion barrier

17.(B) High development and production costs

18.(B) Mimic the body's natural rhythms

19.(C) pH-sensitive polymers

20.(B) Prolong the residence time of the drug at the absorption site

CHAPTER – 2

DOSAGE FORMS FOR PERSONALIZED MEDICINE

INTRODUCTION:

Personalized medicine, also known as precision medicine, tailors medical treatment to the individual characteristics of each patient. The approach considers factors like genetics, environment, and lifestyle. A crucial aspect of personalized medicine is the customization of dosage forms to achieve the optimal therapeutic outcome for individual patients. This introduction will cover the concept, significance, types, technologies, and challenges of personalized dosage forms in medicine.

Concept and Significance

Personalized Dosage Forms: These are specifically designed pharmaceutical forms that consider the unique needs of individual patients. The goal is to enhance efficacy, reduce side effects, and improve patient compliance by adjusting the dosage, release rate, and formulation of medications.

Significance:

1. **Enhanced Efficacy**: Tailoring the dosage to an individual's genetic profile or specific condition can significantly improve the effectiveness of the treatment.

2. **Reduced Side Effects**: Personalized doses can minimize adverse reactions by avoiding underdosing or overdosing.

3. **Improved Compliance**: Customizing the form, such as making it easier to swallow or altering the flavor, can increase patient adherence to the medication regimen.

Types of Personalized Dosage Forms

1. **Oral Dosage Forms:**

a. **Tablets and Capsules**: Customized in terms of dosage strength, shape, and release profiles (immediate-release, sustained-release, etc.).

b. **Liquids:** Adjusted concentrations to match individual dosage requirements, often used for pediatric or geriatric patients.

2. **Injectable Dosage Forms:**

   a. **Prefilled Syringes**: Personalized dosages based on patient-specific needs.

   b. **Implant**s: Long-acting implants that release medication over an extended period tailored to the patient's condition.

3. **Topical Dosage Forms:**

   a. **Creams, Gels, and Patches**: Custom formulations based on the specific skin condition and absorption characteristics of the patient.

4. **Inhalation Dosage Forms:**

   a. **Nebulizers and Inhalers**: Custom formulations and dosages for respiratory conditions.

5. **Transdermal Patches:**

   a. Customizable in terms of drug load and release characteristics to suit individual therapeutic needs.

Technologies for Personalized Dosage Forms

1. **3D Printing:**

   a. Allows for the creation of complex and precise dosage forms with customized shapes, sizes, and release profiles.

   b. **Example:** 3D printed tablets can be designed to release drugs at specific rates tailored to the patient's metabolism.

2. **Microfabrication:**

   a. Techniques such as micro-needles or micro-chips for controlled drug delivery.

b. **Example:** Micro-needles for painless transdermal delivery of vaccines or drugs.

3. **Nanotechnology:**

   a. Nanoparticles can be designed for targeted drug delivery, ensuring the drug reaches the specific site of action.

   b. **Example:** Liposomes or polymeric nanoparticles loaded with drugs for targeted cancer therapy.

4. **Pharmacogenomics:**

   a. Using genetic information to determine the most effective drug and dose for a patient.

   b. **Example**: Testing for specific genetic markers to guide the choice and dosage of drugs in cancer therapy.

5. **Wearable Devices:**

   a. Devices that monitor physiological parameters and adjust drug delivery in real-time.

   b. **Example**: Insulin pumps that adjust insulin delivery based on continuous glucose monitoring.

Challenges in Personalized Dosage Forms

1. **Regulatory Hurdles:**

   a. Personalized dosage forms often face complex regulatory pathways to ensure safety and efficacy.

   b. **Example**: Each customized product may require extensive clinical testing.

2. **Cost and Accessibility:**

   a. Developing and manufacturing personalized dosage forms can be expensive, impacting accessibility for patients.

   b. **Example**: High costs associated with genetic testing and specialized manufacturing equipment.

3. **Complex Manufacturing:**

a. The need for advanced technologies and precise control in manufacturing processes.

b. **Example:** 3D printing requires specialized equipment and expertise.

4. **Data Management:**

a. Handling and interpreting large volumes of patient-specific data to tailor treatments.

b. **Example**: Integrating genetic data, lifestyle information, and environmental factors.

5. **Ethical and Privacy Issues:**

a. Concerns related to the collection and use of personal health information.

b. **Example**: Ensuring patient consent and data security.

DEFINITION OF DOSAGE FORMS FOR PERSONALIZED MEDICINE

Dosage Forms for Personalized Medicine refer to the customized pharmaceutical preparations designed to deliver the appropriate dose of medication tailored to an individual's specific characteristics, such as their genetic makeup, lifestyle, medical history, and other personal health factors. The primary goal is to optimize therapeutic outcomes, minimize adverse effects, and improve patient compliance by personalizing the medication form and dosage.

Key Components of Dosage Forms for Personalized Medicine

1. **Customization:**

a. Dosage forms are specifically tailored to match the unique physiological and genetic profiles of individual patients. This customization can involve adjusting the dosage strength, form, and release mechanism of the medication.

2. **Precision:**

a. The precise calibration of medication dosage to match an individual's metabolic rate, enzyme activity, and disease state. This ensures the most effective therapeutic concentration of the drug is achieved and maintained in the patient's system.

3. Formulation Variability:

a. Utilizing different forms of drug delivery (e.g., tablets, capsules, injections, topical applications) that are best suited to the patient's needs and preferences. Each form can be engineered to optimize absorption, distribution, metabolism, and excretion.

4. Technology Integration:

a. Employing advanced technologies such as 3D printing, nanotechnology, and pharmacogenomics to create and deliver these personalized dosage forms. These technologies enable precise manufacturing and customization at the molecular level.

5. Patient-Centric Approach:

a. Focusing on the patient's overall experience with the medication, including factors like ease of administration, dosing schedule, and sensory preferences (e.g., taste, texture).

Detailed Aspects of Personalized Dosage Forms

1. Oral Dosage Forms:

a. **Tablets and Capsules**: Designed with varying release profiles such as immediate-release, delayed-release, or sustained-release to match the patient's metabolic needs. Dosages can be precisely controlled to avoid under or over-medication.

b. Liquid Forms: Concentrations can be adjusted to provide the exact dosage needed, often used for children or elderly patients who may have difficulty swallowing pills.

2. Injectable Dosage Forms:

a. **Prefilled Syringes and Autoinjectors**: Custom dosages based on specific patient requirements. They can be designed for ease of use by the patient or healthcare provider.

b. **Implants**: These provide long-term drug release, customized to the patient's condition and the required duration of therapy.

3. **Topical Dosage Forms:**

a. **Creams, Gels, and Patches**: Formulated to deliver medication directly through the skin to the targeted area. Dosage and formulation can be adjusted for optimal absorption and efficacy.

4. **Inhalation Dosage Forms:**

a. **Nebulizers and Inhalers**: Custom formulations for respiratory conditions, ensuring the correct dosage and particle size for optimal lung deposition and absorption.

5. **Transdermal Patches:**

a. Customized in terms of the drug load and release characteristics to provide a controlled and sustained delivery of medication through the skin.

6. **Advanced Drug Delivery Systems:**

a. **3D Printing**: Enables the creation of highly specific dosage forms with complex structures and precise drug layering for controlled release.

b. **Nanotechnology**: Utilizes nanoparticles for targeted drug delivery, reducing side effects and improving drug efficacy by directing the medication precisely where it is needed.

c. **Pharmacogenomics**: Involves using genetic information to guide the choice and dosage of drugs, ensuring the most effective and safe treatment plan based on the patient's genetic profile.

Benefits of Personalized Dosage Forms

1. **Increased Therapeutic Efficacy:**

a. By tailoring the drug dosage to the individual, the treatment is more likely to achieve the desired therapeutic outcomes.

2. Reduced Adverse Effects:

a. Custom dosages minimize the risk of side effects associated with standard dosages, as the medication is fine-tuned to the patient's needs.

3. Improved Patient Compliance:

a. Medications that are easier to take and better suited to a patient's preferences increase the likelihood of adherence to the prescribed regimen.

4. Optimized Resource Utilization:

a. Reducing the trial-and-error approach often associated with finding the right medication and dosage for a patient.

Challenges and Considerations

1. Regulatory and Manufacturing Complexity:

a. Personalized dosage forms must undergo rigorous testing and regulatory approval, which can be time-consuming and costly.

2. Cost and Accessibility:

a. The expense associated with producing customized medications can be high, potentially limiting access for some patients.

3. Technological and Logistical Barriers:

a. Implementing the necessary technologies and processes for personalized medicine requires significant investment and expertise.

4. Ethical and Privacy Concerns:

a. Handling and using personal genetic and health information must be managed with strict ethical standards and robust data protection measures.

PHARMACOGENETICS

Pharmacogenetics is the study of how an individual's genetic makeup affects their response to drugs. This field is pivotal in the development of personalized medicine, as it allows for the customization of drug therapies to match a patient's genetic profile, thereby optimizing efficacy and minimizing adverse effects. In the context of dosage forms, pharmacogenetics plays a crucial role in designing and administering medications that are tailored to the genetic characteristics of each patient.

Role of Pharmacogenetics in Personalized Medicine

1. **Genetic Variability in Drug Metabolism:**
   a. **CYP450 Enzymes**: Variants in genes encoding cytochrome P450 enzymes (e.g., CYP2D6, CYP2C19) affect how drugs are metabolized. For instance, individuals with certain CYP2D6 variants may metabolize drugs too quickly or too slowly, necessitating dosage adjustments.
   b. **UDP-glucuronosyltransferase (UGT):** Variants in UGT genes can affect the glucuronidation process, influencing drug clearance and necessitating dosage modifications.

2. **Genetic Influence on Drug Targets:**
   a. **Receptor Polymorphisms**: Variations in genes encoding drug receptors can affect drug efficacy. For example, genetic differences in β-adrenergic receptors can influence responses to beta-blockers.
   b. **Enzyme Targets**: Genetic variations in enzymes that are drug targets can alter drug effectiveness. For example, variations in VKORC1 affect warfarin sensitivity.

3. **Drug Transporters:**
   a. Genetic variations in transporter proteins (e.g., P-glycoprotein) can influence drug absorption and distribution, impacting the effective concentration of the drug at the site of action.

Impact on Dosage Forms

1. **Oral Dosage Forms:**

   a. **Tablets and Capsules**: Pharmacogenetic data can guide the creation of oral dosage forms with customized strengths and release profiles. For instance, slow metabolizers might require lower doses or extended-release formulations to avoid toxicity.

   b. **Liquid Forms**: Adjusted concentrations based on metabolic rate and enzyme activity can ensure precise dosing for pediatric or elderly patients.

2. **Injectable Dosage Forms:**

   a. **Prefilled Syringes**: Dosages can be personalized based on genetic tests that predict how quickly a patient will metabolize a drug.

   b. **Long-acting Injectables**: Formulations can be tailored to release the drug over a period that matches the patient's metabolic rate and therapeutic needs.

3. **Topical and Transdermal Dosage Forms:**

   a. **Patches and Creams**: The rate of drug absorption through the skin can be customized based on genetic data, ensuring consistent and appropriate drug levels in the bloodstream.

4. **Inhalation Dosage Forms:**

   a. **Nebulizers and Inhalers**: Customized formulations for respiratory conditions can be developed based on the patient's genetic profile, optimizing drug delivery and efficacy.

Technologies Facilitating Pharmacogenetic Applications

1. **Genetic Testing:**

   a. **Single Nucleotide Polymorphism (SNP) Analysis**: Identifies genetic variations that affect drug metabolism and response.

   b. **Whole Genome Sequencing**: Provides comprehensive genetic data to guide personalized therapy.

2. Bioinformatics:

a. **Data Integration**: Combines genetic information with clinical data to predict drug responses and optimal dosages.

b. **Predictive Modeling:** Uses algorithms to simulate how different genetic profiles will respond to various drugs and dosages.

3. 3D Printing:

a. **Custom Dosage Forms**: 3D printing allows for the creation of complex, patient-specific dosage forms based on pharmacogenetic data, ensuring precise drug delivery and release profiles.

4. Nanotechnology:

a. **Targeted Drug Delivery**: Nanoparticles can be engineered to deliver drugs directly to specific cells or tissues, reducing side effects and improving efficacy based on genetic predispositions.

Benefits of Pharmacogenetics in Dosage Forms

1. Enhanced Efficacy:

a. Tailored dosages ensure that patients receive the optimal amount of medication, enhancing therapeutic outcomes.

2. Reduced Adverse Effects:

a. Personalized dosages help avoid overdosing or underdosing, minimizing the risk of side effects and improving patient safety.

3. Improved Patient Compliance:

a. Customized dosage forms that align with a patient's genetic profile can reduce the frequency of dosing and improve the ease of administration, leading to better adherence.

4. Optimized Resource Utilization:

a. Reduces the trial-and-error approach often used in prescribing medications, leading to faster and more effective treatment.

Challenges and Considerations

1. Complexity of Genetic Data:

a. Interpreting genetic data and integrating it into clinical practice requires significant expertise and advanced technology.

2. **Regulatory and Ethical Issues:**

   a. Ensuring that genetic information is used ethically and that patient privacy is protected is paramount. Regulatory frameworks need to be established to oversee the use of pharmacogenetic data.

3. **Cost and Accessibility:**

   a. Genetic testing and the development of personalized dosage forms can be expensive, potentially limiting access for some patients.

4. **Integration into Healthcare Systems:**

   Incorporating pharmacogenetics into routine clinical practice requires changes in healthcare infrastructure, including education for healthcare providers and updates to electronic health records.

CATEGORIES OF PATIENTS FOR PERSONALIZED MEDICINES

Personalized medicine aims to tailor medical treatment to the individual characteristics of each patient, and different categories of patients can benefit from personalized dosage forms. This categorization considers factors such as age, genetic profile, disease state, lifestyle, and other specific health conditions. Here are the detailed categories:

1. Pediatric Patients

Characteristics:

a. Children have different metabolic rates, body compositions, and developmental stages compared to adults.

b. Dosage forms need to be age-appropriate, easy to administer, and palatable.

Personalized Dosage Forms:

a. **Oral Liquids and Suspensions**: Adjustable concentrations to ensure precise dosing based on weight and age.

b. **Chewable Tablets**: Flavored and smaller-sized tablets for ease of administration.

c. **Dissolvable Strips**: Quick-dissolve formulations for rapid drug delivery without the need for swallowing pills.

2. Geriatric Patients

Characteristics:

a. Older adults often have multiple comorbidities and may take several medications (polypharmacy).

b. Changes in physiology, such as reduced renal and hepatic function, necessitate dosage adjustments.

Personalized Dosage Forms:

a. **Extended-Release Tablets and Capsules**: To reduce dosing frequency and enhance compliance.

b. **Transdermal Patches**: Non-invasive and provide sustained drug release.

c. **Liquid Formulations**: Easier to swallow and allow precise dose adjustments.

3. Patients with Genetic Variations

Characteristics:

a. Genetic polymorphisms can significantly affect drug metabolism, efficacy, and safety.

b. Requires pharmacogenetic testing to identify specific genetic markers.

Personalized Dosage Forms:

a. **Custom-Dosed Tablets**: Based on metabolic rate (e.g., fast or slow metabolizers).

b. **Targeted Drug Delivery Systems**: Such as nanoparticles designed for specific genetic profiles to improve efficacy and reduce side effects.

c. **Microchips:** Implantable devices that release drugs in response to specific biomarkers.

4. Patients with Chronic Diseases

Characteristics:

a. Conditions like diabetes, hypertension, and chronic pain require long-term medication management.

b. Need for stable and sustained drug delivery to maintain therapeutic levels.

Personalized Dosage Forms:

a. **Insulin Pumps and Patches**: For continuous glucose monitoring and insulin delivery in diabetic patients.

b. **Sustained-Release Capsules**: For consistent medication levels in conditions like hypertension.

c. **Implantable Devices**: For chronic pain management, providing continuous analgesic release.

5. Patients with Rare Diseases

Characteristics:

a. Rare diseases often require specialized treatment regimens.

b. Customization is crucial due to the variability in disease presentation and progression.

Personalized Dosage Forms:

a. **Orphan Drug Formulations**: Tailored to specific rare diseases with unique dosing needs.

b. **Biologics**: Such as monoclonal antibodies, designed for specific genetic mutations or disease pathways.

c. **Gene Therapy**: Personalized vectors delivering therapeutic genes to correct genetic disorders.

6. Oncology Patients

Characteristics:

a. Cancer treatments often require precise targeting of tumor cells while minimizing damage to healthy tissue.

b. Dosages are influenced by factors like tumor genetics and patient's overall health.

Personalized Dosage Forms:

a. **Targeted Therapies**: Drugs designed to target specific genetic mutations in tumors.

b. **3D Printed Tablets**: Custom-designed to release anticancer drugs at controlled rates.

c. **Injectable Nanoparticles**: For delivering chemotherapy directly to tumor sites, reducing systemic toxicity.

7. Pregnant Patients

Characteristics:

a. Pregnancy induces significant physiological changes that affect drug pharmacokinetics and dynamics.

b. Medication must be safe for both mother and fetus.

Personalized Dosage Forms:

a. **Adjustable-Dose Tablets**: To safely manage conditions like hypertension or diabetes during pregnancy.

b. **Topical Applications**: Minimizing systemic absorption to reduce fetal exposure.

c. **Nutritional Supplements**: Custom-formulated to address specific deficiencies without exceeding safe limits.

8. Patients with Allergies and Sensitivities

Characteristics:

a. Allergic reactions and sensitivities to excipients or certain drug compounds.

b. Necessitates avoidance of allergens in drug formulations.

Personalized Dosage Forms:

a. **Hypoallergenic Formulations**: Free from common allergens like lactose, gluten, or specific dyes.

b. **Compounded Medications**: Custom-made by pharmacists to exclude specific allergens.

c. **Topical Formulations**: For localized treatment, reducing systemic exposure and allergen risk.

9. Patients with Lifestyle and Dietary Preferences

Characteristics:

a. Vegetarians, vegans, and those with specific dietary restrictions.

b. Requires medications that comply with lifestyle choices without compromising efficacy.

Personalized Dosage Forms:

a. **Gelatin-Free Capsules**: Suitable for vegetarians and vegans.

b. **Sugar-Free Formulations**: For diabetic patients or those avoiding sugar.

c. **Flavor-Enhanced Tablets**: To improve compliance among patients with taste preferences.

CUSTOMIZED DRUG DELIVERY SYSTEMS

Customized drug delivery systems are essential for tailoring medications to meet the unique needs of individual patient categories. These systems ensure optimal therapeutic outcomes by considering factors such as age, genetic profile, disease state, lifestyle, and personal preferences. Here's a detailed overview of how customized drug delivery systems are applied across various patient categories in personalized medicine:

1. Pediatric Patients

Challenges:

a. Children have varying metabolic rates, developmental stages, and sensitivities to drugs.

b. Medication must be easy to administer and palatable.

Customized Drug Delivery Systems:

a. **Mini Tablets and Multiparticulates**: Small-sized tablets that are easy for children to swallow. Multiparticulates can be sprinkled on food.

b. **Flavor-Enhanced Liquids**: Palatable liquid formulations that encourage adherence.

c. **Oral Dissolvable Films**: Thin films that dissolve quickly in the mouth, providing an easy and convenient method of drug delivery.

d. **Transdermal Patches**: Suitable for delivering drugs over extended periods, reducing the need for frequent dosing.

2. Geriatric Patients

Challenges:

a. Older adults often have reduced organ function and multiple comorbidities, requiring precise dosage adjustments.

b. Difficulty in swallowing and adherence issues.

Customized Drug Delivery Systems:

a. **Extended-Release Tablets**: These provide a steady release of medication, reducing the need for frequent dosing.

b. **Transdermal Patches**: Offer consistent drug delivery and are easier to use for those with difficulty swallowing pills.

c. **Liquid Formulations**: Simplify administration and allow for easy dose adjustments.

d. **Multi-Drug Blister Packs**: Organized packaging that helps manage polypharmacy by simplifying complex regimens.

3. Patients with Genetic Variations

Challenges:

Genetic differences affect drug metabolism, efficacy, and safety.

Customized Drug Delivery Systems:

a. **Pharmacogenetically Tailored Tablets**: Dosage and formulation adjusted based on genetic tests.

b. **Micro-Encapsulation**: Protects drugs from rapid metabolism, allowing controlled release tailored to the patient's metabolic profile.

c. **Nanoparticle**s: Enable targeted delivery, reducing side effects and improving efficacy by delivering drugs directly to specific cells or tissues.

4. Patients with Chronic Diseases

Challenges:

Requires long-term medication with consistent therapeutic levels.

Customized Drug Delivery Systems:

a. **Implantable Pumps:** Provide continuous and adjustable delivery of medications like insulin or pain relievers.

b. **Sustained-Release Capsules**: Ensure steady medication levels over extended periods.

c. **Inhalation Systems**: For respiratory conditions, inhalers and nebulizers can be tailored to deliver precise doses.

d. **Transdermal Systems**: Patches that provide consistent drug release, useful for conditions like chronic pain or hypertension.

5. Patients with Rare Diseases

Challenges:

Need for specialized treatment regimens and precise dosing.

Customized Drug Delivery Systems:

a. **Orphan Drug Formulations**: Customized to meet specific needs of rare disease treatments.

b. **Gene Therapy Vectors**: Deliver therapeutic genes to correct genetic disorders.

c. **Biologics**: Tailored formulations of monoclonal antibodies and other biologics designed for specific rare diseases.

6. Oncology Patients

Challenges:

Cancer treatments need precise targeting to minimize damage to healthy cells.

Customized Drug Delivery Systems:

a. **Targeted Therapies**: Drugs designed to interact with specific genetic mutations in cancer cells.

b. **3D Printed Dosage Forms**: Customized shapes and release profiles to deliver drugs directly to tumors.

c. **Injectable Nanoparticles**: Targeted delivery systems that release chemotherapy drugs directly at the tumor site, reducing systemic toxicity.

7. Pregnant Patients

Challenges:

Ensuring safety for both mother and fetus, considering physiological changes during pregnancy.

Customized Drug Delivery Systems:

a. **Adjustable-Dose Tablets**: Enable safe management of conditions like hypertension or diabetes during pregnancy.

b. **Topical Applications**: Reduce systemic exposure, minimizing risk to the fetus.

c. **Controlled-Release Systems**: Ensure stable drug levels, crucial for managing chronic conditions without harming the fetus.

8. Patients with Allergies and Sensitivities

Challenges:

Need to avoid allergens in drug formulations.

Customized Drug Delivery Systems:

a. **Hypoallergenic Formulations**: Free from common allergens such as lactose, gluten, or specific dyes.

b. **Compounded Medications**: Custom-made to exclude allergens and meet specific patient needs.

c. **Topical Formulations**: Provide localized treatment, reducing the risk of systemic allergic reactions.

9. Patients with Lifestyle and Dietary Preferences

Challenges:

Medications need to align with lifestyle choices without compromising efficacy.

Customized Drug Delivery Systems:

a. **Gelatin-Free Capsules**: Suitable for vegetarians and vegans.

b. **Sugar-Free Formulations**: Appropriate for diabetic patients or those avoiding sugar.

c. **Flavor-Enhanced Tablets**: Improve compliance among patients with taste preferences.

d. **Ethical and Halal/Kosher Formulations**: Meeting dietary restrictions without affecting treatment efficacy.

BIOELECTRONIC MEDICINES

Bioelectronic medicines represent a cutting-edge approach in personalized medicine, involving the use of electronic devices to modulate biological processes and treat diseases. These devices can provide precise, targeted treatment, often with fewer side effects compared to traditional pharmaceuticals. Here's a detailed overview of how bioelectronic medicines are applied across various patient categories in personalized medicine:

1. Pediatric Patients

Challenges:

Children may have conditions that are difficult to manage with traditional drugs due to their rapid growth and development.

Bioelectronic Solutions:

a. **Neurostimulation Devices**: For conditions like epilepsy, devices that provide targeted brain stimulation can reduce seizure frequency without the need for high doses of medication.

b. **Wearable Monitors**: Continuous monitoring devices that track vital signs and provide data for personalized treatment adjustments.

2. Geriatric Patients

Challenges:

Older adults often have multiple chronic conditions and are more sensitive to drug side effects.

Bioelectronic Solutions:

a. **Pacemakers and Defibrillators**: Advanced models that not only regulate heart rhythms but also collect data to adjust therapy automatically.

b. **Neuromodulation Devices**: For pain management in conditions like arthritis or neuropathy, these devices can provide targeted pain relief without systemic side effects.

3. Patients with Genetic Variations

Challenges:

Genetic differences can significantly affect drug metabolism and response.

Bioelectronic Solutions:

a. **Gene Therapy Delivery Systems**: Devices that deliver genetic material precisely to target cells, allowing for personalized gene editing and therapy.

b. **Biosensors:** Implanted sensors that monitor metabolic and genetic markers to provide real-time data for adjusting treatments.

4. Patients with Chronic Diseases

Challenges:

Long-term management requires consistent and effective treatment.

Bioelectronic Solutions:

a. **Insulin Pumps with Continuous Glucose Monitoring (CGM):** For diabetes management, these systems provide real-time blood glucose data and adjust insulin delivery accordingly.

b. **Cardiac Resynchronization Therapy (CRT) Devices**: For heart failure patients, these devices coordinate the heart's pumping action, improving efficiency and reducing symptoms.

5. Patients with Rare Diseases

Challenges:

Limited treatment options and the need for highly specific therapies.

Bioelectronic Solutions:

a. **Implantable Drug Delivery Systems**: These systems can deliver precise doses of rare or experimental drugs directly to target tissues, improving efficacy and reducing side effects.

b. **Neuromodulation Devices**: Used for rare neurological disorders, providing targeted treatment that can be adjusted based on patient response.

6. Oncology Patients

Challenges:

Cancer treatment requires targeting of tumor cells while minimizing damage to healthy cells.

Bioelectronic Solutions:

a. **Tumor-Treating Fields (TTFields)**: These are electric fields that disrupt cancer cell division, used alongside traditional therapies for enhanced effectiveness.

b. **Smart Drug Delivery Systems**: Devices that release chemotherapy drugs in response to specific biomarkers, ensuring targeted treatment and reducing systemic exposure.

7. Pregnant Patients

Challenges:

Treatment must be safe for both the mother and the developing fetus.

Bioelectronic Solutions:

a. **Fetal Monitoring Devices**: Non-invasive devices that continuously monitor fetal health and development, providing data to adjust maternal treatments as needed.

b. **Biofeedback Devices**: Used for managing conditions like hypertension and gestational diabetes through lifestyle interventions and real-time monitoring.

8. Patients with Allergies and Sensitivities

Challenges:

Need to avoid allergens and manage hypersensitivity reactions.

Bioelectronic Solutions:

a. **Allergy Management Systems**: Devices that monitor and predict allergic reactions, providing early warnings and enabling timely interventions.

b. **Implantable Antihistamine Pumps**: Deliver antihistamines in a controlled manner to prevent severe allergic reactions.

9. Patients with Lifestyle and Dietary Preferences

Challenges:

Medications need to align with lifestyle choices without compromising efficacy.

Bioelectronic Solutions:

a. **Wearable Fitness and Health Trackers**: Devices that monitor physical activity, nutrition, and vital signs, helping tailor lifestyle interventions and medication plans.

b. **Personalized Digital Health Assistants**: Apps and devices that integrate with bioelectronic medicines to provide customized health advice and treatment reminders.

3D PRINTING OF PHARMACEUTICALS

3D printing, or additive manufacturing, is revolutionizing the field of pharmaceuticals by enabling the creation of customized dosage forms tailored to individual patient needs. This technology offers unparalleled precision in drug formulation and dosage customization, making it ideal for personalized medicine. Here's a detailed overview of how 3D printing is applied across various patient categories in personalized medicine:

1. Pediatric Patients

Challenges:

a. Children require precise dosages that can vary significantly based on age, weight, and developmental stage.

b. Medications must be palatable and easy to administer.

3D Printing Solutions:

a. **Custom-Dosed Tablets**: 3D printing allows for the precise adjustment of drug dosages to meet the specific needs of pediatric patients.

b. **Chewable and Flavored Tablets**: Tailored to be more palatable for children, enhancing adherence.

c. **Rapidly Dissolving Films**: Thin films that dissolve quickly in the mouth, providing an easy-to-administer dosage form without the need for swallowing pills.

2. Geriatric Patients

Challenges:

a. Older adults often have multiple comorbidities, leading to complex medication regimens.

b. Swallowing difficulties and variable metabolic rates necessitate personalized dosages and forms.

3D Printing Solutions:

a. **Polypill Formulations**: Combining multiple medications into a single pill to simplify regimens and improve adherence.

b. **Extended-Release Tablets**: Custom-designed to release medication over an extended period, reducing dosing frequency.

c. **Easily Swallowable Forms**: Creating tablets with shapes and textures that are easier to swallow.

3. Patients with Genetic Variations

Challenges:

Genetic differences can significantly influence drug metabolism and efficacy, requiring highly individualized dosages.

3D Printing Solutions:

a. **Genetically-Tailored Tablets**: Adjusted dosages and release profiles based on genetic testing to optimize efficacy and minimize side effects.

b. **Multiparticulate Systems**: Enabling a combination of immediate and controlled-release profiles tailored to the patient's metabolic rate.

4. Patients with Chronic Diseases

Challenges:

Long-term management often requires stable and consistent drug delivery.

3D Printing Solutions:

a. **Sustained-Release Formulations**: Customizable release profiles to maintain therapeutic levels over extended periods.

b. **Implantable Devices**: 3D-printed implants that can deliver drugs directly to target areas, reducing the need for frequent dosing.

c. **Personalized Dosage Forms**: Tailored dosages to meet the specific needs of patients with conditions like diabetes, hypertension, and chronic pain.

5. Patients with Rare Diseases

Challenges:

Rare diseases often require specialized and precise treatment regimens, which are not readily available in standard forms.

3D Printing Solutions:

a. **Orphan Drug Formulations**: Customized production of medications for rare diseases, including precise dosages and unique formulations.

b. **Patient-Specific Tablets**: Creating formulations based on individual patient profiles and the specific progression of the rare disease.

6. Oncology Patients

Challenges:

Cancer treatments need to be precisely targeted to minimize damage to healthy tissues while effectively treating the tumor.

3D Printing Solutions:

a. **Targeted Drug Delivery Systems**: Designing tablets or capsules that release the drug directly at the tumor site.

b. **Multi-Layer Tablets**: Combining different drugs and release profiles within a single tablet to optimize cancer therapy.

c. **Patient-Specific Dosages**: Adjusting dosages based on the patient's response to treatment and genetic profile.

7. Pregnant Patients

Challenges:

Ensuring the safety and efficacy of medications for both the mother and the developing fetus.

3D Printing Solutions:

a. **Custom-Dosed Tablets**: Ensuring precise dosages that are safe for both mother and fetus.

b. **Controlled-Release Systems**: Providing steady medication levels to manage chronic conditions without frequent dosing.

c. **Nutritional Supplements**: Tailored to address specific deficiencies without exceeding safe limits.

8. Patients with Allergies and Sensitivities

Challenges:

Avoiding allergens and managing sensitivities in drug formulations.

3D Printing Solutions:

a. **Allergen-Free Tablets**: Customized formulations that exclude specific allergens.

b. **Compounded Medications**: Creating medications that meet individual allergy and sensitivity needs.

c. **Topical Formulations**: Customizable for local application, reducing systemic exposure and allergic reactions.

9. Patients with Lifestyle and Dietary Preferences

Challenges:

Medications need to align with lifestyle choices and dietary restrictions without compromising efficacy.

3D Printing Solutions:

a. **Gelatin-Free Capsules**: Suitable for vegetarians and vegans.

b. **Sugar-Free Formulations**: Appropriate for diabetic patients or those avoiding sugar.

c. **Personalized Flavors and Textures**: Enhancing compliance by catering to individual taste preferences.

TELEPHARMACY

Telepharmacy, the delivery of pharmaceutical care through telecommunications, plays a significant role in personalized medicine by providing remote access to pharmacy services. This approach can be particularly beneficial in ensuring that personalized medication needs are met, regardless of a patient's location. Here's a detailed overview of how telepharmacy is applied across various patient categories in personalized medicine:

1. Pediatric Patients

Challenges:

Children require specific dosages that need careful monitoring and adjustment.

Telepharmacy Solutions:

a. **Remote Consultations**: Pharmacists can provide virtual consultations to parents, ensuring accurate dosing and adherence.

b. **Medication Management Apps**: Tools that help track dosing schedules and provide reminders, tailored to pediatric needs.

c. **Educational Support**: Online resources and guidance for parents on medication administration and side effect monitoring.

2. Geriatric Patients

Challenges:

Older adults often have multiple medications, complex regimens, and may face mobility issues.

Telepharmacy Solutions:

a. **Medication Reconciliation**: Virtual reviews of medication regimens to avoid drug interactions and optimize therapy.

b. **Home Delivery Services**: Coordinated through telepharmacy to ensure timely delivery of medications.

c. **Telemonitoring**: Use of remote monitoring devices to track health parameters and adjust medications as needed.

3. Patients with Genetic Variations

Challenges:

Genetic differences affect drug metabolism and response, requiring personalized treatment plans.

Telepharmacy Solutions:

a. **Pharmacogenetic Counseling**: Remote counseling sessions to discuss genetic test results and implications for medication therapy.

b. **Customized Medication Plans**: Personalized plans developed and adjusted through telepharmacy consultations based on genetic profiles.

c. **Continuous Monitoring**: Use of telehealth tools to monitor treatment efficacy and side effects in real time.

4. Patients with Chronic Diseases

Challenges:

Long-term management requires consistent monitoring and medication adjustments.

Telepharmacy Solutions:

a. **Regular Check-ins**: Scheduled virtual appointments to assess treatment progress and make necessary adjustments.

b. **Adherence Support**: Apps and reminders to help patients maintain their medication regimen.

c. **Remote Health Monitoring**: Devices that send health data to pharmacists for ongoing assessment and medication optimization.

5. Patients with Rare Diseases

Challenges:

Rare diseases often require specialized medications that are not widely available.

Telepharmacy Solutions:

a. **Access to Specialists**: Virtual consultations with pharmacists who specialize in rare diseases and orphan drugs.

b. **Coordination with Specialty Pharmacies**: Ensuring access to necessary medications through remote communication.

c. **Education and Support**: Providing patients and caregivers with detailed information about their treatment and managing side effects.

6. Oncology Patients

Challenges:

Cancer treatments often involve complex regimens and severe side effects.

Telepharmacy Solutions:

a. **Symptom Management**: Remote consultations to help manage side effects and provide supportive care.

b. **Medication Adherence Programs**: Tools to ensure patients follow their treatment protocols.

c. **Personalized Treatment Adjustments**: Regular virtual assessments to tailor therapy based on patient response and side effects.

7. Pregnant Patients

Challenges:

Ensuring the safety of both mother and fetus while managing chronic conditions.

Telepharmacy Solutions:

a. **Prenatal Counseling**: Remote sessions to discuss medication safety and necessary adjustments during pregnancy.

b. **Nutritional Guidance**: Virtual support for managing diet and supplements during pregnancy.

c. **Monitoring and Adjustments:** Regular virtual follow-ups to track health parameters and adjust medications as needed.

8. Patients with Allergies and Sensitivities

Challenges:

Avoiding allergens and managing hypersensitivities in medications.

Telepharmacy Solutions:

a. **Customized Consultations**: Remote sessions to discuss and identify safe medication options.

b. **Allergy Management Plans**: Personalized plans and emergency action plans developed and communicated through telepharmacy.

c. **Education and Alerts**: Providing information about potential allergens in medications and alternative options.

9. Patients with Lifestyle and Dietary Preferences

Challenges:

Medications need to align with lifestyle choices and dietary restrictions.

Telepharmacy Solutions:

a. **Tailored Medication Plans**: Virtual consultations to create medication plans that respect dietary and lifestyle choices.

b. **Support and Counseling**: Ongoing virtual support to address any concerns and adjust medications as needed.

c. **Access to Resources**: Providing information and resources about medication options that align with patients' preferences.

Multiple Choice Questions (MCQs) from the Context

1. What is the main goal of personalized medicine?

    A) To create a uniform approach to treatment

    B) To reduce the cost of healthcare

    C) To tailor medical treatment to individual characteristics

    D) To simplify drug formulations

2. Which dosage form is often used for pediatric patients due to ease of administration?

    A) Tablets

    B) Capsules

    C) Liquids

    D) Patches

3. What technology allows for the creation of complex and precise dosage forms in personalized medicine?

    A) Nanotechnology

    B) Pharmacogenomics

    C) 3D Printing

    D) Microfabrication

4. Which aspect of pharmacogenetics is crucial for designing personalized dosage forms?

    A) Analyzing lifestyle choices

    B) Understanding genetic influence on drug metabolism

    C) Monitoring environmental conditions

    D) Assessing socioeconomic status

5. What is a key benefit of using nanoparticles in personalized dosage forms?

    A) Increased cost-effectiveness

B) Simplified manufacturing processes

C) Targeted drug delivery

D) Enhanced flavor profiles

6. Which regulatory challenge is associated with personalized dosage forms?

    A) Reduced need for clinical testing

    B) Simplified approval pathways

    C) Complex regulatory pathways

    D) Faster market access

7. What does pharmacogenomics use to determine the most effective drug and dose for a patient?

    A) Patient's age and weight

    B) Genetic information

    C) General population data

    D) Traditional methods

8. Which type of dosage form is designed for ease of use by the patient or healthcare provider?

    A) Oral liquids

    B) Chewable tablets

    C) Prefilled syringes

    D) Creams

9. What is a primary challenge in the manufacturing of personalized dosage forms?

    A) Basic technology requirements

    B) Lower costs of production

    C) Advanced technology and precise control

    D) Reduced data management needs

10. How does bioelectronic medicine primarily help patients?

    A) By using traditional pharmaceuticals

    B) By modulating biological processes through electronic devices

C) By reducing the need for any medical intervention

D) By completely replacing all forms of medication

11. Which patient category might require dosage forms that consider rapid growth and development?

A) Geriatric patients

B) Oncology patients

C) Pediatric patients

D) Patients with chronic diseases

12. Which technology is used to create dosage forms that release drugs at specific sites in the body?

A) 3D Printing

B) Microfabrication

C) Wearable devices

D) Nanotechnology

13. What feature do transdermal patches offer in personalized medicine?

A) Rapid systemic release

B) Flavor enhancement

C) Controlled and sustained drug delivery

D) High-cost production

14. Why is genetic testing important in personalized medicine?

A) It determines the patient's blood type

B) It helps in designing custom exercise plans

C) It assists in selecting the right dietary supplements

D) It guides the choice and dosage of drugs

15. Which form of technology assists in monitoring physiological parameters and adjusting drug delivery?

A) Bioinformatics

B) 3D Printing

C) Wearable devices

D) Microfabrication

16. What advantage does microfabrication offer in drug delivery?

   A) Increased drug absorption through large devices

   B) General drug delivery without specificity

   C) Controlled release through micro-scale devices

   D) Use in large-scale pharmaceutical manufacturing

17. Why is telepharmacy important in personalized medicine?

   A) It provides a traditional approach to patient care

   B) It offers remote access to pharmacy services

   C) It encourages self-medication

   D) It decreases the importance of pharmacists

18. Which dosage form is particularly beneficial for patients with swallowing difficulties?

   A) Injectable solutions

   B) Tablets

   C) Liquids

   D) Hard capsules

19. What does the integration of pharmacogenomics and 3D printing facilitate?

   A) Decreased customization in drug delivery

   B) Creation of standard drug dosages

   C) Personalized drug profiles based on genetic data

   D) Simplification of complex drug formulations

20. What is a significant challenge in applying pharmacogenetics in clinical practice?

   A) Easy accessibility of genetic data

   B) Low cost of genetic testing

   C) Complexity of genetic data interpretation

   D) Quick regulatory approvals

Short Answer Type Questions (Subjective)

1. What is personalized medicine and how does it differ from traditional medical practices?
2. Describe two benefits of customizing dosage forms in personalized medicine.
3. Explain the role of 3D printing in the development of personalized dosage forms.
4. What are the primary challenges faced by regulatory bodies when approving personalized dosage forms?
5. How does nanotechnology contribute to personalized medicine?
6. Detail how pharmacogenomics can influence the choice and dosage of drugs in personalized medicine.
7. What are some ethical concerns associated with the use of patient-specific data in personalized medicine?
8. Discuss the impact of wearable devices on the management of chronic diseases in personalized medicine.
9. Why is it important to adjust medication dosages for pediatric patients in personalized medicine?
10. How do inhalation dosage forms benefit patients with respiratory conditions in personalized medicine?
11. Describe the importance of bioinformatics in pharmacogenetics.
12. What advantages do prefilled syringes offer in personalized medication delivery?
13. Why is genetic testing significant in the context of personalized medicine?
14. What is a transdermal patch and how is it customized for personalized therapy?
15. How can bioelectronic devices be used to treat chronic diseases?
16. Explain how telepharmacy plays a role in personalized medicine.

17. Discuss the significance of dosage customization in geriatric patients with multiple comorbidities.

18. How do oral dissolvable films work, and why are they suitable for pediatric use?

19. What challenges are associated with manufacturing personalized dosage forms?

20. How do lifestyle and dietary preferences influence the customization of medication in personalized medicine?

Long Answer Type Questions (Subjective)

1. Discuss the various types of dosage forms used in personalized medicine and how they cater to the specific needs of different patient categories.

2. Explain the technological advancements that have facilitated the development of personalized dosage forms, such as 3D printing and nanotechnology, and their impact on patient care.

3. Evaluate the role of pharmacogenetics in personalized medicine, specifically how genetic differences affect drug metabolism and how this knowledge is used to tailor drug therapies.

4. Describe the regulatory and ethical challenges faced in the implementation of personalized dosage forms and how these challenges are being addressed.

5. Assess the importance of patient-centric approaches in the formulation of personalized medications, and how this influences therapeutic outcomes and patient compliance.

6. Analyze the challenges and benefits of integrating wearable technology and bioelectronic medicines into personalized healthcare strategies.

7. Detail the process of developing customized drug delivery systems for rare diseases and the role of genetic information in this process.

8. Discuss how telepharmacy enhances the delivery of personalized medicine and the benefits it brings to patients with limited access to healthcare facilities.

9. Examine the use of bioinformatics in personalized medicine, particularly in predicting drug responses and developing personalized treatment plans.

10. Explore the future trends and potential developments in personalized medicine, particularly in the areas of drug delivery and patient monitoring.

Answer Key for the MCQs

1. (C) To tailor medical treatment to individual characteristics
2. (C) Liquids
3. (C) 3D Printing
4. (B) Understanding genetic influence on drug metabolism
5. (C) Targeted drug delivery
6. (C) Complex regulatory pathways
7. (B) Genetic information
8. (C) Prefilled syringes
9. (C) Advanced technology and precise control
10. (B) By modulating biological processes through electronic devices
11. (C) Pediatric patients
12. (D) Nanotechnology
13. (C) Controlled and sustained drug delivery
14. (D) It guides the choice and dosage of drugs
15. (C) Wearable devices
16. (C) Controlled release through micro-scale devices
17. (B) It offers remote access to pharmacy services
18. (C) Liquids
19. (C) Personalized drug profiles based on genetic data
20. (C) Complexity of genetic data interpretation

CHAPTER – 3

RATE CONTROLLED DRUG DELIVERY SYSTEMS

INTRODUCTION:

Rate-controlled drug delivery systems (RCDDS) are advanced pharmaceutical technologies designed to deliver medications at a predetermined and controlled rate, enhancing therapeutic efficacy and minimizing side effects. This approach ensures that the drug concentration remains within the therapeutic window for an extended period, improving patient compliance and optimizing clinical outcomes. Here's a detailed introduction to RCDDS:

Key Concepts of Rate-Controlled Drug Delivery Systems

1. **Definition:** RCDDS are formulations or devices that release drugs at a controlled, predictable rate over a specified period. This control can be achieved through various mechanisms and technologies.

2. **Advantages:**

    a. **Improved Therapeutic Efficacy**: Maintains drug levels within the therapeutic window.

    b. **Reduced Side Effects**: Avoids peaks and troughs in drug concentration.

    c. **Enhanced Patient Compliance**: Reduces the frequency of dosing.

    d. **Optimized Pharmacokinetics**: Provides consistent drug absorption and distribution.

Mechanisms of Rate Control

1. **Diffusion-Controlled Systems:**

    a. **Reservoir Systems**: Drug core surrounded by a polymer membrane that controls the release rate. Examples include transdermal patches.

b. **Matrix Systems:** Drug dispersed uniformly in a polymer matrix. The release rate is controlled by the diffusion of the drug through the matrix material.

2. Dissolution-Controlled Systems:

a. **Encapsulation:** Drug is coated with a material that dissolves slowly in bodily fluids, controlling the drug release rate.

b. **Matrix Dissolution:** Drug is dispersed in a slowly dissolving matrix. The rate of matrix dissolution controls drug release.

3. Osmotically Controlled Systems:

a. **Osmotic Pumps:** Utilize osmotic pressure to drive the drug out of a semipermeable membrane at a controlled rate. Examples include the OROS (Osmotic-controlled Release Oral delivery System) tablets.

4. Erosion-Controlled Systems:

a. **Surface Erosion:** The drug is released as the polymer matrix erodes over time.

b. **Bulk Erosion:** The entire matrix degrades uniformly, releasing the drug.

5. Ion-Exchange Systems:

a. Utilize ion-exchange resins to control the drug release rate. The drug is bound to the resin and released upon exchange with ions in the gastrointestinal tract.

Types of Rate-Controlled Drug Delivery Systems

1. Oral Controlled-Release Systems:

a. **Tablets and Capsules:** Designed with specific polymers or coatings to control the release rate in the gastrointestinal tract.

b. **Gastroretentive Systems:** Formulations that remain in the stomach for an extended period to release the drug at a controlled rate.

2. **Transdermal Systems:**

   a. **Patches**: Adhere to the skin and release the drug through the skin into the bloodstream. Controlled by diffusion through the polymer matrix and skin.

3. **Implantable Systems:**

   a. **Biodegradable Implants**: Placed subcutaneously and release the drug as the matrix erodes.

   b. **Non-biodegradable Implants**: Use mechanical pumps or diffusion mechanisms for long-term drug delivery.

4. **Injectable Systems:**

   a. **Microspheres**: Biodegradable polymer spheres that release the drug over time as they degrade.

   b. **Nanoparticles**: Designed to release the drug at a controlled rate and target specific tissues or cells.

Challenges and Future Directions

1. **Challenges:**

   a. **Formulation Complexity**: Designing systems that provide consistent and predictable release rates.

   b. **Manufacturing:** Scaling up the production of RCDDS while maintaining quality and uniformity.

   c. **Regulatory Approval:** Ensuring safety, efficacy, and stability of the drug delivery system.

2. **Future Directions:**

   a. **Smart Drug Delivery**: Incorporating sensors and feedback mechanisms to adjust the drug release rate based on real-time physiological parameters.

   b. **Targeted Delivery**: Enhancing the ability of RCDDS to deliver drugs to specific tissues or cells, improving therapeutic outcomes.

   c. **Biodegradable Polymers**: Developing new polymers that provide better control over drug release and degrade safely within the body.

PRINCIPLES OF RATE CONTROLLED DRUG DELIVERY SYSTEMS

Rate-controlled drug delivery systems (RCDDS) are based on several fundamental principles that ensure the consistent and predictable release of drugs over time. Understanding these principles is crucial for designing effective RCDDS. Here are the key principles in detail:

1. Diffusion-Controlled Release

Reservoir Systems:

   a. **Principle:** Drug diffusion through a polymer membrane.

   b. **Mechanism:** The drug is encapsulated in a core surrounded by a rate-controlling polymer membrane. The drug diffuses through the membrane at a rate determined by the membrane's properties and the concentration gradient.

   c. **Example**s: Transdermal patches, ocular inserts.

Matrix Systems:

   a. **Principle**: Drug diffusion through a polymer matrix.

   b. **Mechanism**: The drug is uniformly dispersed within a polymer matrix. Release occurs as the drug molecules diffuse out of the matrix material.

   c. **Examples**: Hydrophilic matrix tablets, controlled-release capsules.

2. Dissolution-Controlled Release

Encapsulation Dissolution:

   a. **Principle**: Controlled dissolution of the drug coating.

   b. **Mechanism**: The drug is coated with a material that dissolves slowly in bodily fluids. The dissolution rate of the coating controls the release of the drug.

   c. **Examples:** Sugar-coated tablets, certain controlled-release capsules.

Matrix Dissolution:

   a. **Principle:** Controlled dissolution of the polymer matrix.

b. **Mechanism**: The drug is embedded in a matrix that dissolves over time, releasing the drug at a controlled rate.

c. **Examples**: Hydrogel-based systems, biodegradable implants.

3. Osmotically Controlled Release

Osmotic Pumps:

a. **Principle:** Osmotic pressure-driven drug release.

b. **Mechanism**: The drug is enclosed in a semi-permeable membrane along with an osmotic agent. Water enters the device through the membrane, creating osmotic pressure that pushes the drug solution out through a delivery orifice.

c. **Example**s: OROS (Osmotic-controlled Release Oral delivery System) tablets.

4. Erosion-Controlled Release

Surface Erosion:

a. **Principle**: Surface degradation of the polymer matrix.

b. **Mechanism:** The drug is released as the outer layer of the matrix erodes in a controlled manner.

c. **Examples**: Poly(ortho esters), certain biodegradable polymer systems.

Bulk Erosion:

a. **Principle:** Uniform degradation of the polymer matrix.

b. **Mechanism**: The entire matrix degrades at a uniform rate, releasing the drug uniformly over time.

c. **Examples:** Polylactic acid (PLA) and polyglycolic acid (PGA) based systems.

5. Ion-Exchange Systems

a. **Principle**: Ion-exchange resin controlled drug release.

b. **Mechanism**: The drug is bound to an ion-exchange resin and released in exchange for ions present in the gastrointestinal tract or other body fluids.

c. **Examples:** Ion-exchange resin tablets, certain oral controlled-release formulations.

6. Swelling-Controlled Release

a. **Principle:** Polymer swelling-controlled drug diffusion.

b. **Mechanism:** The polymer matrix swells upon contact with bodily fluids, increasing the mesh size of the polymer network and allowing the drug to diffuse out at a controlled rate.

c. **Examples:** Hydrogel-based delivery systems, gastroretentive formulations.

7. Complexation-Controlled Release

a. **Principle:** Drug release controlled by complex formation and dissociation.

b. **Mechanism:** The drug forms a reversible complex with another molecule (e.g., cyclodextrins). The release rate is controlled by the dissociation of the complex.

c. **Examples:** Cyclodextrin inclusion complexes, certain injectable formulations.

Key Factors Influencing Rate-Controlled Drug Delivery

a. **Polymer Properties:** The choice of polymer (biodegradable vs. non-biodegradable, hydrophilic vs. hydrophobic) significantly affects the release rate and mechanism.

b. **Drug Properties:** Solubility, molecular weight, and stability of the drug influence its release kinetics.

c. **Environmental Factors:** pH, temperature, and presence of enzymes can affect the release rate from RCDDS.

d. **Device Design:** Geometry and structure of the delivery system, including membrane thickness, matrix composition, and surface area, are crucial for controlling drug release.

FUNDAMENTALS OF RATE CONTROLLED DRUG DELIVERY SYSTEMS

Understanding the fundamentals of rate-controlled drug delivery systems (RCDDS) is essential for developing effective and efficient drug delivery formulations. Here's a detailed exploration of these fundamentals:

1. Purpose of Rate Control

a. **Maintaining Therapeutic Levels**: Ensures that drug concentrations in the body remain within the therapeutic window for extended periods, optimizing efficacy.

b. **Minimizing Side Effects**: Avoids rapid fluctuations in drug levels, reducing the likelihood of adverse reactions.

c. **Improving Patient Compliance:** Reduces dosing frequency and improves convenience for patients, leading to better adherence to treatment regimens.

2. Drug Release Kinetics

a. **Zero-Order Release**: Constant rate of drug release over time, independent of concentration. Achieved through mechanisms such as matrix erosion or osmotic pumps.

b. **First-Order Release**: Rate of drug release decreases exponentially over time. Common in diffusion-controlled systems.

c. **Sigmoidal Release**: Initial lag phase followed by a sustained release period. Often seen in dissolution-controlled systems.

3. Mechanisms of Rate Control

a. **Diffusion-Based Systems**: Drug molecules diffuse through a barrier, such as a polymer membrane or matrix, at a controlled rate.

b. **Dissolution-Based Systems**: Drug release is controlled by the dissolution rate of the formulation, such as coatings or matrices.

c. **Osmotic Systems**: Utilize osmotic pressure gradients to control drug release, typically through osmotic pumps or tablets.

d. **Erosion-Based Systems**: Drug release occurs as the delivery system erodes or degrades over time, releasing encapsulated drug molecules.

e. **Ion-Exchange Systems**: Drug release is governed by ion exchange between the formulation and the surrounding environment.

4. Factors Influencing Rate Control

a. **Physicochemical Properties of the Drug**: Solubility, molecular weight, and stability affect drug release kinetics.

b. **Properties of Excipients and Polymers**: Choice of polymers, additives, and coatings can influence drug release rates.

c. **Environmental Conditions**: pH, temperature, and presence of enzymes in the physiological environment can impact drug release.

d. **Device Design**: Geometry, surface area, and porosity of the delivery system affect drug release kinetics.

5. Types of Rate-Controlled Drug Delivery Systems

a. **Oral Formulations**: Including tablets, capsules, and multiparticulate systems designed for controlled release in the gastrointestinal tract.

b. **Transdermal Patches**: Deliver drugs through the skin for systemic absorption, maintaining constant plasma concentrations.

c. **Implantable Devices**: Biodegradable or non-biodegradable implants for sustained release of drugs over extended periods.

d. **Injectable Formulations**: Microspheres, liposomes, or nanoparticles designed for controlled release upon administration.

6. Characterization Techniques

a. **In vitro Release Studies:** Measure drug release from formulations under controlled laboratory conditions.

b. **In vivo Pharmacokinetic Studies:** Assess drug absorption, distribution, metabolism, and excretion in animal models or human subjects.

c. **Physicochemical Analysis**: Characterize the physical and chemical properties of drug formulations, including particle size, surface morphology, and drug-polymer interactions.

7. Regulatory Considerations

a. **Bioequivalence Studies**: Demonstrate that a rate-controlled formulation is equivalent to a reference product in terms of pharmacokinetic parameters.

b. **Stability Testing**: Assess the stability of formulations under various storage conditions to ensure product quality and shelf-life.

c. **Safety and Efficacy Evaluation**: Conduct preclinical and clinical studies to evaluate the safety and efficacy of rate-controlled drug delivery systems.

TYPES OF RATE CONTROLLED DRUG DELIVERY SYSTEMS

Rate-controlled drug delivery systems (RCDDS) encompass various technologies and formulations designed to release drugs at a predetermined rate over time. These systems offer several advantages, including improved therapeutic outcomes, reduced side effects, and enhanced patient compliance. Here's a detailed exploration of the types of RCDDS:

1. Oral Controlled-Release Systems

a. **Matrix Tablets and Capsules**: Drug is dispersed in a polymer matrix that controls drug release by diffusion. Examples include hydrophilic and hydrophobic matrix tablets.

b. **Coated Tablets**: Drug is coated with a polymer that regulates drug release. Types include enteric-coated tablets and sustained-release coatings.

c. **Gastroretentive Systems**: Formulations designed to prolong gastric residence time, ensuring controlled drug release. Examples include floating systems and mucoadhesive formulations.

d. **Osmotic Controlled-Release Systems**: Utilize osmotic pressure gradients to deliver drugs at a controlled rate. Examples include OROS (Osmotic-Controlled Release Oral Delivery System) tablets.

2. Transdermal Delivery Systems

- **Patches**: Deliver drugs through the skin for systemic absorption. The drug is released from the patch in a controlled manner over a specified period.
- **Transdermal Gels**: Drug-containing gels applied to the skin for controlled release of medications.
- **Transdermal Films**: Thin films applied to the skin, releasing drugs at a controlled rate.

3. Injectable Controlled-Release Systems

a. **Microspheres and Nanoparticles**: Biodegradable polymer particles loaded with drugs for controlled release upon injection.

b. **Implants**: Subcutaneously implanted devices designed to release drugs over an extended period. Examples include biodegradable and non-biodegradable implants.

4. Inhalation Systems

a. **Metered-Dose Inhalers (MDIs):** Deliver aerosolized drugs to the lungs for systemic or local effects, providing controlled drug delivery.

b. **Dry Powder Inhalers (DPIs):** Deliver micronized drug particles to the lungs, ensuring controlled drug release.

5. Implantable Controlled-Release Systems

a. **Drug-Eluting Stents**: Stents coated with a drug-polymer matrix to prevent restenosis after angioplasty, providing controlled drug release at the site of action.

b. **Contraceptive Implants**: Subdermal implants releasing hormones at a controlled rate for long-term contraception.

6. Intravaginal Systems

a. **Vaginal Rings**: Flexible rings inserted into the vagina, releasing hormones or other drugs at a controlled rate for contraception, hormone replacement therapy, or treatment of vaginal infections.

7. Gastrointestinal Delivery Systems

a. **Colon-Specific Delivery Systems**: Designed to release drugs in the colon for the treatment of colonic diseases. Examples include pH-sensitive coatings and time-dependent formulations.

b. **Enteric-Coated Formulations**: Protect drugs from degradation in the acidic environment of the stomach, ensuring drug release in the intestine.

8. Ocular Delivery Systems

a. **Ocular Inserts**: Thin, drug-loaded inserts placed in the conjunctival sac for controlled drug release to the eye.

b. **Intraocular Implants**: Implants placed in the eye for sustained release of drugs to treat conditions such as glaucoma or macular degeneration.

ACTIVATION OF RATE CONTROLLED DRUG DELIVERY SYSTEMS

Activation mechanisms in rate-controlled drug delivery systems (RCDDS) are crucial as they determine when and how the drug is released from the formulation. These systems are designed to ensure controlled and predictable drug release, often triggered by specific stimuli or conditions. Here's a detailed exploration of the activation mechanisms in RCDDS:

1. Passive Activation

a. **Diffusion-Based Systems**: Drug release occurs passively through diffusion, driven by concentration gradients.

b. **Erosion-Based Systems**: Release is activated by the gradual erosion or degradation of the delivery system over time.

c. **Dissolution-Based Systems**: Activation relies on the dissolution of a coating or matrix material, allowing drug release to commence.

2. Stimuli-Responsive Activation

a. **pH-Responsive Systems**: Drug release is triggered by changes in pH. For example, formulations designed to release drugs specifically in the acidic environment of the stomach or the alkaline environment of the intestines.

b. **Temperature-Responsive Systems**: Activation occurs in response to changes in temperature, such as those experienced in the body's various compartments. Thermosensitive polymers undergo a phase transition, leading to drug release.

c. **Enzyme-Responsive Systems**: Release is activated by the presence of specific enzymes in the biological environment. For example, drug release from liposomal formulations triggered by enzymes present in tumors or inflamed tissues.

d. **Redox-Responsive Systems**: Activation is triggered by changes in redox potential. These systems release drugs in response to variations in the oxidative state of tissues or cells.

e. **Mechanical Activation**: Release is activated by mechanical forces, such as pressure or shear stress. Examples include microneedle patches or implantable devices activated by physical manipulation.

3. Externally Triggered Activation

a. **Magnetic Field-Activated Systems**: Drug release is activated by an external magnetic field, which triggers the movement or deformation of magnetic components within the formulation.

b. **Ultrasound-Activated Systems**: Activation occurs in response to ultrasound waves, leading to changes in the structure or properties of the drug delivery system.

c. **Light-Activated Systems**: Release is triggered by exposure to specific wavelengths of light. Light-sensitive molecules or materials undergo a photoreaction, initiating drug release.

4. Biological Activation

a. **Target-Specific Activation**: Activation occurs upon interaction with specific biological targets, such as receptors or antigens. This mechanism ensures localized drug release at the site of action.

b. **Biochemical Activation**: Release is activated by biochemical processes within the body, such as metabolic pathways or signaling cascades.

5. Programmed Activation

a. **Time-Dependent Activation**: Release is activated after a predetermined time interval, allowing for delayed or sustained drug delivery.

b. **Sequential Activation**: Multiple activation mechanisms are employed sequentially, allowing for precise control over drug release kinetics.

MODULATED DRUG DELIVERY SYSTEMS

Modulated drug delivery systems, a subset of rate-controlled drug delivery systems (RCDDS), offer the capability to adjust drug release rates over time according to specific patterns or requirements. These systems provide a more sophisticated approach to drug delivery, allowing for customized dosing regimens and optimized therapeutic outcomes. Here's a detailed exploration of modulated drug delivery systems within the context of RCDDS:

1. Purpose of Modulated Drug Delivery

i. **Tailored Therapy**: Allows for the delivery of drugs at varying rates or doses to match the fluctuating needs of patients or specific disease conditions.

ii. **Optimized Pharmacokinetics**: Mimics physiological drug release patterns, leading to improved drug absorption, distribution, metabolism, and excretion.

iii. **Reduced Side Effects**: Enables the administration of drugs at lower doses or during specific times, minimizing adverse effects while maintaining therapeutic efficacy.

iv. **Enhanced Patient Compliance**: Provides convenient dosing regimens, reducing the frequency of administration and improving patient adherence to treatment.

2. Types of Modulated Drug Delivery Systems

a. Pulsatile Drug Delivery Systems

i. **Principle**: Drug release occurs as discrete pulses or bursts at predefined intervals, mimicking natural physiological rhythms.

ii. **Applications:** Suitable for drugs with circadian or pulsatile release patterns, such as hormones or medications targeting conditions with periodic symptoms (e.g., asthma, angina).

iii. **Mechanisms**: Utilizes swellable polymers, osmotic pumps, or reservoir systems with timed release mechanisms.

b. Chronotherapeutic Drug Delivery Systems

i. **Principle**: Drug release is synchronized with the body's circadian rhythms to optimize therapeutic outcomes.

ii. **Applications**: Ideal for diseases exhibiting time-dependent symptoms or variations in drug metabolism, such as cardiovascular diseases, arthritis, or asthma.

iii. **Mechanisms:** Incorporates time-delayed release formulations, controlled by pH, osmotic pressure, or environmental stimuli.

c. On-Demand Drug Delivery Systems

i. **Principle:** Drug release is triggered in response to specific physiological cues or patient actions.

ii. **Applications**: Used for pain management, contraception, or acute conditions requiring immediate drug delivery upon symptom onset.

iii. **Mechanisms**: Employ stimuli-responsive materials, such as pH-sensitive polymers, temperature-sensitive hydrogels, or enzyme-triggered systems.

d. Programmed Drug Delivery Systems

i. **Principle**: Drug release is programmed to follow a predetermined temporal profile or sequence, allowing for tailored dosing regimens.

ii. **Applications**: Suitable for diseases requiring complex treatment protocols, such as cancer chemotherapy or hormone replacement therapy.

iii. **Mechanisms**: Utilizes multilayered or multiparticulate formulations with varying release kinetics, controlled by different mechanisms.

3. Design Considerations

a. **Release Kinetics**: Selection of appropriate release mechanisms and polymers to achieve the desired release profile.

b. **Triggering Mechanisms**: Incorporation of stimuli-responsive components or external triggers to initiate drug release.

c. **Dosing Regimens**: Determination of optimal dosing intervals, durations, and drug concentrations based on therapeutic requirements and patient preferences.

d. **Formulation Stability**: Ensuring stability and compatibility of the formulation components to maintain the desired release profile over the intended duration.

4. Challenges and Future Directions

a. **Complexity**: Designing and manufacturing modulated drug delivery systems with precise control over release kinetics and response triggers.

b. **Regulatory Approval**: Demonstrating safety, efficacy, and reproducibility of modulated drug delivery systems for clinical use.

c. **Personalized Medicine**: Integration of modulated drug delivery with patient-specific factors, such as genetics, metabolism, and lifestyle, for optimized therapy.

d. **Emerging Technologies**: Exploration of novel materials, nanotechnology, and advanced engineering approaches to enhance the functionality and performance of modulated drug delivery systems.

MECHANICALLY ACTIVATED

Mechanically activated rate-controlled drug delivery systems (RCDDS) rely on physical manipulation or mechanical forces to trigger or modulate drug release. These systems offer unique advantages in terms of precise control over drug release kinetics and targeted delivery. Here's a detailed exploration of mechanically activated RCDDS:

1. Principle of Mechanical Activation

Mechanically activated RCDDS are designed to release drugs in response to specific mechanical stimuli, such as pressure, shear stress, or deformation. These stimuli can be applied externally or internally to the drug delivery system, leading to controlled drug release.

2. Types of Mechanically Activated RCDDS

a. Microneedle Patches

i. **Principle**: Microneedles, typically made of biocompatible polymers or metals, penetrate the skin's outer layers, delivering drugs directly into the underlying tissue layers.

ii. **Activation:** Application of slight pressure or insertion into the skin triggers the dissolution or diffusion of drug-loaded microneedles, facilitating controlled drug release.

b. Implantable Devices

i. **Principle**: Biocompatible implants, such as reservoirs, capsules, or pellets, are placed subcutaneously or within body tissues.

ii. **Activation:** External pressure or mechanical manipulation of the implant triggers drug release by deforming the implant structure or rupturing a membrane barrier.

c. Hydrogels and Responsive Polymers

i. **Principle:** Hydrogels and responsive polymers undergo volume changes or structural transitions in response to mechanical stimuli.

ii. **Activation:** Mechanical deformation or compression of the hydrogel matrix induces drug release by altering its porosity, swelling behavior, or polymer chain conformation.

d. Compression-Activated Tablets

i. **Principle:** Tablets containing drug-loaded reservoirs or compartments are designed to release drugs upon compression or deformation.

ii. **Activation**: Crushing or compressing the tablet disrupts the compartments, allowing drug release through diffusion or erosion mechanisms.

e. Osmotic Pump Systems

i. **Principle**: Osmotic pumps utilize osmotic pressure to drive drug release through a semipermeable membrane.

ii. **Activation:** External pressure applied to the osmotic pump device triggers drug release by compressing the internal reservoir or altering membrane permeability.

3. Applications of Mechanically Activated RCDDS

a. **Pain Management**: Microneedle patches and implantable devices offer controlled delivery of analgesic drugs directly to pain sites, providing localized relief.

b. **Contraception**: Intrauterine devices (IUDs) or implantable contraceptive systems are activated mechanically for controlled release of hormones over extended periods.

c. **Wound Healing**: Hydrogel-based dressings or patches respond to mechanical deformation at the wound site, releasing growth factors or antimicrobial agents to promote healing.

d. **Orthopedic Treatments**: Implantable devices activated by mechanical stress or pressure release drugs locally to treat inflammatory or degenerative joint conditions.

4. Advantages of Mechanically Activated RCDDS

a. **Site-Specific Delivery**: Enables targeted drug delivery to specific anatomical sites or tissues, minimizing systemic exposure and side effects.

b. **Precise Control**: Offers precise control over drug release kinetics, allowing for customized dosing regimens tailored to patient needs.

c. **Enhanced Compliance**: Simplifies drug administration and improves patient adherence by providing convenient and user-friendly dosage forms.

d. **Reduced Toxicity**: Minimizes systemic drug exposure and potential toxicity by delivering drugs directly to the site of action.

5. Challenges and Considerations

a. **Biocompatibility**: Ensuring compatibility of materials with biological tissues to prevent adverse reactions or tissue damage.

b. **Mechanical Stability**: Designing mechanically activated systems that withstand mechanical forces without compromising drug stability or formulation integrity.

c. **Regulatory Approval**: Meeting regulatory requirements for safety, efficacy, and performance of mechanically activated RCDDS for clinical use.

PH ACTIVATED

pH-activated rate-controlled drug delivery systems (RCDDS) are designed to release drugs in response to changes in pH levels within the body. These systems offer precise control over drug release kinetics, enabling targeted delivery to specific physiological environments or tissues. Here's a detailed exploration of pH-activated RCDDS:

1. Principle of pH Activation

pH-activated RCDDS exploit variations in pH levels within different physiological compartments, such as the stomach, intestines, or intracellular environments. Changes in pH trigger alterations in the formulation's properties, leading to controlled drug release.

2. Types of pH-Activated RCDDS

a. Enteric-Coated Formulations

i. **Principle**: Enteric coatings are pH-sensitive polymers that remain intact in the acidic environment of the stomach but dissolve in the alkaline pH of the intestines.

ii. **Activation:** Upon reaching the small intestine, the enteric coating dissolves, allowing drug release in the less acidic environment.

b. pH-Responsive Polymers

i. **Principle:** pH-sensitive polymers undergo conformational changes or solubility alterations in response to changes in pH.

ii. **Activation:** When exposed to specific pH levels, these polymers swell, dissolve, or undergo phase transitions, triggering drug release.

c. Gastric Retentive Systems

i. **Principle:** Formulations are designed to remain in the stomach for prolonged periods, where pH levels are acidic.

ii. **Activation**: Upon exposure to the acidic gastric environment, the formulation undergoes changes, such as swelling or erosion, leading to controlled drug release.

d. pH-Responsive Hydrogels

i. **Principle**: Hydrogels composed of pH-sensitive polymers respond to changes in pH by altering their swelling behavior or network structure.

ii. **Activation**: pH changes induce swelling or collapse of the hydrogel, facilitating drug release.

e. Microbial-Derived Systems

i. **Principle:** Some microorganisms produce enzymes that can degrade pH-sensitive materials, leading to drug release.

ii. **Activation:** Upon encountering specific microbial populations in the gastrointestinal tract, enzymatic degradation of the formulation occurs, triggering drug release.

3. Applications of pH-Activated RCDDS

a. **Gastrointestinal Disorders**: Targeted delivery of drugs to the intestines for the treatment of conditions such as inflammatory bowel disease, ulcerative colitis, or Crohn's disease.

b. **Oral Vaccines**: pH-activated formulations enable the delivery of antigens to the intestinal mucosa, enhancing immune responses for vaccination purposes.

c. **Colon-Specific Drug Delivery**: pH-activated systems deliver drugs to the colon for the treatment of diseases such as colon cancer or colonic infections.

4. Advantages of pH-Activated RCDDS

a. **Targeted Delivery:** Enables precise delivery of drugs to specific regions of the gastrointestinal tract, maximizing therapeutic efficacy and minimizing systemic exposure.

b. **Reduced Side Effects**: Minimizes gastrointestinal irritation or degradation of acid-labile drugs by avoiding release in the stomach.

c. **Enhanced Stability**: Protects drugs from degradation in the acidic stomach environment, preserving their integrity until reaching the target site.

5. Challenges and Considerations

a. **Formulation Stability**: Ensuring stability and integrity of pH-sensitive materials throughout manufacturing, storage, and administration.

b. **Optimization of Release Kinetics**: Fine-tuning the pH-responsive properties of the formulation to achieve the desired drug release profile.

c. **Patient Variability**: Accounting for interindividual variations in gastrointestinal pH levels and transit times when designing pH-activated RCDDS.

ENZYME ACTIVATED

Enzyme-activated rate-controlled drug delivery systems (RCDDS) are designed to release drugs in response to specific enzymes present in biological environments. These systems offer targeted drug delivery, providing controlled release only in tissues or cells where the required enzyme activity is present. Here's a detailed exploration of enzyme-activated RCDDS:

1. Principle of Enzyme Activation

Enzyme-activated RCDDS utilize enzymes as triggers to initiate or modulate drug release. These enzymes catalyze specific biochemical reactions within the drug delivery system, leading to changes in its structure or properties, thereby facilitating drug release.

2. Types of Enzyme-Activated RCDDS

a. Enzyme-Sensitive Polymers

i. **Principle**: Polymers are designed to contain peptide sequences or chemical moieties that are susceptible to enzymatic cleavage.

ii. **Activation**: Upon exposure to the target enzyme, such as proteases, lipases, or glycosidases, the polymer undergoes cleavage, leading to drug release.

b. Prodrug Systems

i. **Principle**: Drugs are conjugated to inactive prodrug moieties, which are selectively activated by specific enzymes.

ii. **Activation**: Enzymatic cleavage of the prodrug by the target enzyme releases the active drug molecule.

c. Enzyme-Responsive Nanoparticles

i. **Principle:** Nanoparticles are designed to encapsulate drugs and enzyme-sensitive components, such as peptide linkers or cross-linkers.

ii. **Activation:** Enzymatic degradation of the nanoparticle matrix by the target enzyme triggers drug release.

d. Enzyme-Triggered Hydrogels

i. **Principle:** Hydrogels contain enzyme-sensitive cross-linking motifs or polymer chains that undergo enzymatic degradation.

ii. **Activation:** Exposure to the target enzyme results in hydrogel degradation, facilitating drug release.

3. Applications of Enzyme-Activated RCDDS

a. **Cancer Therapy:** Enzyme-activated systems enable targeted drug delivery to tumor tissues, where elevated levels of certain enzymes (e.g., matrix metalloproteinases) are present.

b. **Inflammatory Diseases:** Enzyme-responsive formulations deliver anti-inflammatory drugs to inflamed tissues, where enzymes (e.g., elastase, hyaluronidase) play a role in tissue degradation.

c. **Tissue Engineering:** Enzyme-triggered hydrogels facilitate controlled release of growth factors or cytokines in tissue engineering applications, promoting cell proliferation and tissue regeneration.

4. Advantages of Enzyme-Activated RCDDS

a. **Targeted Delivery:** Ensures drug release occurs specifically in tissues or cells where the target enzyme activity is elevated, minimizing off-target effects.

b. **Enhanced Specificity:** Provides precise control over drug release kinetics, leading to improved therapeutic efficacy and reduced systemic toxicity.

c. **Tailored Therapy:** Allows for personalized treatment strategies by selecting enzymes and substrates tailored to individual patient profiles or disease states.

5. Challenges and Considerations

a. **Enzyme Variability**: Consideration of interindividual variability in enzyme expression levels and activity profiles when designing enzyme-activated RCDDS.

b. **Formulation Stability**: Ensuring stability and integrity of enzyme-sensitive components throughout manufacturing, storage, and administration.

c. **Regulatory Approval**: Meeting regulatory requirements for safety, efficacy, and reproducibility of enzyme-activated RCDDS for clinical use.

OSMOTIC ACTIVATED DRUG DELIVERY SYSTEMS FEEDBACK

Osmotic-activated drug delivery systems represent a sophisticated approach to controlled drug release, relying on osmotic pressure differentials to regulate drug delivery. These systems offer precise control over release rates, independent of physiological factors such as pH or enzyme activity. Here's a detailed exploration of osmotic-activated drug delivery systems within the context of rate-controlled drug delivery systems:

1. Principle of Osmotic Activation

Osmotic-activated drug delivery systems function based on the principle of osmosis, where water permeates through a semipermeable membrane from an area of low solute concentration to an area of high solute concentration. This osmotic pressure differential is harnessed to control drug release from the delivery system.

2. Components of Osmotic-Activated Drug Delivery Systems

a. Core Formulation

i. Contains the drug formulation to be delivered.

ii. Often includes osmotic agents or osmotically active compounds to create an osmotic pressure gradient.

b. Semipermeable Membrane

i. Surrounds the core formulation.

ii. Permits the passage of water while restricting the passage of drug molecules and other large solutes.

c. Osmotic Agent

i. Added to the core formulation to create an osmotic pressure gradient across the semipermeable membrane.

ii. Common osmotic agents include salts (e.g., sodium chloride), sugars (e.g., sucrose), or polymers (e.g., polyethylene glycol).

3. Activation Mechanism

a. Osmotic Pressure Gradient

i. Water influx into the osmotic-activated system occurs due to the higher osmotic pressure inside the system compared to the surrounding environment.

ii. This influx of water generates hydrostatic pressure within the system, leading to the expansion of the core formulation and subsequent drug release through an orifice or porous membrane.

b. Controlled Release Mechanism

i. The release rate of the drug is controlled by the properties of the semipermeable membrane and the design of the delivery system.

ii. Factors such as membrane permeability, membrane thickness, and orifice size influence the rate of water influx and, consequently, the rate of drug release.

4. Applications of Osmotic-Activated Drug Delivery Systems

a. **Oral Controlled Release**: Osmotic-activated systems are widely used in oral drug delivery to achieve sustained release profiles, minimizing dosing frequency and improving patient compliance.

b. **Transdermal Delivery**: Osmotic-activated patches can be applied to the skin for controlled release of drugs, offering steady plasma concentrations over extended periods.

c. **Ocular Delivery:** Ophthalmic inserts or implants utilizing osmotic activation provide controlled release of drugs to the eye, enhancing therapeutic efficacy and minimizing side effects.

5. Advantages of Osmotic-Activated Drug Delivery Systems

a. **Precise Control**: Offers precise control over drug release kinetics, ensuring consistent and predictable release rates over time.

b. **Independence from Physiological Factors**: Release rates are not affected by physiological factors such as pH, enzyme activity, or gastrointestinal transit time.

c. **Tailored Release Profiles**: Allows for customization of release profiles to match specific therapeutic needs, including zero-order release or pulsatile release.

6. Challenges and Considerations

a. **System Design Complexity**: Designing osmotic-activated systems requires careful consideration of formulation components, membrane properties, and system geometry to achieve desired release profiles.

b. **Regulatory Approval:** Ensuring compliance with regulatory standards for safety, efficacy, and reproducibility of osmotic-activated drug delivery systems.

c. **Compatibility with Drug Formulations**: Compatibility of drugs with osmotic agents and membrane materials must be assessed to prevent drug degradation or alteration of release kinetics.

REGULATED DRUG DELIVERY SYSTEMS; PRINCIPLES & FUNDAMENTALS

Regulated drug delivery systems form a critical subset of rate-controlled drug delivery systems (RCDDS), designed to ensure precise control over drug release kinetics. These systems are governed by specific principles and fundamentals to achieve targeted and controlled drug delivery. Here's a detailed exploration:

1. Principles of Regulated Drug Delivery Systems:

a. Controlled Release Kinetics:

   i. **Zero-Order Release**: Ensures a constant rate of drug release over time, independent of concentration.

   ii. **First-Order Release:** Rate of drug release decreases exponentially over time.

   iii. **Pulsatile Release**: Drug release occurs as discrete pulses or bursts at predefined intervals.

   iv. **Sigmoidal Release**: Initial lag phase followed by a sustained release period.

b. Trigger Mechanisms:

   i. **Physical Stimuli**: Such as temperature, pressure, or mechanical forces.

   ii. **Chemical Stimuli**: Such as pH, enzymatic activity, or redox potential.

   iii. **Biological Stimuli**: Targeting specific receptors, antigens, or cell types.

c. Formulation Design:

   i. **Core/Matrix Formulations**: Drug is dispersed within a polymer matrix or core, controlling release through diffusion or erosion mechanisms.

   ii. **Coated Systems**: Drug is coated with a polymer membrane or film, controlling release through dissolution or permeation barriers.

   iii. **Implantable Devices**: Biodegradable or non-biodegradable implants for sustained release over extended periods.

   iv. **Osmotic Systems**: Utilize osmotic pressure gradients to control drug release, typically through osmotic pumps or tablets.

2. Fundamentals of Regulated Drug Delivery Systems:

a. Kinetics of Drug Release:

   i. **Fick's Law of Diffusion**: Governs the rate of drug diffusion through a barrier.

   ii. **Matrix Erosion Kinetics**: Describes the erosion or degradation of polymer matrices and its effect on drug release.

iii. **Dissolution Rate:** Determines the rate at which drug molecules dissolve from a solid dosage form.

b. Drug-Polymer Interactions:

i. **Polymer Selection**: Choice of polymers based on their compatibility with the drug, desired release profile, and regulatory considerations.

ii. **Drug Loading**: Optimization of drug loading to ensure uniform distribution and controlled release.

c. Characterization Techniques:

i. **In vitro Release Studies**: Measure drug release from formulations under controlled laboratory conditions.

ii. **Physicochemical Analysis**: Characterize the physical and chemical properties of drug formulations, including particle size, surface morphology, and drug-polymer interactions.

iii. **In vivo Pharmacokinetic Studies**: Assess drug absorption, distribution, metabolism, and excretion in animal models or human subjects.

3. Regulatory Considerations:

a. **Bioequivalence Studies**: Demonstrate that a regulated drug delivery system is equivalent to a reference product in terms of pharmacokinetic parameters.

b. **Stability Testing**: Assess the stability of formulations under various storage conditions to ensure product quality and shelf-life.

c. **Safety and Efficacy Evaluation**: Conduct preclinical and clinical studies to evaluate the safety and efficacy of regulated drug delivery systems.

Multiple Choice Questions (MCQs) from the Context

1. What is the primary function of rate-controlled drug delivery systems (RCDDS)?

    A) To deliver drugs at random rates

B) To minimize therapeutic efficacy

C) To deliver medications at a predetermined and controlled rate

D) To maximize drug toxicity

2. Which system uses osmotic pressure to drive the drug out of a semipermeable membrane at a controlled rate?

A) Diffusion-controlled systems

B) Dissolution-controlled systems

C) Osmotic pumps

D) Ion-exchange systems

3. What advantage does the reservoir system of RCDDS have?

A) Increased side effects

B) Unpredictable drug release

C) Maintains drug levels within the therapeutic window

D) High frequency of dosing

4. Which type of RCDDS involves a drug core surrounded by a polymer membrane?

A) Matrix systems

B) Reservoir systems

C) Injectable systems

D) Transdermal systems

5. What is a common application of osmotically controlled systems like OROS tablets?

A) Topical application

B) Rectal insertion

C) Oral delivery

D) Inhalation

6. Which mechanism describes a drug release system where the drug is dispersed uniformly in a polymer matrix?

A) Surface erosion

B) Diffusion through matrix systems

C) Osmotic pressure control

D) Ion exchange

7. What is one of the future directions for RCDDS mentioned in the text?

    A) Reducing drug delivery accuracy

    B) Decreasing the control over drug release

    C) Incorporating sensors and feedback mechanisms

    D) Simplifying drug delivery systems

8. Which RCDDS mechanism involves using a material that slowly dissolves in bodily fluids to control the drug release rate?

    A) Diffusion-controlled encapsulation

    B) Dissolution-controlled encapsulation

    C) Osmotically controlled release

    D) Erosion-controlled release

9. What type of RCDDS is designed to remain in the stomach for an extended period to release the drug at a controlled rate?

    A) Gastroretentive systems

    B) Transdermal patches

    C) Injectable microspheres

    D) Oral controlled-release systems

10. Which RCDDS is used for delivering medication through the skin into the bloodstream?

    A) Oral tablets

    B) Transdermal patches

    C) Inhalation systems

    D) Injectable systems

11. What is the primary challenge in designing systems that provide consistent and predictable release rates?

    A) Formulation simplicity

B) High production costs

C) Formulation complexity

D) Lack of regulatory pathways

12. Which type of erosion-controlled system degrades the entire matrix uniformly?

A) Surface erosion

B) Bulk erosion

C) Ion-exchange

D) Diffusion-controlled

13. Which type of drug delivery system uses ion-exchange resins to control drug release?

A) Osmotic systems

B) Diffusion-controlled systems

C) Ion-exchange systems

D) Erosion-controlled systems

14. What describes a transdermal RCDDS?

A) Tablets and capsules

B) Patches adhering to the skin

C) Biodegradable implants

D) Microsphere injections

15. What is the main advantage of the ion-exchange systems for RCDDS?

A) High cost-effectiveness

B) Ease of manufacturing

C) Drug is bound to the resin and released upon exchange with ions

D) Immediate drug release

16. What future direction involves enhancing RCDDS to deliver drugs to specific tissues or cells?

A) Reducing therapeutic efficacy

B) Targeted delivery

C) Simplification of regulatory approvals

D) Development of less durable materials

17. What is a significant barrier to the broader adoption of RCDDS?

A) Lack of technology

B) High efficacy and safety

C) Complex regulatory pathways

D) Reduced research interest

18. Which of the following is a benefit of using biodegradable polymers in RCDDS?

A) They increase the frequency of dosing.

B) They provide better control over drug release.

C) They prevent the drug from reaching the targeted site.

D) They extend the duration of clinical testing.

19. Which type of controlled-release system is particularly useful for targeting drug delivery to the colon?

A) Transdermal systems

B) Osmotic pumps

C) Gastroretentive systems

D) Colon-specific delivery systems

20. Which activation mechanism in RCDDS is triggered by temperature changes?

A) pH-responsive

B) Enzyme-responsive

C) Temperature-responsive

D) Mechanical-responsive

Short Answer Type Questions

1. Define rate-controlled drug delivery systems (RCDDS) and explain their purpose.

2. What are the primary advantages of using RCDDS over traditional drug delivery methods?

3. Describe the mechanism of drug release in diffusion-controlled systems.

4. How do dissolution-controlled systems regulate the release of drugs?

5. Explain the role of osmotic pressure in osmotically controlled drug delivery systems.

6. What is the principle of ion-exchange systems in controlling drug release?

7. List and describe two types of erosion-controlled drug delivery systems.

8. Compare and contrast oral controlled-release systems and transdermal systems.

9. What challenges are associated with the development of RCDDS?

10. How do pH-responsive systems activate drug release?

11. Describe the principle of mechanically activated RCDDS.

12. What is the significance of enzyme-activated drug delivery systems?

13. Explain the concept of modulated drug delivery systems and their applications.

14. What are the main design considerations for creating effective RCDDS?

15. How does the physicochemical property of a drug influence its release kinetics in RCDDS?

16. What are gastrointestinal delivery systems and how do they work?

17. Describe one example of an implantable controlled-release system.

18. What role do environmental conditions play in influencing drug release from RCDDS?

19. Explain the concept of zero-order release kinetics.

20. How do osmotic-activated drug delivery systems function?

Long Answer Type Questions

1. Discuss the different mechanisms employed by rate-controlled drug delivery systems to ensure the consistent and predictable release of drugs.

2. Explain the various types of oral controlled-release systems and how they enhance patient compliance and therapeutic efficacy.

3. Describe the role and mechanism of transdermal patches in delivering medications through the skin. Include examples.

4. Evaluate the challenges and future directions of rate-controlled drug delivery systems, particularly focusing on smart drug delivery and targeted delivery.

5. Discuss the activation mechanisms used in RCDDS, including both passive and stimuli-responsive activation.

6. Explain the principles and applications of mechanically activated rate-controlled drug delivery systems.

7. Describe the concept of enzyme-activated drug delivery systems and discuss their advantages and potential applications in medicine.

8. Explain how modulated drug delivery systems provide tailored therapy and discuss the types of these systems with examples.

9. Discuss the impact of environmental conditions and device design on the effectiveness of rate-controlled drug delivery systems.

10. Analyze the regulatory considerations and challenges faced in the development and approval of rate-controlled drug delivery systems.

Answer Key for the MCQs

1. (C) To deliver medications at a predetermined and controlled rate

2. (C) Osmotic pumps

3. (C) Maintains drug levels within the therapeutic window

4. (B) Reservoir systems

5. (C) Oral delivery

6. (B) Diffusion through matrix systems

7. (C) Incorporating sensors and feedback mechanisms

8. (B) Dissolution-controlled encapsulation

9. (A) Gastroretentive systems

10.(B) Transdermal patches

11.(C) Formulation complexity

12.(B) Bulk erosion

13.(C) Ion-exchange systems

14.(B) Patches adhering to the skin

15.(C) Drug is bound to the resin and released upon exchange with ions

16.(B) Targeted delivery

17.(C) Complex regulatory pathways

18.(B) They provide better control over drug release

19.(D) Colon-specific delivery systems

20.(C) Temperature-responsive

CHAPTER – 4

GASTRO-RETENTIVE DRUG DELIVERY SYSTEMS

INTRODUCTION

Overview

Gastro-retentive drug delivery systems (GRDDS) are designed to prolong the retention of the dosage form within the gastrointestinal (GI) tract, particularly in the stomach, thereby enhancing the bioavailability of drugs that have a narrow absorption window in the upper part of the GI tract. These systems offer a promising approach for controlled drug delivery, leading to improved therapeutic efficacy and patient compliance.

Objectives of GRDDS

1. **Prolonged Gastric Retention**: Extend the duration the drug stays in the stomach.

2. **Improved Bioavailability**: Enhance the absorption of drugs that are primarily absorbed in the stomach or upper part of the small intestine.

3. **Reduced Dosing Frequency**: Enable controlled release of the drug over an extended period, reducing the need for frequent dosing.

4. **Enhanced Patient Compliance**: Simplify dosing regimens, which improves adherence to the medication schedule.

Types of Gastro-Retentive Systems

1. **Floating Drug Delivery Systems (FDDS):** These systems remain buoyant on gastric fluid, increasing gastric retention time.

    i. **Effervescent Systems**: Generate gas (CO_2) upon contact with gastric fluids, making the dosage form float.

    ii. **Non-effervescent Systems**: Utilize low-density polymers to keep the dosage form afloat.

2. **Swelling and Expanding Systems**: These systems swell or expand in the stomach, preventing them from passing through the pylorus.

    i. **Hydrogels:** Swell upon contact with gastric fluids.

    ii. **Expandable Devices**: Physically expand in the stomach to a size larger than the pyloric opening.

3. **Mucoadhesive Systems**: Adhere to the gastric mucosa, thereby retaining the dosage form in the stomach for a longer period.

    i. **Polymer**s: Use mucoadhesive polymers that stick to the gastric lining.

4. **High-Density Systems**: These systems are denser than gastric fluids and sink to the bottom of the stomach, remaining in the gastric region.

    i. **Barium Sulfate**: Often used to increase density.

5. **Magnetic Systems**: Utilize a small internal magnet and an external magnet to control the position of the dosage form within the stomach.

Mechanisms of GRDDS

1. **Floating Mechanism**: By maintaining buoyancy, these systems counteract the peristaltic movements and gastric emptying, remaining in the stomach for prolonged periods.

2. **Swelling and Expansion**: These systems increase in size upon contact with gastric fluids, preventing their passage through the pyloric sphincter.

3. **Adhesion to Mucosa**: Mucoadhesive systems adhere to the mucosal lining of the stomach, resisting gastric emptying.

4. **Density-based Retention**: High-density systems settle at the bottom of the stomach, remaining unaffected by gastric emptying dynamics.

Advantages of GRDDS

1. **Improved Drug Bioavailability**: Especially for drugs absorbed in the upper GI tract.

2. **Controlled Drug Release**: Allows for sustained and controlled drug release over extended periods.

3. **Reduced Dosing Frequency**: Enhances patient convenience and compliance.

4. **Targeted Delivery**: Ideal for local treatment in the stomach (e.g., Helicobacter pylori infection).

5. **Minimized Fluctuations in Drug Concentration**: Provides a steady plasma drug concentration.

Limitations and Challenges

1. **Variable Gastric Emptying Rates**: Can affect the consistency of drug delivery.

2. **Gastric Fluid Variability**: Differences in pH and enzymatic activity can impact drug release and absorption.

3. **Food Effects**: Presence of food can alter gastric retention and drug release profiles.

4. **Patient Variability**: Differences in gastric motility and anatomy among individuals.

5. **Formulation Complexity**: Developing a GRDDS requires sophisticated technology and expertise.

Applications

1. **Chronotherapy**: Timing drug release to match biological rhythms.

2. **Antibiotic Treatment**: Prolonged delivery for infections like H. pylori.

3. **Drugs with Absorption Windows**: Ideal for drugs absorbed in the upper GI tract (e.g., riboflavin, levodopa).

4. **Local Stomach Treatment**: For conditions like peptic ulcers and gastritis.

PRINCIPLE OF GASTRO-RETENTIVE DRUG DELIVERY SYSTEMS

The primary principle behind Gastro-Retentive Drug Delivery Systems (GRDDS) is to prolong the residence time of the drug dosage form in the stomach and the upper part of the gastrointestinal (GI) tract. This is achieved through various mechanisms that counteract the natural gastric emptying process. Here, we delve into the principles, mechanisms, and factors influencing the functionality of GRDDS in detail.

Key Principles

1. **Extended Gastric Retention Time:**
   i. GRDDS are designed to remain in the stomach for an extended period, enhancing the absorption of drugs with narrow absorption windows in the upper GI tract.

2. **Control of Drug Release:**
   i. By maintaining the drug in the stomach, GRDDS provide controlled and sustained release, ensuring a consistent drug level in the systemic circulation over time.

3. **Targeted Delivery:**
   i. GRDDS can deliver drugs directly to the site of action within the stomach, making them particularly useful for treating local conditions like peptic ulcers.

Mechanisms of GRDDS

1. **Floating Systems:**
   i. **Effervescent Systems**: These contain gas-generating agents like sodium bicarbonate that react with gastric acid to produce carbon dioxide, which gets trapped in a gel matrix, making the dosage form buoyant.
   ii. **Non-Effervescent Systems**: Use low-density polymers that swell upon contact with gastric fluids, maintaining the dosage form on the surface of the stomach contents.

2. **Swelling and Expanding Systems:**
   i. These systems are designed to swell upon contact with gastric fluids, significantly increasing in size to prevent passing through the pylorus.
   ii. **Hydrogels**: Absorb water and expand.

iii.   **Expandable Devices**: Use polymers that unfold to a larger size once in the stomach.

3. Mucoadhesive Systems:

i.   Utilize bioadhesive polymers that adhere to the gastric mucosa, prolonging the residence time of the drug delivery system in the stomach.

ii.   Common mucoadhesive polymers include chitosan, carbopol, and polycarbophil.

4. High-Density Systems:

i.   Formulated to have a higher density than gastric fluids, these systems settle at the bottom of the stomach, avoiding premature evacuation.

ii.   Materials like barium sulfate or zinc oxide are used to increase density.

5. Magnetic Systems:

i.   Incorporate a small internal magnet within the dosage form and an external magnet worn by the patient to control and retain the position of the drug delivery system in the stomach.

Factors Influencing GRDDS Performance

1. Gastric Motility:

i.   Gastric motility patterns vary with fasting and fed states, influencing the transit time of the dosage form. GRDDS must be designed to withstand these variations.

2. Gastric pH:

i.   The pH of the stomach can influence drug solubility and stability. GRDDS must ensure drug release is not adversely affected by acidic conditions.

3. Gastric Emptying Rate:

i. The rate at which the stomach empties its contents into the small intestine affects drug release and absorption. Factors like meal composition, size, and timing can alter this rate.

4. Food Effects:

i. The presence of food can delay gastric emptying, increase gastric retention time, and affect drug release. GRDDS can leverage this effect to enhance performance.

5. Patient Factors:

i. Variability in gastric physiology among patients, such as differences in gastric pH, motility, and disease states, can impact the effectiveness of GRDDS.

Design Considerations for GRDDS

1. Polymer Selection:

i. Choosing the right polymer is critical for ensuring buoyancy, swelling, mucoadhesion, or density. Biocompatible and biodegradable polymers are preferred.

2. Dosage Form Shape and Size:

i. The shape and size of the dosage form should be optimized to ensure it can be easily ingested and retained in the stomach without causing discomfort.

3. Drug Properties:

i. The physicochemical properties of the drug, such as solubility and stability in gastric conditions, must be considered when designing GRDDS.

4. Release Kinetics:

i. The drug release profile should be tailored to provide a controlled and sustained release, maintaining therapeutic drug levels over the desired period.

CONCEPTS OF GASTRO-RETENTIVE DRUG DELIVERY SYSTEMS

The core concepts of Gastro-Retentive Drug Delivery Systems (GRDDS) revolve around enhancing the retention time of drug formulations within the stomach. This extension is critical for drugs with a narrow absorption window, low solubility at high pH, or those targeting specific sites within the stomach. Below are the detailed concepts underlying GRDDS:

1. Prolonged Gastric Retention

The primary concept of GRDDS is to extend the duration the drug formulation stays in the stomach. This is crucial for:

i. **Narrow Absorption Window**: Drugs absorbed primarily in the upper part of the GI tract.

ii. **Local Treatment**: Conditions requiring drug action in the stomach (e.g., H. pylori infections).

iii. **Enhanced Solubility**: Drugs with better solubility in acidic environments.

2. Mechanisms for Retention

To achieve prolonged gastric retention, GRDDS employ several mechanisms:

1. **Floating Systems:**

    i. **Effervescent Systems**: Utilize gas-generating agents like sodium bicarbonate that react with gastric acid, producing CO_2 that causes the dosage form to float.

    ii. **Non-Effervescent Systems**: Use polymers like hydroxypropyl methylcellulose (HPMC) that swell in gastric fluids, decreasing density and maintaining buoyancy.

2. **Swelling and Expanding Systems:**

    i. **Hydrogels:** These polymers swell significantly upon contact with gastric fluids, increasing in size to prevent passing through the pyloric sphincter.

ii. **Expandable Devices**: Mechanically expand to a size larger than the pyloric opening once they reach the stomach.

3. **Mucoadhesive Systems:**

   i. **Bioadhesive Polymers**: Utilize polymers (e.g., chitosan, carbopol) that adhere to the gastric mucosa, ensuring prolonged gastric residence.

4. **High-Density Systems:**

   i. **Dense Materials**: Use materials like barium sulfate to increase the density of the dosage form, making it sink to the bottom of the stomach and resist gastric emptying.

5. **Magnetic Systems:**

   i. **Internal and External Magnets**: Incorporate small internal magnets in the dosage form and external magnets to control and maintain the position within the stomach.

3. Control of Drug Release

GRDDS are designed to provide controlled and sustained drug release, which is vital for:

   i. **Steady Plasma Drug Concentrations**: Avoids peaks and troughs in drug levels.

   ii. **Reduced Dosing Frequency**: Enhances patient compliance by reducing the number of doses needed per day.

   iii. **Targeted Therapy**: Improves the efficacy of treatments targeting specific regions of the stomach or upper GI tract.

4. Bioavailability Enhancement

By extending the time the drug remains in the stomach, GRDDS enhance the bioavailability of drugs that:

   i. **Are Absorbed in the Upper GI Tract**: Such as riboflavin, furosemide, and ciprofloxacin.

ii. **Have Stability Issues in Alkaline pH**: Drugs that degrade in the higher pH of the intestine can benefit from prolonged stomach residence.

5. Formulation Strategies

The development of GRDDS involves sophisticated formulation strategies to optimize performance:

i. **Polymer Selection**: Choosing appropriate polymers for buoyancy, swelling, adhesion, or density is critical.

ii. **Dosage Form Design**: The shape, size, and physical characteristics of the dosage form must be tailored to ensure retention and patient comfort.

iii. **Drug Properties**: The solubility, stability, and release profile of the drug must be compatible with the GRDDS approach.

6. Physiological Considerations

Understanding the physiological environment of the stomach is crucial for designing effective GRDDS:

i. **Gastric Motility**: Varies between fasting and fed states, influencing the residence time of the dosage form.

ii. **Gastric pH**: Affects drug solubility and stability; GRDDS should be stable in the acidic environment.

iii. **Gastric Emptying Rate**: Affected by food intake, meal size, and composition, which can impact drug release and absorption.

iv. **Patient Variability**: Differences in gastric physiology among patients must be considered during the design and testing of GRDDS.

ADVANTAGES OF GASTRO-RETENTIVE DRUG DELIVERY SYSTEMS

Gastro-Retentive Drug Delivery Systems (GRDDS) offer several significant advantages, making them an attractive option for enhancing the therapeutic efficacy and patient compliance of certain medications. Below is a detailed exploration of the key benefits associated with GRDDS:

1. Improved Bioavailability

i. **Enhanced Absorption**: Drugs with a narrow absorption window in the upper part of the gastrointestinal (GI) tract benefit from prolonged gastric retention, leading to improved bioavailability.

ii. **Acidic Environment Stability**: Drugs that are more soluble or stable in the acidic pH of the stomach (e.g., certain weakly basic drugs) exhibit better absorption and efficacy when retained longer in the stomach.

2. Controlled and Sustained Drug Release

i. **Steady Drug Levels**: GRDDS can maintain steady plasma drug concentrations over extended periods, avoiding the peaks and troughs associated with immediate-release formulations.

ii. **Reduced Dosing Frequency**: By providing a sustained release of the drug, GRDDS reduce the need for frequent dosing, enhancing patient adherence to medication regimens.

3. Enhanced Patient Compliance

i. **Convenience**: With fewer doses required per day, patients find it easier to follow their treatment plans.

ii. **Improved Quality of Life:** Consistent therapeutic effects without the need for multiple daily doses contribute to better management of chronic conditions.

4. Localized Effect in the Stomach

i. **Targeted Therapy:** GRDDS are particularly useful for treating stomach-specific conditions such as peptic ulcers, gastritis, and Helicobacter pylori infections.

ii. **Reduced Systemic Side Effects**: Localized drug action minimizes systemic exposure and associated side effects.

5. Minimized Drug Degradation

i. **Protection from Intestinal Environment**: Drugs that are unstable or degrade in the higher pH of the intestines are protected by remaining in the stomach.

ii. **Improved Efficacy**: Stability in the acidic environment of the stomach ensures that the drug remains effective over the intended period.

6. Better Management of Conditions Requiring Chronotherapy

i. **Timing Drug Release**: GRDDS can be designed to release drugs in sync with the body's circadian rhythms, improving the management of conditions like hypertension and arthritis, where symptoms vary over a 24-hour period.

7. Flexibility in Formulation

i. **Versatility**: GRDDS can be formulated using various approaches (e.g., floating, swelling, mucoadhesive systems), allowing for tailored drug delivery solutions based on the specific needs of the drug and the therapeutic requirements.

ii. **Innovative Delivery**: Advanced technologies such as magnetic systems offer novel ways to control drug positioning and release within the stomach.

8. Application to a Wide Range of Drugs

i. **Weakly Basic Drugs**: Drugs that exhibit poor solubility at higher pH levels benefit significantly from prolonged exposure to the stomach's acidic environment.

ii. **Low Dose and Potent Drugs**: GRDDS are ideal for drugs requiring precise dosing and controlled release, especially when high potency and low doses are involved.

9. Potential for Reduced Side Effects

i. **Localized Drug Action**: Reducing the systemic exposure of drugs by targeting the stomach can lead to fewer side effects and improved patient tolerability.

ii. **Controlled Release**: Gradual drug release prevents high peak plasma concentrations, which can be associated with adverse effects.

10. Enhanced Therapeutic Efficacy

i. **Optimized Drug Utilization**: Prolonged and controlled release ensures that the drug is released at the optimal rate and site, maximizing therapeutic benefits.

ii. **Improved Symptom Control**: Consistent drug levels help in better management of chronic conditions, leading to better symptom control and patient outcomes.

DISADVANTAGES OF GASTRO-RETENTIVE DRUG DELIVERY SYSTEMS

While Gastro-Retentive Drug Delivery Systems (GRDDS) offer numerous benefits, they also come with several challenges and disadvantages. These drawbacks can impact their effectiveness, patient compliance, and overall therapeutic outcomes. Below is a detailed discussion of the key disadvantages associated with GRDDS:

1. Variable Gastric Emptying Rates

i. **Inter-Individual Variability**: Differences in gastric emptying rates among patients can lead to inconsistent drug release and absorption.

ii. **Influence of Food**: The presence of food, its composition, and meal size can significantly alter gastric emptying rates, impacting the performance of GRDDS.

2. Gastric pH Variability

i. **pH Differences**: Variations in gastric pH, influenced by factors such as age, diet, and disease states (e.g., achlorhydria), can affect drug solubility and stability, leading to unpredictable drug release profiles.

3. Patient-Dependent Factors

i. **Gastric Motility Disorders**: Conditions like gastroparesis (delayed gastric emptying) can hinder the performance of GRDDS.

ii. **Inter-Patient Variability**: Differences in gastric physiology among patients can lead to varied therapeutic outcomes, making it challenging to standardize dosing regimens.

4. Limited to Specific Drugs

i. **Drug Characteristics**: GRDDS are suitable only for drugs that are stable and soluble in the acidic environment of the stomach and those with narrow absorption windows in the upper GI tract. Drugs absorbed in the lower intestines or colon are not suitable for GRDDS.

5. Complex Formulation Requirements

i. **Development and Manufacturing**: Formulating GRDDS requires sophisticated technology and expertise, increasing the complexity and cost of development and manufacturing.

ii. **Polymer Selection**: Choosing the right polymer for buoyancy, swelling, mucoadhesion, or density can be challenging and requires extensive research and development.

6. Potential for Dose Dumping

i. **Risk of Rapid Release**: If the GRDDS fails to function as intended (e.g., due to premature disintegration or mechanical failure), it can lead to rapid drug release (dose dumping), causing toxicity or reduced therapeutic efficacy.

7. Adverse Reactions

i. **Gastrointestinal Irritation**: Prolonged contact of the dosage form with the gastric mucosa can cause irritation or damage, particularly if the formulation contains irritant excipients or high drug concentrations.

ii. **Patient Discomfort**: Swelling or expanding systems may cause a feeling of fullness or discomfort in some patients.

8. Complicated Regulatory Approval

i. **Regulatory Challenges**: The novel nature and complexity of GRDDS formulations can pose challenges in obtaining regulatory approval.

Extensive testing is required to demonstrate safety, efficacy, and consistent performance.

9. Potential Impact of Disease States

i. **GI Diseases**: Conditions such as peptic ulcers, Crohn's disease, or other gastrointestinal disorders can impact the performance and safety of GRDDS.

ii. **Altered Physiology**: Changes in the GI tract's structure or function due to disease can affect the retention and release profile of the drug.

10. Limited to Oral Administration

i. **Mode of Delivery**: GRDDS are specifically designed for oral administration and are not suitable for drugs that require parenteral, transdermal, or other non-oral routes of administration.

11. Environmental and Lifestyle Factors

i. **Lifestyle Influences**: Factors such as smoking, alcohol consumption, and stress can influence gastric motility and pH, potentially affecting GRDDS performance.

ii. **Dietary Habits**: Variations in diet, including the consumption of high-fat or highly fibrous meals, can impact the retention and release characteristics of GRDDS.

MODULATION OF GI TRANSIT TIME APPROACHES TO EXTEND GI TRANSIT

Modulating the gastrointestinal (GI) transit time is a critical strategy in the design of Gastro-Retentive Drug Delivery Systems (GRDDS). The primary goal is to extend the residence time of the drug formulation in the stomach and upper GI tract, ensuring prolonged drug release and absorption. Here are detailed approaches employed to modulate and extend GI transit time in GRDDS:

1. Floating Drug Delivery Systems (FDDS)

Floating systems are designed to remain buoyant on gastric fluids, thereby prolonging gastric residence time.

i. **Effervescent Systems:**

    a. **Mechanism**: Utilize gas-generating agents like sodium bicarbonate, citric acid, or tartaric acid. These agents react with gastric acid to produce carbon dioxide, which is trapped in the hydrocolloid matrix, causing the dosage form to float.

    b. **Example**: Effervescent tablets and capsules.

ii. **Non-Effervescent Systems:**

    a. **Mechanism:** Utilize swellable polymers like hydroxypropyl methylcellulose (HPMC), polyacrylates, or polysaccharides that swell upon contact with gastric fluids, decreasing the density of the system and keeping it afloat.

    b. **Example**: Alginate beads, floating matrix tablets.

2. Swelling and Expanding Systems

These systems swell significantly or expand in size upon contact with gastric fluids, preventing their passage through the pyloric sphincter.

i. **Hydrogels:**

    a. **Mechanism**: Use superabsorbent polymers that can swell to several times their original volume. The swollen system remains in the stomach for an extended period due to its increased size.

    b. **Example**: Polyvinyl alcohol (PVA), polyethylene oxide (PEO).

ii. **Expandable Devices:**

    a. **Mechanism**: Devices designed to unfold or expand to a size that prevents gastric emptying. These devices can be made from shape memory polymers or unfoldable structures.

    b. **Example**: Geometrically expandable systems.

3. Mucoadhesive Systems

Mucoadhesive systems adhere to the gastric mucosa, thereby extending the gastric residence time.

   i.   **Mucoadhesive Polymers:**

      a. **Mechanism**: Polymers such as chitosan, carbopol, and polycarbophil interact with the mucin layer covering the mucosal epithelium. This interaction involves hydrogen bonding, electrostatic attraction, or hydrophobic interactions.

      b. **Example:** Mucoadhesive tablets and films.

4. High-Density Systems

High-density systems are designed to sink and remain at the bottom of the stomach.

   i.   **High-Density Materials:**

      a. **Mechanism:** Formulations with a density higher than gastric fluids (usually greater than 1.5 g/cm^3) sink to the bottom of the stomach and resist being swept away by peristaltic movements.

      b. **Example:** Use of dense materials like barium sulfate, zinc oxide.

5. Magnetic Systems

Magnetic systems utilize an external magnetic field to control the position of the dosage form within the stomach.

   i.   **Internal Magnets:**

      a. **Mechanism:** Incorporate small magnets within the dosage form and use an external magnet placed over the stomach area to retain the dosage form in the stomach.

      b. **Example**: Magnetically controlled tablets.

6. Bioadhesive Systems

Bioadhesive systems adhere to the mucosal surfaces of the GI tract.

   i.   **Bioadhesive Polymers:**

a. **Mechanism**: Use polymers that can bind to the mucosal surface through various interactions, extending the GI transit time.

b. **Example:** Bioadhesive tablets and patches using polymers like polycarbophil, hyaluronic acid.

7. Superporous Hydrogel Systems

These systems are characterized by their fast-swelling properties.

i. **Superporous Hydrogels:**

a. **Mechanism**: Contain interconnected pores that absorb water rapidly, leading to quick swelling and prolonged retention in the stomach.

b. **Example**: Superporous hydrogel composites.

8. Raft-Forming Systems

Raft-forming systems create a viscous cohesive gel in contact with gastric fluids.

i. **Raft-Forming Agents:**

a. **Mechanism**: Typically composed of alginic acid and sodium bicarbonate. Upon contact with gastric acid, a gel-like raft forms that floats on the gastric contents, preventing the reflux and prolonging the drug's presence in the stomach.

b. **Example**: Alginates in antacid formulations.

BUCCAL DRUG DELIVERY SYSTEMS

Buccal Drug Delivery Systems and Gastro-Retentive Drug Delivery Systems (GRDDS) are distinct approaches within the realm of advanced drug delivery, each targeting different anatomical sites and utilizing unique mechanisms for drug release and absorption. Below, we detail the principles, mechanisms, advantages, and challenges of Buccal Drug Delivery Systems within the context of Gastro-Retentive Drug Delivery Systems.

Key Concepts

1. **Buccal Mucosa:**

i. The buccal mucosa is well-vascularized, providing a rich supply of blood vessels that facilitates rapid drug absorption directly into the systemic circulation, bypassing the first-pass metabolism in the liver.

2. Drug Absorption:

i. Drugs administered via the buccal route can be absorbed through the buccal mucosal membrane, entering the systemic circulation more directly than oral administration.

Mechanisms of Buccal Drug Delivery

1. Bioadhesion:

i. **Bioadhesive Polymers**: These systems use bioadhesive polymers such as chitosan, polyvinyl alcohol, and carbopol to adhere to the buccal mucosa, allowing prolonged retention and enhanced absorption.

ii. **Examples**: Bioadhesive patches, tablets, and films.

2. Permeation Enhancers:

i. **Mechanism**: Permeation enhancers are substances that increase the permeability of the buccal mucosa, facilitating greater drug absorption.

ii. **Examples:** Use of surfactants, bile salts, and fatty acids.

3. Mucoadhesive Drug Delivery Systems:

i. **Mechanism**: Utilize polymers that adhere to the mucin layer covering the buccal mucosa, ensuring the drug remains in contact with the absorption site for extended periods.

ii. **Examples:** Mucoadhesive buccal films and tablets.

Advantages of Buccal Drug Delivery

1. Bypass First-Pass Metabolism:

i. Drugs absorbed through the buccal mucosa bypass the hepatic first-pass effect, leading to increased bioavailability.

2. **Rapid Onset of Action:**
   i. Direct absorption into the systemic circulation results in a quicker onset of action compared to oral administration.

3. **Improved Patient Compliance:**
   i. Non-invasive and easy administration makes buccal delivery a patient-friendly option, especially for those who have difficulty swallowing pills.

4. **Controlled and Sustained Release:**
   i. Buccal drug delivery systems can be designed to release the drug in a controlled and sustained manner, ensuring prolonged therapeutic effects.

5. **Localized Treatment:**
   i. Suitable for local treatment of oral conditions, such as mouth ulcers and fungal infections.

Challenges of Buccal Drug Delivery

1. **Limited Absorption Area:**
   i. The surface area available for drug absorption in the buccal mucosa is relatively small compared to the GI tract.

2. **Mucosal Barrier:**
   i. The presence of saliva and the mucosal barrier can limit drug permeability and absorption.

3. **Patient Factors:**
   i. Variability in the salivary flow and mucosal health among patients can affect the consistency of drug absorption.

4. **Taste and Irritation:**
   i. Unpleasant taste or irritation at the site of application can affect patient compliance.

Integration of Buccal Systems within GRDDS Context

Although Buccal Drug Delivery Systems and GRDDS target different sites and use different mechanisms, there are some parallels and potential integrations:

1. **Mucoadhesion:**
    i. Both systems often utilize mucoadhesive polymers to prolong the residence time of the drug at the absorption site, whether in the buccal cavity or the stomach.

2. **Controlled Release:**
    i. Both delivery systems aim to provide controlled and sustained release of drugs to improve therapeutic outcomes.

3. **Patient Compliance:**
    i. Enhancing patient compliance through non-invasive delivery methods and reducing dosing frequency is a common goal of both systems.

4. **Bypass of Certain Barriers:**
    i. Buccal systems bypass hepatic first-pass metabolism, while GRDDS aim to maintain drugs in the stomach for drugs that benefit from gastric retention or are unstable in the intestinal environment.

PRINCIPLE OF MUCO ADHESION

Mucoadhesion is a key strategy used in Gastro-Retentive Drug Delivery Systems (GRDDS) to prolong the retention time of a dosage form in the gastrointestinal (GI) tract. By adhering to the mucosal lining of the stomach, these systems can enhance the bioavailability and efficacy of drugs with narrow absorption windows or those targeting specific sites within the stomach. Below is a detailed exploration of the principle of mucoadhesion in GRDDS.

Fundamental Concepts of Mucoadhesion

1. **Mucoadhesion:**

a. **Definition**: Mucoadhesion refers to the adhesion of a drug delivery system to the mucosal surface of the GI tract, particularly the stomach, to extend its retention time and improve drug absorption.

b. **Mechanism:** This adhesion is achieved through the interaction between the mucoadhesive polymers in the drug delivery system and the mucin layer covering the gastric mucosa.

2. **Mucosal Surface:**

a. **Composition**: The mucosal lining is composed of a layer of mucus, primarily consisting of glycoproteins known as mucins, water, electrolytes, enzymes, and lipids.

b. **Role in Mucoadhesion**: The mucus layer provides the substrate to which the mucoadhesive drug delivery systems adhere.

Mechanisms of Mucoadhesion

Mucoadhesion occurs through a series of steps, generally classified into two main stages: the contact stage and the consolidation stage.

1. **Contact Stage:**

a. **Wet Adhesion**: The dosage form comes into contact with the mucosal surface, often facilitated by the presence of moisture, which allows the mucoadhesive polymers to hydrate and swell.

b. **Initial Contact**: Physical forces such as electrostatic attraction, van der Waals forces, and hydrogen bonding help in the initial attachment of the dosage form to the mucus layer.

2. **Consolidation Stage:**

a. **Interpenetration and Bonding**: The hydrated mucoadhesive polymers interpenetrate with the mucin network, forming stronger bonds through various interactions:

   i. **Hydrogen Bonding**: Between the functional groups of the polymer and the mucin glycoproteins.

ii. **Electrostatic Interactions**: Between charged groups on the polymer and the mucus.

iii. **Hydrophobic Interactions**: Between hydrophobic regions of the polymer and the mucosal surface.

b. **Entanglement**: Polymer chains can entangle with the glycoprotein chains in the mucus, further stabilizing the attachment.

Mucoadhesive Polymers

The choice of polymer is crucial for effective mucoadhesion. Commonly used mucoadhesive polymers include:

1. **Natural Polymers:**

    i. **Chitosan:** Positively charged, interacts strongly with the negatively charged mucosal surface.

    ii. **Alginate**: Forms a gel in the presence of divalent cations, providing a mucoadhesive matrix.

2. **Synthetic Polymers:**

    i. **Polyacrylic Acid (Carbopol):** Swells significantly in the presence of water, forming strong hydrogen bonds with mucin.

    ii. **Hydroxypropyl Methylcellulose (HPMC):** Hydrophilic and forms a gel upon hydration, adhering to the mucosal surface.

3. **Semi-Synthetic Polymers:**

    i. **Cellulose Derivatives**: Such as methylcellulose and ethylcellulose, which swell and adhere to the mucosa.

Advantages of Mucoadhesive GRDDS

1. **Prolonged Gastric Retention:**

    i. Enhanced residence time in the stomach ensures that the drug remains in the optimal absorption site for a longer period, improving bioavailability.

2. **Localized Drug Action:**

i. Ideal for drugs targeting stomach-specific conditions, providing localized treatment and reduced systemic side effects.

3. **Controlled Release:**

i. Mucoadhesive systems can be designed for controlled and sustained drug release, ensuring a consistent therapeutic effect over an extended period.

4. **Improved Patient Compliance:**

i. By reducing the frequency of dosing due to sustained drug release, patient adherence to the medication regimen can be improved.

Challenges and Considerations

i. **Mucus Turnover:**

a. The natural turnover of mucus in the stomach can affect the duration of mucoadhesion and, consequently, the retention time of the dosage form.

ii. **Environmental Factors:**

a. Variations in pH, presence of food, and gastric motility can impact the effectiveness of mucoadhesive systems.

iii. **Patient Variability:**

a. Differences in mucus composition and thickness among individuals can lead to variability in drug delivery performance.

iv. **Potential for Irritation:**

a. Prolonged contact of the mucoadhesive system with the gastric mucosa may cause irritation or discomfort in some patients.

ADVANTAGES OF BUCCAL DRUG DELIVERY SYSTEMS

Buccal Drug Delivery Systems and Gastro-Retentive Drug Delivery Systems (GRDDS) are both advanced approaches to drug delivery, each offering unique advantages for specific applications. Below, we detail the advantages of Buccal Drug Delivery Systems and explore how their principles and benefits can complement the goals of GRDDS.

Advantages of Buccal Drug Delivery Systems

1. Bypass of First-Pass Metabolism

i. **Direct Systemic Absorption**: Drugs administered buccally are absorbed directly into the bloodstream through the buccal mucosa, bypassing the hepatic first-pass metabolism. This can significantly increase the bioavailability of drugs that are extensively metabolized by the liver.

ii. **Example**: Drugs such as nitroglycerin, which are subject to substantial first-pass metabolism, show enhanced bioavailability when administered buccally.

2. Rapid Onset of Action

i. **Fast Absorption**: The rich vascularization of the buccal mucosa allows for rapid drug absorption, leading to a quick onset of action. This is particularly advantageous for drugs requiring immediate therapeutic effects.

ii. **Example:** Analgesics and antianginal medications that need to act quickly can benefit from buccal administration.

3. Improved Patient Compliance

i. **Ease of Administration**: Buccal drug delivery is non-invasive and can be more convenient for patients compared to injections or swallowing tablets, especially for those who have difficulty swallowing (dysphagia).

ii. **Discreet and Comfortable**: Buccal systems, such as films and tablets, are easy to use and can be administered discreetly, enhancing patient comfort and compliance.

4. Avoidance of Gastrointestinal Issues

i. **Protection from GI Environment**: Drugs that are unstable, poorly absorbed, or degraded in the harsh acidic environment of the stomach or by digestive enzymes benefit from buccal administration.

ii. **Example:** Peptide and protein drugs that are susceptible to enzymatic degradation in the GI tract can be effectively delivered via the buccal route.

5. Localized Treatment

i. **Targeted Therapy**: Buccal delivery is advantageous for local treatment of conditions in the oral cavity, such as oral infections, ulcers, and pain relief.

ii. **Example:** Topical anesthetics and antifungal agents used for oral conditions can be directly applied to the buccal mucosa for effective localized treatment.

6. Reduced Side Effects

i. **Lower Dosing Requirements**: Enhanced bioavailability and targeted delivery can lead to lower required doses, potentially reducing systemic side effects.

ii. **Example**: Medications like hormone therapies can achieve therapeutic levels with lower doses when administered buccally, minimizing side effects.

Complementary Advantages within the Context of GRDDS

While buccal drug delivery and GRDDS operate in different regions of the GI tract and employ different mechanisms, their principles can complement each other in the broader scope of advanced drug delivery:

1. Enhanced Bioavailability

i. **Synergistic Approaches**: Combining the bioavailability benefits of buccal delivery with the targeted and prolonged release properties of GRDDS can optimize overall therapeutic outcomes for certain drugs.

ii. **Example:** A patient may use a buccal delivery system for immediate relief of symptoms while a GRDDS provides sustained release of medication for ongoing treatment.

2. Patient-Centric Designs

i. **Improved Compliance and Flexibility**: Both systems offer non-invasive, patient-friendly options that can be tailored to individual patient needs, enhancing adherence and treatment effectiveness.

ii. **Example**: For chronic conditions requiring both immediate and sustained drug levels, a combination of buccal and gastro-retentive formulations could be employed.

3. Targeted Delivery and Reduced Dosage Frequency

i. **Localized and Prolonged Action**: GRDDS provide prolonged gastric retention for drugs targeting the stomach, while buccal delivery offers rapid systemic absorption. Together, they can reduce the need for frequent dosing.

ii. **Example**: In diseases requiring both localized treatment in the stomach and rapid systemic action, such as certain types of gastrointestinal cancers or infections, using both delivery systems strategically can maximize therapeutic effects.

4. Avoidance of GI Degradation

i. **Protection from Enzymatic Degradation**: Drugs that are sensitive to gastric enzymes can be protected using buccal delivery for systemic absorption, while GRDDS can deliver drugs stable in the stomach for localized treatment.

ii. **Example**: Insulin, which is degraded in the GI tract, can be delivered buccally for systemic effects, while GRDDS can be used for stable compounds needing extended gastric retention.

DISADVANTAGES OF BUCCAL DRUG DELIVERY SYSTEMS

While Buccal Drug Delivery Systems offer several advantages, they also come with specific limitations and challenges that can impact their effectiveness and application. Understanding these disadvantages is crucial for optimizing drug delivery strategies. Here, we explore the disadvantages of Buccal Drug

Delivery Systems in detail and discuss their relevance in the context of Gastro-Retentive Drug Delivery Systems (GRDDS).

1. Limited Absorption Area

i. **Small Surface Area**: The buccal mucosa provides a relatively small surface area for drug absorption compared to the extensive surface area of the gastrointestinal (GI) tract.

    a. **Impact**: This limitation can reduce the total amount of drug that can be absorbed, making it unsuitable for drugs requiring large doses.

2. Mucosal Barrier

i. **Mucus Layer:** The buccal mucosa is covered by a mucus layer that can act as a barrier to drug absorption.

    a. **Impact:** This barrier can limit the rate and extent of drug penetration, affecting bioavailability.

    b. **Example**: Hydrophilic drugs may have difficulty crossing the hydrophobic mucus barrier.

3. Saliva Production

i. **Constant Saliva Flow**: Continuous production and presence of saliva in the oral cavity can dilute and wash away the drug, reducing the contact time with the mucosal surface.

    a. **Impact:** This can lead to inconsistent drug absorption and reduced therapeutic effectiveness.

    b. **Example:** Drugs that require prolonged contact with the mucosa may have their efficacy compromised by saliva.

4. Taste and Mouthfeel

i. **Unpleasant Taste**: Many drugs have a bitter or unpleasant taste, which can be challenging to mask in buccal formulations.

    a. **Impact**: This can lead to poor patient compliance, especially for long-term treatments.

b. **Example**: Bitter-tasting drugs may need additional excipients or flavoring agents to improve acceptability.

5. Irritation and Sensitivity

i. **Mucosal Irritation**: Prolonged contact of certain drugs or excipients with the buccal mucosa can cause irritation or sensitivity.

a. **Impact:** This can lead to discomfort, ulceration, or allergic reactions, negatively affecting patient compliance.

b. **Example**: Drugs with acidic or alkaline pH may cause mucosal irritation.

6. Variable Drug Absorption

i. **Inter-Patient Variability**: Differences in the thickness of the mucosal layer, saliva composition, and enzymatic activity can lead to variability in drug absorption among different patients.

a. **Impact**: This variability can result in inconsistent therapeutic outcomes and dosing challenges.

7. Short Retention Time

i. **Limited Residence Time**: The natural movements of the mouth, such as chewing, speaking, and swallowing, can dislodge the buccal dosage form, reducing its retention time.

a. **Impact**: This can compromise the sustained release and absorption of the drug.

b. **Example**: Buccal patches or films may not remain in place long enough to deliver the desired dose.

Disadvantages in the Context of GRDDS

When comparing and integrating the disadvantages of Buccal Drug Delivery Systems within the context of GRDDS, several points of distinction and overlap emerge:

1. Target Site Differences

i. **Different Anatomical Targets**: Buccal systems target the oral mucosa, while GRDDS aim to retain drugs in the stomach. Each system faces unique challenges based on their target sites.

   a. **Impact:** The disadvantages specific to each system do not generally overlap, as they operate in different parts of the GI tract.

2. Absorption and Bioavailability

i. **Absorption Challenges**: Both systems aim to improve bioavailability, but buccal systems face barriers like limited surface area and saliva dilution, whereas GRDDS deal with variable gastric emptying and pH differences.

   a. **Impact**: Understanding these distinct challenges is crucial for selecting the appropriate delivery system for a specific drug.

3. Patient Compliance

i. **Compliance Issues**: Buccal systems may suffer from taste issues and mucosal irritation, while GRDDS may cause gastric discomfort or require complex administration.

   a. **Impact**: Both systems need to address patient comfort and ease of use to ensure compliance.

MECHANISM OF DRUG PERMEATION

The mechanism of drug permeation in Gastro-Retentive Drug Delivery Systems (GRDDS) involves the controlled release of the drug from the dosage form, followed by its absorption across the gastrointestinal (GI) mucosa. GRDDS are designed to prolong the residence time of drugs in the stomach or upper GI tract, allowing for sustained release and enhanced absorption. Here's a detailed explanation of the mechanisms involved:

1. Drug Release Mechanisms in GRDDS:

a. Matrix Systems:

i. **Matrix Formation**: In matrix-based GRDDS, the drug is uniformly dispersed within a polymeric matrix.

ii. **Swelling and Erosion**: Upon contact with gastric fluids, the polymer matrix swells, forming a gel layer around the dosage form. This gel layer controls drug release by diffusion and erosion.

iii. **Diffusion**: The dissolved drug diffuses through the swollen matrix and the gel layer, gradually releasing into the surrounding gastric fluids.

iv. **Erosion:** Over time, the polymer matrix undergoes erosion due to the action of gastric fluids, releasing the entrapped drug particles.

b. Floating Systems:

i. **Buoyancy:** Floating GRDDS are designed to float on the gastric fluids, prolonging their residence time in the stomach.

ii. **Gas Generation**: Effervescent agents within the dosage form react with gastric acid to generate carbon dioxide gas. This gas gets trapped in the dosage form, reducing its density and causing it to float.

iii. **Drug Release**: While floating, the dosage form releases the drug either through diffusion from a matrix or through erosion of a floating layer, allowing for controlled drug release.

c. Bioadhesive Systems:

i. **Mucoadhesion:** Bioadhesive polymers present in the dosage form adhere to the mucosal lining of the stomach.

ii. **Retention**: This adhesion prolongs the residence time of the dosage form in the stomach, enhancing drug absorption.

iii. **Drug Release**: The drug is released from the bioadhesive dosage form through diffusion, erosion, or desorption, depending on the formulation design.

2. Drug Permeation Mechanisms in GRDDS:

a. Diffusion:

i. **Passive Diffusion**: Most drugs permeate across the GI mucosa through passive diffusion, driven by concentration gradients.

ii. **Concentration Gradient**: The drug molecules dissolve in the gastric fluids and diffuse across the mucosal epithelial cells into the bloodstream.

iii. **Factors Affecting Diffusion**: Factors such as drug solubility, molecular size, lipid solubility, and pH gradient influence the rate and extent of drug diffusion.

b. Paracellular Transport:

i. **Interstitial Pathway**: Some drugs may permeate through the tight junctions between epithelial cells via paracellular transport.

ii. **Limited Contribution**: Paracellular transport usually contributes minimally to drug absorption due to the tightness of the epithelial cell junctions.

c. Carrier-Mediated Transport:

i. **Active Transport**: Certain drugs utilize carrier proteins or transporters to facilitate their absorption across the mucosal membrane.

ii. **Specific Binding**: The drug binds to specific transporter proteins present on the epithelial cell membrane, allowing for facilitated transport into the bloodstream.

iii. **Energy Requirement**: Active transport often requires energy expenditure in the form of ATP hydrolysis.

d. Endocytosis:

i. **Vesicular Transport**: Large molecules or particles may be absorbed through endocytosis, where the cell membrane invaginates to engulf the drug-containing vesicles.

ii. **Transcellular Transport**: Endocytosed vesicles are transported across the epithelial cell and released into the interstitial space.

METHODS OF FORMULATION OF BUCCAL DRUG DELIVERY SYSTEMS

Formulating Buccal Drug Delivery Systems within the framework of Gastro-Retentive Drug Delivery Systems (GRDDS) requires careful consideration of both buccal and gastric retention properties. These systems aim to deliver drugs through the buccal mucosa while ensuring prolonged retention in the stomach for localized or systemic effects. Here's a detailed overview of the methods used in the formulation of Buccal Drug Delivery Systems within GRDDS:

1. Film-Based Systems:

a. Mucoadhesive Films:

i. **Composition**: These films consist of mucoadhesive polymers such as hydroxypropyl methylcellulose (HPMC), sodium alginate, chitosan, and polyvinyl alcohol (PVA).

ii. **Formulation**: Polymers are dissolved or dispersed in a solvent along with the drug and other excipients. The solution is then cast into thin films using methods like solvent casting or hot-melt extrusion.

iii. **Mucoadhesion Enhancement**: Addition of mucoadhesive enhancers such as Carbopol, guar gum, or xanthan gum can improve adhesion to the buccal mucosa.

b. Dissolvable Films:

i. **Composition**: These films are typically made of water-soluble polymers such as hydroxypropyl cellulose (HPC), pullulan, or polyvinylpyrrolidone (PVP).

ii. **Formulation**: The polymers, drug, and other excipients are dissolved in a suitable solvent, and the solution is cast into films. Upon administration, the film dissolves in saliva, releasing the drug for absorption.

iii. **Rapid Drug Release**: Dissolvable films offer rapid drug release and can be advantageous for drugs requiring immediate onset of action.

2. Tablet-Based Systems:

a. Mucoadhesive Tablets:

i. **Composition**: Tablets contain mucoadhesive polymers along with the drug and other excipients.

ii. **Formulation**: Mucoadhesive polymers such as chitosan, Carbopol, or HPMC are mixed with the drug and compressed into tablets using direct compression or wet granulation methods.

iii. **Extended Contact Time**: Mucoadhesive tablets adhere to the buccal mucosa, allowing for prolonged drug release and absorption.

b. Floating Tablets:

i. **Composition**: These tablets contain floating agents such as gas-generating agents (e.g., sodium bicarbonate) or low-density materials (e.g., microcrystalline cellulose).

ii. **Formulation**: Tablets are formulated using effervescent excipients or by incorporating low-density materials to ensure buoyancy in gastric fluids.

iii. **Prolonged Gastric Retention**: Floating tablets remain buoyant in the stomach, prolonging their residence time and enhancing drug absorption.

3. Gel-Based Systems:

a. Mucoadhesive Gels:

i. **Composition**: These gels contain mucoadhesive polymers dispersed in a suitable gel-forming base such as Carbopol gel or Pluronic gel.

ii. **Formulation**: Mucoadhesive polymers are dispersed or dissolved in the gel base along with the drug and other excipients. The gel is then applied to the buccal mucosa using a syringe or applicator.

iii. **Site-Specific Application**: Mucoadhesive gels allow for targeted delivery to specific areas of the buccal cavity, ensuring prolonged drug contact with the mucosa.

b. Thermosensitive Gels:

i. **Composition**: These gels undergo sol-gel transition in response to temperature changes, forming a gel at body temperature.

ii. **Formulation**: Thermosensitive polymers such as Pluronic F-127 or poloxamer are dissolved in a liquid state along with the drug and other excipients. Upon administration, the gel forms at the site of application, providing sustained drug release.

iii. **Ease of Application**: Thermosensitive gels offer ease of administration and can adhere to the buccal mucosa, prolonging drug contact time.

4. Patch-Based Systems:

a. Mucoadhesive Patches:

i. **Composition**: These patches consist of mucoadhesive polymers embedded in a backing layer.

ii. **Formulation:** Mucoadhesive polymers are dispersed or dissolved in a suitable adhesive matrix along with the drug and other excipients. The formulation is then coated onto a backing layer to form the patch.

iii. **Extended Release**: Mucoadhesive patches adhere to the buccal mucosa, allowing for controlled and sustained drug release over an extended period.

b. Dissolvable Patches:

i. **Composition**: These patches are made of water-soluble polymers.

ii. **Formulation**: Water-soluble polymers such as pullulan or PVP are cast into thin films along with the drug and other excipients. The films are then cut into patches of appropriate size.

iii. **Rapid Dissolution**: Dissolvable patches disintegrate upon contact with saliva, releasing the drug for absorption through the buccal mucosa.

EVALUATIONS OF BUCCAL DRUG DELIVERY SYSTEMS

Evaluating the performance and effectiveness of Buccal Drug Delivery Systems within the context of Gastro-Retentive Drug Delivery Systems (GRDDS) requires comprehensive assessments covering various aspects such as drug release, absorption, retention, safety, and patient acceptability. Here's a detailed exploration of the evaluations conducted for Buccal Drug Delivery Systems in GRDDS:

1. Drug Release Studies:

a. In vitro Release Testing:

i. **Dissolution Studies**: Evaluate the release profile of the drug from buccal dosage forms using simulated gastric fluids.

ii. **Apparatus**: Conduct dissolution tests using USP apparatus, typically employing paddle or basket methods.

iii. **Sampling**: Collect samples at predetermined time intervals and analyze drug release using analytical techniques such as UV-Vis spectroscopy or HPLC.

b. Drug Release Kinetics:

i. **Model Fitting**: Fit release data to various mathematical models (e.g., zero-order, first-order, Higuchi, Korsmeyer-Peppas) to determine the mechanism and kinetics of drug release.

ii. **Comparison**: Compare the release kinetics of different formulations to optimize the formulation parameters.

2. Mucoadhesion Studies:

a. Mucoadhesive Strength:

i. **Mechanical Testing**: Measure the force required to detach mucoadhesive formulations from the buccal mucosa using instruments like texture analyzers.

ii. **Ex vivo Studies**: Conduct mucoadhesion studies using excised animal or human buccal tissue to evaluate the adhesive properties.

b. Mucoadhesive Time:

i. **Visual Observation**: Assess the duration of mucoadhesion by visually monitoring the retention of dosage forms on the buccal mucosa over time.

ii. **Quantitative Measurement**: Use image analysis software to quantify the mucoadhesive properties based on the area of contact and duration of adhesion.

3. In vitro Permeation Studies:

a. Permeation Testing:

i. **Transswell Assay**: Use Transwell inserts with buccal mucosa membranes to evaluate drug permeation across the mucosal barrier.

ii. **Sample Analysis**: Analyze samples collected from the acceptor compartment at different time points to quantify drug permeation using suitable analytical methods.

b. Permeation Kinetics:

i. **Permeation Modeling**: Fit permeation data to mathematical models (e.g., Fick's law) to determine the permeation kinetics and permeability coefficient of the drug across the buccal mucosa.

4. Pharmacokinetic Studies:

a. In vivo Absorption Studies:

i. **Animal Models**: Conduct pharmacokinetic studies in animal models (e.g., rats, rabbits) to evaluate the systemic absorption of drugs delivered via buccal GRDDS.

ii. **Blood Sampling**: Collect blood samples at different time points following administration and analyze drug concentrations using validated bioanalytical methods.

b. Bioavailability Assessment:

i. **Comparison**: Compare the pharmacokinetic parameters (e.g., Cmax, Tmax, AUC) of buccal GRDDS with conventional oral formulations to assess the relative bioavailability.

ii. **Statistical Analysis**: Perform statistical tests (e.g., t-test, ANOVA) to determine significant differences between formulations.

5. Gastric Retention Studies:

a. In vivo Retention Studies:

i. **Imaging Techniques**: Employ imaging modalities such as X-ray, scintigraphy, or magnetic resonance imaging (MRI) to visualize and quantify the gastric retention of dosage forms.

ii. **Animal Studies**: Conduct retention studies in animal models to assess the duration of gastric retention and the influence of formulation parameters.

b. Gastrointestinal Motility Assessment:

i. **Motility Studies**: Evaluate gastric emptying rates and intestinal transit times using methods like gastric scintigraphy or gastrointestinal motility monitoring.

ii. **Impact on Retention**: Assess the impact of formulation characteristics (e.g., buoyancy, mucoadhesion) on gastric retention and drug absorption.

6. Safety and Tolerability Assessment:

a. Mucosal Irritation Studies:

i. **Histopathological Evaluation**: Examine buccal tissues for signs of irritation, inflammation, or damage following prolonged exposure to mucoadhesive formulations.

ii. **Animal Studies**: Conduct safety assessments in animal models to evaluate local tissue reactions.

b. Systemic Toxicity Studies:

i. **Acute and Chronic Toxicity**: Investigate the potential systemic toxicity of buccal GRDDS through acute and chronic toxicity studies in animals.

ii. **Organ Histology**: Perform histological examination of vital organs to assess any adverse effects.

7. Patient Acceptability Studies:

a. Patient Surveys and Interviews:

i. **Feedback Collection**: Gather feedback from patients regarding the ease of administration, taste, comfort, and overall experience with buccal GRDDS.

ii. **Questionnaires**: Administer structured questionnaires to assess patient satisfaction and preferences.

b. Usability Testing:

i. **User Experience Evaluation**: Conduct usability testing to evaluate the practicality and user-friendliness of buccal dosage forms, including ease of handling and application.

Multiple-Choice Questions (MCQs)

1. What is the primary goal of Gastro-Retentive Drug Delivery Systems (GRDDS)?
   A) To increase the speed of gastric emptying
   B) To prolong the retention time of drug formulations in the stomach
   C) To decrease the absorption of drugs
   D) To enhance liver metabolism of drugs

2. Which type of GRDDS is designed to float on gastric fluids for prolonged gastric residence?
   A) Swelling and expanding systems
   B) Effervescent systems
   C) High-density systems
   D) Magnetic systems

3. What is the role of mucoadhesive polymers in GRDDS?
   A) To decrease the density of the drug formulation
   B) To enhance the solubility of the drug
   C) To adhere to the gastric mucosa
   D) To act as a buffer against gastric acids

4. Which material is often used in high-density systems to increase the density of the drug delivery system?
   A) Chitosan
   B) Barium sulfate
   C) Sodium bicarbonate

D) Hydroxypropyl methylcellulose (HPMC)

5. What type of system utilizes internal and external magnets to control the position of the dosage form within the stomach?

    A) Floating drug delivery systems

    B) Mucoadhesive systems

    C) Magnetic systems

    D) Effervescent systems

6. Which mechanism does a hydrogel use to remain in the stomach?

    A) Dissolving quickly in gastric acids

    B) Expanding upon contact with gastric fluids

    C) Decreasing its density through a chemical reaction

    D) Using a magnetic field to stay in place

7. What is the primary concept behind prolonging the gastric retention in GRDDS?

    A) To enhance drug absorption by keeping it in the lower GI tract

    B) To facilitate faster drug absorption in the intestines

    C) To extend drug formulation residence time in the stomach

    D) To immediately release the drug into the circulatory system

8. How do effervescent systems in GRDDS generate buoyancy?

    A) By expanding in size

    B) By generating gas upon reaction with gastric acid

    C) By adhering to the stomach wall

    D) By increasing the density of the tablet

9. What is a significant challenge in developing GRDDS formulations?

    A) Simplifying the drug formula to only include active ingredients

    B) Ensuring the drug directly passes through the liver

    C) Developing technology and expertise to create sophisticated systems

    D) Reducing the effectiveness of the drug

10. In what condition are gastro-retentive systems particularly beneficial for delivering medication?

    A) Lower intestine conditions

    B) Liver diseases

    C) Helicobacter pylori infections in the stomach

    D) Pancreatic issues

11. What impact can food have on gastro-retentive drug delivery systems?

    A) No impact as GRDDS are not affected by gastric contents

    B) It can delay gastric emptying and enhance performance

    C) It can cause rapid disintegration of the system

    D) It decreases the retention time of the drug delivery system

12. Which type of polymer is often used for mucoadhesive systems in GRDDS?

    A) Polyvinyl alcohol (PVA)

    B) Sodium chloride

    C) Chitosan

    D) Zinc oxide

13. What is the mechanism of drug release from swellable polymer systems in GRDDS?

    A) The drug is released through passive diffusion as the polymer degrades.

    B) Drugs are pumped out using a small mechanical pump within the system.

    C) The polymer contracts and squeezes the drug out in a controlled manner.

    D) The polymer dissolves entirely in gastric fluids releasing the drug.

14. What is the primary advantage of controlled drug release in GRDDS?

    A) It allows for instant drug levels in the plasma.

    B) It minimizes drug interactions with food.

    C) It maintains steady plasma drug concentrations over time.

D) It enhances the flavor of the drug formulation.

15. Which condition can variably affect the performance of GRDDS due to differences in anatomy and physiology?

    A) Cardiac conditions

    B) Gastric motility and anatomy variations among individuals

    C) Respiratory issues

    D) Skin diseases

16. Why are high-density systems used in GRDDS?

    A) To float on the gastric fluid

    B) To sink and stay in the lower parts of the stomach

    C) To disintegrate quickly

    D) To adhere to the stomach walls

17. Which formulation complexity is often a challenge in GRDDS development?

    A) Creating a visually appealing system

    B) Ensuring rapid drug action

    C) Developing sophisticated technology and expertise

    D) Finding natural ingredients

18. Which approach does not describe a method used by GRDDS to prolong drug retention in the stomach?

    A) Creating a high-density system that sinks to the bottom of the stomach

    B) Using a magnet to attract the dosage form to the stomach wall

    C) Heating the dosage form to activate absorption

    D) Employing a mucoadhesive polymer

19. What role does the pH of gastric fluids play in GRDDS?

    A) It has no significant effect on the system.

    B) It can influence drug solubility and stability.

    C) It serves to deactivate the drug as quickly as possible.

    D) It enhances the flavor of the drug formulation.

20. What is a potential downside of gastro-retentive systems regarding patient comfort?

    A) They are always flavored to mask the drug taste.

    B) They can cause gastrointestinal irritation or discomfort.

    C) They change color when reacting with gastric fluids.

    D) They can be audibly noticeable within the stomach.

Short Answer Type Questions (Subjective)

1. What are Gastro-Retentive Drug Delivery Systems (GRDDS)?

2. Describe the main objective of GRDDS.

3. What is the principle mechanism by which floating drug delivery systems operate?

4. Explain how effervescent systems in GRDDS generate buoyancy.

5. What role do high-density systems play in GRDDS?

6. How do mucoadhesive systems contribute to drug retention in the stomach?

7. Mention two materials used in high-density systems and their purpose.

8. What are the key advantages of employing magnetic systems in GRDDS?

9. How does the presence of food affect the performance of GRDDS?

10. Discuss the importance of polymer selection in the development of GRDDS.

11. What factors influence the gastric emptying rate and how do they impact GRDDS?

12. Describe how GRDDS can enhance the bioavailability of certain drugs.

13. Explain the concept of chronotherapy in relation to GRDDS.

14. How does gastric pH variability affect drug release and absorption in GRDDS?

15. Why is patient variability a significant challenge in the effectiveness of GRDDS?

16. What are the potential risks associated with the dose dumping phenomenon in GRDDS?

17. Describe the role of mucoadhesion in enhancing drug delivery in GRDDS.

18. Explain how environmental factors can affect the functionality of mucoadhesive systems.

19. What are the therapeutic advantages of localized drug action in GRDDS?

20. Discuss the challenges faced in obtaining regulatory approval for GRDDS.

Long Answer Type Questions (Subjective)

1. Elaborate on the different types of gastro-retentive systems and how each type functions to prolong gastric retention.

2. Discuss the mechanisms and materials used in swellable and expanding systems in GRDDS and their impact on drug delivery efficacy.

3. Explain the role of mucoadhesive systems in GRDDS, including the types of polymers used and their interactions with the gastric mucosa.

4. Describe the process and challenges involved in the formulation of GRDDS, emphasizing the importance of drug properties and release kinetics.

5. Analyze the impact of physiological factors like gastric motility and pH on the performance of GRDDS, and how these systems can be optimized to address these factors.

6. Discuss the advantages of GRDDS in the management of diseases requiring chronotherapy, providing examples of how drug release timing can be crucial.

7. Evaluate the limitations and disadvantages of GRDDS, particularly focusing on the challenges posed by variable gastric emptying rates and patient-dependent factors.

8. Describe the integration of buccal and gastro-retentive drug delivery systems, highlighting how they can complement each other to enhance therapeutic outcomes.

9. Explore the potential of GRDDS in targeting stomach-specific diseases, such as Helicobacter pylori infections, and how these systems improve treatment efficacy.

10. Discuss the future prospects of GRDDS technology in pharmaceutical development and patient care, considering the ongoing research and technological advancements.

Answer Key

1. B) To prolong the retention time of drug formulations in the stomach
2. B) Effervescent systems
3. C) To adhere to the gastric mucosa
4. B) Barium sulfate
5. C) Magnetic systems
6. B) Expanding upon contact with gastric fluids
7. C) To extend drug formulation residence time in the stomach
8. B) By generating gas upon reaction with gastric acid
9. C) Developing technology and expertise to create sophisticated systems
10. C) Helicobacter pylori infections in the stomach
11. B) It can delay gastric emptying and enhance performance
12. C) Chitosan
13. A) The drug is released through passive diffusion as the polymer degrades.
14. C) It maintains steady plasma drug concentrations over time.
15. B) Gastric motility and anatomy variations among individuals
16. B) To sink and stay in the lower parts of the stomach
17. C) Developing sophisticated technology and expertise

18.C) Heating the dosage form to activate absorption

19.B) It can influence drug solubility and stability.

20.B) They can cause gastrointestinal irritation or discomfort.

CHAPTER – 5

OCULAR DRUG DELIVERY SYSTEMS

INTRODUCTION:

Overview

Ocular drug delivery systems are specialized methods designed to deliver therapeutic agents directly to the eye. The unique anatomy and physiology of the eye pose significant challenges to effective drug delivery, necessitating innovative solutions to treat various ocular conditions. These systems aim to overcome barriers such as tear production, blinking, and limited permeability of the corneal epithelium.

Anatomy of the Eye and Barriers to Drug Delivery

The eye's unique anatomy and physiology present significant challenges to effective drug delivery. To develop efficient ocular drug delivery systems, it is crucial to understand the eye's structure and the specific barriers that impede drug penetration.

Anatomy of the Eye

The eye can be divided into two main segments: the anterior segment and the posterior segment. Each segment comprises various tissues and fluids that serve as barriers to drug delivery.

1. **Anterior Segment:**
    a. **Cornea:** The transparent, dome-shaped surface that covers the front of the eye.
    b. **Conjunctiva**: A thin, transparent tissue covering the white part of the eye and the inside of the eyelids.
    c. **Aqueous Humor**: The clear fluid filling the space between the cornea and the lens.
    d. **Iris**: The colored part of the eye that controls the size of the pupil.

e. **Ciliary Body**: Produces aqueous humor and contains the muscle that controls the shape of the lens.

f. **Lens:** A transparent, flexible structure that focuses light on the retina.

2. Posterior Segment:

a. **Vitreous Humor**: A gel-like substance filling the space between the lens and the retina.

b. **Retina:** The light-sensitive tissue lining the back of the eye.

c. **Choroid:** A vascular layer between the retina and the sclera, providing oxygen and nutrients to the retina.

d. **Sclera**: The white, fibrous outer layer of the eyeball.

e. **Optic Nerve**: Transmits visual information from the retina to the brain.

Barriers to Drug Delivery

1. Pre-Corneal Barriers:

a. **Tear Film:**

i. **Rapid Turnover**: Tears are continuously produced and drained, diluting and washing away drugs.

ii. **Tear Volume**: Limits the amount of drug that can be retained on the ocular surface.

iii. **Blinking**: Physically removes drug formulations from the ocular surface.

2. Corneal Barrier:

a. **Multilayered Structure**: Comprises five layers, each presenting unique challenges:

i. **Epithelium**: The outermost layer, with tight junctions limiting the penetration of hydrophilic drugs.

ii. **Bowman's Layer**: An acellular layer that adds to the structural barrier.

iii. **Stroma**: Hydrophilic, collagenous layer restricting lipophilic drug penetration.

iv. **Descemet's Membrane**: A thin but tough layer providing additional resistance.

v. **Endothelium**: The innermost layer, less restrictive but still a barrier.

3. **Conjunctival Barrier:**

   a. **Vascularization**: High blood flow can lead to rapid drug clearance.

   b. **Lymphatic Drainage**: Removes drugs from the ocular surface, reducing bioavailability.

4. **Scleral Barrier:**

   a. **Dense Collagen Fibers**: Hinder the diffusion of large molecules.

   b. **Vascular Permeability**: Though more permeable than the cornea, still presents a significant barrier.

5. **Blood-Aqueous Barrier:**

   a. **Tight Junctions**: In the ciliary epithelium and iris vasculature, limiting drug entry from the blood into the aqueous humor.

   b. **Active Efflux Mechanisms**: Proteins such as P-glycoprotein pump drugs out, reducing intraocular drug levels.

6. **Vitreous Barrier:**

   a. **Gel-Like Structure**: Slows the diffusion of drugs, particularly large or hydrophobic molecules.

   b. **Limited Drug Movement**: Drugs must diffuse through this dense medium to reach the retina.

7. **Blood-Retinal Barrier:**

   a. **Outer Blood-Retinal Barrier**: Formed by the retinal pigment epithelium (RPE), with tight junctions restricting drug entry.

b. **Inner Blood-Retinal Barrier**: Composed of tight junctions between endothelial cells of retinal capillaries, further limiting drug access.

8. **Efflux Transporters:**

   a. **Active Transport Mechanisms**: Proteins like P-glycoprotein in various ocular tissues actively expel drugs, reducing their effectiveness.

Strategies to Overcome Barriers

To enhance drug delivery to the eye, various strategies are employed, each targeting specific barriers:

1. **Prodrugs**: Modify drug molecules to enhance penetration, converting to active forms within the eye.
2. **Nanoparticles**: Encapsulate drugs to protect them from degradation and enhance penetration.
3. **Mucoadhesive Polymers**: Increase residence time by adhering to the ocular surface.
4. **Permeation Enhancers**: Temporarily disrupt tight junctions to facilitate drug entry.
5. **Implantable Devices**: Provide sustained release of drugs directly at the site of action.
6. **In Situ Gels**: Form gels upon contact with the eye, prolonging drug release.
7. **Microneedles**: Create microchannels for drug delivery, enhancing permeability.
8. **Contact Lenses**: Release drugs slowly over time, maintaining therapeutic levels.

Types of Ocular Drug Delivery Systems

Ocular drug delivery systems are designed to overcome the unique barriers posed by the anatomy and physiology of the eye. These systems aim to enhance drug bioavailability, prolong therapeutic effects, and improve patient compliance. Below are detailed descriptions of the various types of ocular drug delivery systems:

1. Topical Delivery Systems

    a. Eye Drops and Solutions:

        i. **Usage:** Common for treating anterior segment diseases like conjunctivitis, dry eye, and glaucoma.

        ii. **Advantages:** Easy to administer and non-invasive.

        iii. **Limitations:** Poor bioavailability (less than 5%), rapid tear turnover, and limited corneal penetration.

    b. Ointments and Gels:

        i. **Usage:** Provide prolonged contact time with the ocular surface, useful for conditions like blepharitis and post-surgical care.

        ii. **Advantages:** Enhanced residence time and drug stability.

        iii. **Limitations:** Blurred vision and patient discomfort.

2. Periocular Delivery Systems

    a. Subconjunctival Injections:

        i. **Usage:** Administered into the space between the conjunctiva and the sclera, used for delivering drugs to the anterior and posterior segments.

        ii. **Advantages:** Higher drug concentrations at the site of action.

        iii. **Limitations:** Invasive and may require clinical administration.

    b. Peribulbar and Retrobulbar Injections:

        i. **Usage:** Administered around or behind the eyeball, often used for anesthesia or delivering drugs to the posterior segment.

ii. **Advantage**s: Effective delivery to deeper ocular tissues.

iii. **Limitations**: Invasive with risks of complications like globe perforation or optic nerve damage.

3. Intraocular Delivery Systems

a. Intravitreal Injections:

i. **Usage**: Directly injected into the vitreous humor, used for retinal diseases like age-related macular degeneration (AMD) and diabetic retinopathy.

ii. **Advantages**: Direct delivery to the posterior segment, bypassing barriers.

iii. **Limitations**: Invasive with risks of infection, retinal detachment, and hemorrhage.

b. Implantable Devices:

i. Biodegradable Implants:

i. **Usage**: Slowly release drugs over time and degrade naturally.

ii. **Examples**: Ozurdex (dexamethasone implant) for macular edema.

iii. **Advantages:** Sustained drug release and minimal need for repeated injections.

iv. **Limitations**: Surgical insertion required, and possible inflammation or adverse reactions.

ii. Non-biodegradable Implants:

i. **Usage**: Provide long-term drug release but need surgical removal after depletion.

ii. **Examples:** Retisert (fluocinolone acetonide implant) for chronic uveitis.

iii. **Advantages**: Long-lasting drug release.

iv. **Limitation**s: Need for surgical insertion and removal.

4. Advanced Delivery Systems

    a. Nanoparticles:

        i.   **Types**: Lipid-based (liposomes, solid lipid nanoparticles), polymeric (PLGA, chitosan), and inorganic (gold, silica).

        ii.   **Usage:** Encapsulate drugs to enhance stability, penetration, and controlled release.

        iii.   **Advantages**: Improved bioavailability, targeted delivery, and prolonged action.

        iv.   **Limitations**: Complex formulation and potential toxicity.

    b. Hydrogels:

        i.   **Usage:** Swell upon contact with ocular fluids, forming a gel that releases drugs over time.

        ii.   **Advantages**: Prolonged residence time and sustained release.

        iii.   **Limitations:** Potential for blurred vision and discomfort.

    c. In Situ Forming Gels:

        i.   **Mechanism**: Liquid formulations that gel upon contact with the ocular surface, triggered by temperature, pH, or ion concentration.

        ii.   **Examples**: Thermosensitive and pH-sensitive gels.

        iii.   **Advantages**: Enhanced residence time and controlled drug release.

        iv.   **Limitations**: Formulation complexity and patient comfort.

    d. Microneedles:

        i.   **Usage**: Tiny needles create microchannels in ocular tissues for drug delivery.

        ii.   **Advantages**: Minimally invasive, precise delivery, and reduced risk compared to conventional injections.

        iii.   **Limitations**: Requires specialized equipment and training.

e. **Contact Lenses:**

   i. **Drug-Loaded Contact Lenses:**

      i. **Usage**: Designed to release drugs slowly over time directly to the cornea and conjunctiva.

      ii. **Advantages**: Sustained release, improved compliance, and reduced side effects.

      iii. **Limitations**: Patient comfort and potential for lens-related complications.

5. Emerging Technologies

a. **Gene Therapy:**

   i. **Usage:** Delivery of genetic material to ocular cells to treat genetic disorders or provide therapeutic proteins.

   ii. **Examples:** Luxturna for RPE65 mutation-associated retinal dystrophy.

   iii. **Advantages**: Potential for long-term or permanent treatment.

   iv. **Limitations:** High cost, regulatory hurdles, and potential for immune reactions.

b. **Biologics:**

   i. **Usage:** Antibodies, peptides, and nucleic acids for targeted therapies, especially for retinal diseases.

   ii. **Advantages:** High specificity and efficacy.

   iii. **Limitations**: Stability, delivery challenges, and potential immunogenicity.

c. **Regenerative Medicine:**

   i. **Stem Cell Therapy:**

      i. **Usage:** Use of stem cells to regenerate damaged ocular tissues.

ii. **Advantages**: Potential to restore vision and ocular function.

iii. **Limitations:** Ethical concerns, regulatory issues, and risk of tumor formation.

d. Smart Drug Delivery Systems:

i. **Mechanism**: Systems that respond to environmental stimuli (e.g., pH, temperature) to release drugs in a controlled manner.

ii. **Advantages**: Precise control over drug release profiles.

iii. **Limitations**: Technological complexity and cost.

Advances and Future Directions

The field of ocular drug delivery is rapidly evolving, driven by the need for more effective, patient-friendly, and targeted therapies. Advances in technology and a deeper understanding of ocular physiology are paving the way for innovative delivery systems that overcome the traditional barriers to ocular drug delivery. Here are the detailed advances and future directions in ocular drug delivery systems:

1. Nanotechnology-Based Delivery Systems

a. Nanoparticles:

i. **Advances:** Use of biodegradable and biocompatible materials such as PLGA (poly(lactic-co-glycolic acid)) and chitosan to encapsulate drugs, enhancing stability, bioavailability, and controlled release.

ii. **Future Directions**: Development of multi-functional nanoparticles that can deliver drugs, genes, or imaging agents simultaneously, providing combined therapeutic and diagnostic (theranostic) capabilities.

b. Liposomes and Niosomes:

i. **Advances**: Improved formulations to enhance drug encapsulation efficiency and stability. Use of surface modifications to target specific ocular tissues.

ii. **Future Directions**: Exploration of stimuli-responsive liposomes and niosomes that release drugs in response to environmental triggers like pH, temperature, or light.

2. In Situ Forming Gels and Hydrogels

a. In Situ Gels:

i. **Advances:** Development of thermosensitive, pH-sensitive, and ion-sensitive gels that transition from liquid to gel upon contact with the ocular surface, enhancing drug residence time and sustained release.

ii. **Future Directions**: Creation of smart in situ gels that respond to specific disease markers or conditions, providing targeted and on-demand drug release.

b. Hydrogels:

i. **Advances**: Use of hydrogels that can encapsulate a wide range of therapeutic agents, including small molecules, proteins, and nucleic acids. Improved biocompatibility and controlled release properties.

ii. **Future Directions**: Integration of hydrogels with electronic components to create "smart" contact lenses that can monitor ocular conditions and deliver drugs accordingly.

3. Implantable and Injectable Devices

a. Biodegradable Implants:

i. **Advances**: Development of implants that provide sustained drug release over months, reducing the need for frequent administration. Use of biodegradable materials to avoid the need for surgical removal.

ii. **Future Directions**: Design of implants that can deliver multiple drugs or have programmable release profiles, responding to the progression of diseases.

b. **Microneedles:**

i. **Advances:** Development of microneedle arrays for minimally invasive drug delivery, enhancing penetration and bioavailability while reducing pain and discomfort.

ii. **Future Directions**: Exploration of dissolvable microneedles that leave no residue, and microneedles capable of delivering biologics, such as peptides, proteins, and genes.

4. Gene and Cell Therapy

a. **Gene Therapy:**

i. **Advances**: Successful clinical trials and FDA approval of gene therapies like Luxturna for treating inherited retinal diseases. Use of viral and non-viral vectors for efficient gene delivery.

ii. **Future Directions**: Development of safer, more efficient gene editing technologies like CRISPR/Cas9 for precise gene correction. Use of gene therapy to treat a broader range of ocular diseases, including age-related macular degeneration and glaucoma.

b. **Cell Therapy:**

i. **Advances**: Use of stem cells to regenerate damaged ocular tissues. Clinical trials demonstrating the potential of cell therapy to restore vision in conditions like retinal degeneration.

ii. **Future Directions**: Development of standardized protocols for stem cell isolation, expansion, and differentiation. Use of induced pluripotent stem cells (iPSCs) for personalized cell therapy.

5. Smart and Responsive Drug Delivery Systems

    a. Stimuli-Responsive Systems:

        i. **Advances**: Development of drug delivery systems that respond to environmental triggers such as pH, temperature, light, or enzymes, providing controlled and targeted drug release.

        ii. **Future Directions**: Integration of biosensors with drug delivery systems to create responsive systems that can release drugs in response to real-time physiological changes, providing on-demand therapy.

    b. Bioelectronic Devices:

        i. **Advances**: Development of contact lenses embedded with microelectronics to monitor ocular conditions and deliver drugs as needed.

        ii. **Future Directions**: Creation of fully integrated bioelectronic systems that can diagnose, monitor, and treat ocular diseases autonomously.

6. Biologics and Biopharmaceuticals

    a. Antibody-Based Therapies:

        i. **Advances:** Use of monoclonal antibodies for treating ocular diseases like AMD and diabetic retinopathy. Development of antibody fragments and bispecific antibodies for enhanced efficacy and targeting.

        ii. **Future Directions**: Exploration of antibody-drug conjugates (ADCs) for targeted delivery of cytotoxic agents to pathological cells in the eye.

    b. Peptide and Protein Therapies:

i. **Advances**: Formulation of peptides and proteins to enhance stability and bioavailability. Use of delivery systems like nanoparticles and hydrogels to protect these molecules and prolong their release.

ii. **Future Directions**: Development of multifunctional peptide-based therapeutics that combine anti-inflammatory, anti-angiogenic, and neuroprotective properties.

7. Personalized Medicine and Precision Therapy

a. Personalized Ocular Therapy:

i. **Advances**: Use of genetic and biomarker analysis to tailor treatments to individual patients, enhancing efficacy and reducing adverse effects.

ii. **Future Directions**: Integration of advanced diagnostics with drug delivery systems to provide personalized and adaptive treatments based on real-time monitoring of disease progression and patient response.

b. Precision Drug Delivery:

i. **Advances:** Development of targeted delivery systems that direct drugs specifically to affected tissues, minimizing systemic exposure and side effects.

ii. **Future Directions**: Use of artificial intelligence and machine learning to optimize drug delivery systems, predicting patient response and adjusting treatments dynamically.

BARRIERS OF DRUG PERMEATION

Delivering drugs to the eye is particularly challenging due to several anatomical and physiological barriers. These barriers can be classified based on the anatomical segments of the eye and their specific properties. Understanding these barriers is crucial for developing effective ocular drug delivery systems.

Tear Film Barrier

The tear film is a critical barrier to drug permeation in ocular drug delivery systems. Understanding its structure, functions, and dynamics is essential for developing effective ocular therapeutics. Here's a detailed look at the tear film barrier and its implications for ocular drug delivery:

Structure of the Tear Film

The tear film is a complex, multilayered structure that covers the surface of the eye, providing lubrication, protection, and a smooth optical surface. It consists of three main layers:

1. **Lipid Layer:**
   a. **Location**: Outermost layer.
   b. **Composition**: Composed of lipids secreted by the meibomian glands.
   c. **Function**: Prevents evaporation of the underlying aqueous layer and provides a smooth surface for the spread of tears.

2. **Aqueous Layer:**
   a. **Location:** Middle layer.
   b. **Composition:** Primarily water with dissolved proteins (enzymes, antibodies), electrolytes, and nutrients.
   c. **Function**: Provides moisture, supplies oxygen and nutrients to the cornea, and has antimicrobial properties.

3. **Mucin Layer:**
   a. **Location**: Innermost layer, adjacent to the corneal and conjunctival epithelium.
   b. **Composition:** Mucins secreted by goblet cells and the epithelial cells of the conjunctiva.
   c. **Function**: Ensures even distribution of the tear film over the ocular surface and stabilizes the tear film.

Functions of the Tear Film

1. **Protection:** Acts as a barrier against environmental pathogens, debris, and toxins.
2. **Lubrication**: Reduces friction between the eyelid and the cornea during blinking.
3. **Optical Clarity**: Maintains a smooth refractive surface necessary for clear vision.
4. **Nutrient Supply**: Delivers essential nutrients and oxygen to the avascular cornea.
5. **Waste Removal**: Helps remove metabolic waste products from the ocular surface.

Dynamics of the Tear Film

1. **Turnover and Renewal**: The tear film is continuously produced and drained, with a turnover rate of about 15-20% per minute. This rapid renewal dilutes and washes away applied drugs, reducing their residence time and bioavailability.
2. **Blinking**: Each blink spreads the tear film over the ocular surface, redistributing and potentially removing topically applied drugs. Blinking also stimulates tear production and drainage.
3. **Drainage**: Tears are drained through the lacrimal puncta into the nasolacrimal duct, further reducing drug retention on the ocular surface.

Barriers to Drug Delivery

1. **Dilution Effect:**
   a. **Challenge:** The continuous production and drainage of tears dilute topically applied drugs, significantly reducing their concentration on the ocular surface.
   b. **Impact:** This leads to low bioavailability, often less than 5% of the applied dose reaches the target tissues.

2. **Rapid Clearance:**

a. **Challenge:** The high turnover rate of the tear film and blinking actions result in the rapid clearance of drugs from the ocular surface.

b. **Impact:** Frequent administration is required to maintain therapeutic drug levels, which can reduce patient compliance.

3. **Limited Volume:**

   a. **Challenge**: The tear film can only hold a limited volume of fluid, approximately 7-10 microliters, whereas a typical eye drop contains about 30-50 microliters.

   b. **Impact**: Excess fluid is quickly drained, and only a small fraction of the administered dose remains on the ocular surface.

4. **Enzymatic Degradation:**

   a. **Challenge**: The aqueous layer contains enzymes such as lysozymes and proteases that can degrade therapeutic agents, particularly proteins and peptides.

   b. **Impact**: Enzymatic activity reduces the efficacy of biologic drugs and necessitates the use of protective delivery systems.

5. **Barrier to Penetration:**

   a. **Challenge**: The mucin layer presents a barrier to the penetration of hydrophobic drugs due to its hydrophilic nature.

   b. **Impact:** Drugs must be formulated to enhance their solubility and penetration through this layer to reach the underlying tissues.

Strategies to Overcome the Tear Film Barrier

1. **Mucoadhesive Polymers:**

   a. **Example**: Chitosan, hyaluronic acid.

   b. **Mechanism:** These polymers adhere to the mucin layer, prolonging the residence time of the drug on the ocular surface.

2. **In Situ Forming Gels:**

   a. **Example:** Thermosensitive gels like Pluronic F127.

    b. **Mechanism:** These formulations transition from liquid to gel upon contact with the ocular surface, increasing drug retention time.

3. **Nanoparticles and Liposomes:**
   a. **Example**: Liposomal formulations, PLGA nanoparticles.
   b. **Mechanism**: Encapsulate drugs to protect them from enzymatic degradation and enhance penetration through the mucin layer.

4. **Prodrug Approach:**
   a. **Example**: Latanoprost.
   b. **Mechanism**: Prodrugs are metabolized into active drugs within the eye, improving penetration and bioavailability.

5. **Controlled Release Systems:**
   a. **Example**: Ocular inserts, contact lenses.
   b. **Mechanism**: These devices provide a sustained release of drugs, reducing the need for frequent administration.

6. **Permeation Enhancers:**
   a. **Example**: Benzalkonium chloride.
   b. **Mechanism**: Temporarily disrupt the mucin layer or epithelial tight junctions to enhance drug penetration.

Corneal Barrier

The cornea is one of the most significant barriers to drug permeation in ocular drug delivery systems due to its unique structure and physiological properties. A detailed understanding of the corneal barrier is essential for developing effective ocular therapies.

Structure of the Cornea

The cornea is a transparent, avascular tissue composed of five distinct layers, each contributing to the barrier function:

1. **Epithelium:**
   a. **Structure:** The outermost layer consisting of 5-7 layers of tightly packed epithelial cells with tight junctions.

b. **Function:** Acts as a primary barrier to drug penetration due to its hydrophobic nature and tight junctions, which restrict the entry of hydrophilic molecules.

2. **Bowman's Layer:**

   a. **Structure**: An acellular, collagen-rich layer beneath the epithelium.

   b. **Function:** Provides structural integrity but does not significantly impede drug permeation.

3. **Stroma:**

   a. **Structure**: The thickest layer, comprising about 90% of the corneal thickness, made of hydrated collagen fibers and keratocytes.

   b. **Function:** Highly hydrophilic, acting as a barrier to lipophilic drugs.

4. **Descemet's Membrane:**

   a. **Structure:** A thin but strong collagenous layer.

   b. **Function**: Adds to the structural strength of the cornea but offers minimal resistance to drug permeation.

5. **Endothelium:**

   a. **Structure:** A single layer of hexagonal cells lining the innermost part of the cornea.

   b. **Function**: Maintains corneal hydration and transparency; while less of a barrier compared to the epithelium, it still plays a role in controlling drug entry into the anterior chamber.

Functions of the Corneal Barrier

1. **Protection**: Shields the inner structures of the eye from pathogens, debris, and harmful substances.

2. **Transparency**: Maintains clarity for vision by being free of blood vessels and regularly arranged collagen fibers.

3. **Selective Permeability**: Regulates the passage of substances to protect the internal ocular environment.

Barriers to Drug Delivery

1. **Physicochemical Barriers:**
   a. **Hydrophobic Epithelium**: The lipophilic nature of the epithelial cell membranes restricts the penetration of hydrophilic drugs.
   b. **Hydrophilic Stroma**: The stromal layer, being hydrophilic, hinders the penetration of lipophilic drugs.

2. **Tight Junctions:**
   a. **Challenge**: Tight junctions between epithelial cells create a physical barrier that limits paracellular transport of drugs.
   b. **Impact:** Only small, lipophilic, and uncharged molecules can easily penetrate through the corneal epithelium.

3. **Enzymatic Degradation:**
   a. **Challenge:** Presence of enzymes in the corneal epithelium that can degrade drugs, particularly peptides and proteins.
   b. **Impact**: Reduces the efficacy of enzymatically labile drugs.

4. **Efflux Transporters:**
   a. **Challenge:** Active efflux mechanisms, such as P-glycoprotein pumps, expel drugs from corneal cells back into the tear film.
   b. **Impact:** Limits the intracellular accumulation of drugs, reducing their effectiveness.

Strategies to Overcome the Corneal Barrier

1. **Prodrugs:**
   a. **Mechanism**: Modify the parent drug to enhance lipophilicity or hydrophilicity, improving corneal penetration. The prodrug is converted to the active form within the cornea or anterior chamber.

b. **Example**: Latanoprost, a prodrug for glaucoma treatment, penetrates the cornea effectively and is converted to its active form in the eye.

2. **Permeation Enhancers:**

   a. **Mechanism**: Temporarily disrupt the tight junctions or alter the lipid structure of the corneal epithelium to enhance drug permeability.

   b. **Examples**: Benzalkonium chloride (BAK) and other surfactants.

   c. **Consideration**s: Potential for irritation and toxicity with long-term use.

3. **Nanoparticles:**

   a. **Mechanism:** Encapsulate drugs in nanoparticles to enhance penetration through the cornea and protect the drug from degradation.

   b. **Types:** Lipid-based nanoparticles, polymeric nanoparticles, and dendrimers.

   c. **Advantages**: Improved bioavailability and sustained release.

4. **Liposomes:**

   a. **Mechanism:** Encapsulate hydrophilic and lipophilic drugs in liposomes to enhance corneal penetration and prolong drug residence time.

   b. **Advantages:** Biocompatibility and ability to carry both hydrophilic and lipophilic drugs.

5. **Cyclodextrins:**

   a. **Mechanism**: Form inclusion complexes with drugs to enhance their solubility and stability, improving corneal penetration.

   b. **Advantages:** Non-toxic and enhance drug bioavailability.

6. **Mucoadhesive Systems:**

a. **Mechanism**: Use mucoadhesive polymers (e.g., chitosan, hyaluronic acid) to increase the contact time of the drug with the corneal surface.

b. **Advantages**: Improved drug retention and penetration.

7. **Hydrogels:**

a. **Mechanism**: Use hydrogels that swell upon contact with ocular fluids, releasing drugs in a controlled manner.

b. **Advantages**: Enhanced residence time and sustained drug release.

8. **In Situ Forming Gels:**

a. **Mechanism**: Form gels upon contact with the ocular surface due to changes in temperature, pH, or ionic strength, prolonging drug retention.

b. **Examples**: Thermosensitive and pH-sensitive gels.

c. **Advantages**: Increased drug bioavailability and patient comfort.

Conjunctival Barrier

The conjunctival barrier is another significant barrier to drug permeation in ocular drug delivery systems. The conjunctiva, a thin, vascularized membrane covering the sclera and the inner surface of the eyelids, plays a crucial role in ocular drug delivery by impacting drug absorption, distribution, and clearance. Here is a detailed examination of the conjunctival barrier and its implications for ocular drug delivery:

Structure of the Conjunctiva

The conjunctiva is divided into three regions:

1. **Palpebral Conjunctiva**: Lines the inner surface of the eyelids.

2. **Bulbar Conjunctiva**: Covers the sclera (white part of the eye).

3. **Forniceal Conjunctiva**: Forms the junction between the palpebral and bulbar conjunctiva.

Histological Features

1. **Epithelium**: The outermost layer, consisting of 2-5 layers of epithelial cells, including goblet cells that secrete mucin.
2. **Stroma (Substantia Propria)**: Composed of loose connective tissue with blood vessels, lymphatics, and immune cells. It consists of:
   a. **Adenoid Layer**: Rich in lymphoid tissue and blood vessels.
   b. **Fibrous Layer**: Contains fibroblasts and collagen fibers, providing structural support.

Functions of the Conjunctiva

1. **Protection**: Acts as a barrier against pathogens and foreign particles.
2. **Lubrication**: Secretes mucin to stabilize the tear film and facilitate eyelid movement.
3. **Immunological Defense**: Contains immune cells that help protect the eye from infections.
4. **Absorption and Clearance**: Plays a role in the absorption and clearance of topically applied drugs.

Barriers to Drug Delivery

1. **Epithelial Barrier:**
   a. **Tight Junctions**: Similar to the corneal epithelium, the conjunctival epithelium has tight junctions that limit paracellular drug transport.
   b. **Lipophilic Nature:** The epithelial cell membranes are lipophilic, restricting the entry of hydrophilic drugs.
2. **Enzymatic Degradation:**
   a. **Enzymes**: The conjunctival epithelium contains enzymes like esterases and proteases that can degrade drugs, particularly peptides and proteins.
3. **Blood and Lymphatic Clearance:**

a. **High Vascularity**: The conjunctiva is highly vascularized, leading to rapid absorption and clearance of drugs into the systemic circulation, which reduces local drug concentration.

b. **Lymphatic Drainage**: Efficient lymphatic drainage further contributes to the rapid clearance of drugs.

4. **Efflux Transporters:**

a. **P-glycoprotein and Other Transporters**: Efflux transporters in the conjunctival epithelium can actively pump drugs out of cells, reducing their intracellular concentration.

5. **Limited Surface Area:**

a. **Surface Area and Volume**: The limited surface area and volume of the conjunctival sac constrain the amount of drug that can be administered topically.

Strategies to Overcome the Conjunctival Barrier

1. **Prodrugs:**

a. **Mechanism**: Prodrugs are designed to enhance lipophilicity or hydrophilicity, improving penetration through the conjunctival epithelium. They are converted to active drugs within the ocular tissues.

b. **Examples**: Prodrugs of acyclovir and ganciclovir for antiviral therapy.

2. **Permeation Enhancers:**

a. **Mechanism**: Permeation enhancers temporarily disrupt the tight junctions or alter the lipid structure of the conjunctival epithelium, enhancing drug permeability.

b. **Examples**: Surfactants like polysorbates, bile salts, and chelating agents like EDTA.

3. **Nanoparticles:**

a. **Mechanism**: Nanoparticles can encapsulate drugs, protecting them from enzymatic degradation and enhancing penetration through the conjunctival barrier.

b. **Types:** Lipid-based nanoparticles, polymeric nanoparticles, dendrimers.

c. **Advantages**: Improved bioavailability, controlled release, and targeting capabilities.

4. **Liposomes:**

   a. **Mechanism:** Liposomes can encapsulate hydrophilic and lipophilic drugs, enhancing their penetration and prolonging their retention time on the ocular surface.

   b. **Advantages**: Biocompatibility and ability to carry various types of drugs.

5. **Mucoadhesive Polymers:**

   a. **Mechanism:** Mucoadhesive polymers, such as chitosan and hyaluronic acid, increase the contact time of drugs with the conjunctival surface, enhancing absorption.

   b. **Advantages**: Improved drug retention and reduced dosing frequency.

6. **Hydrogels and In Situ Forming Gels:**

   a. **Mechanis**m: Hydrogels and in situ forming gels swell upon contact with ocular fluids, releasing drugs in a controlled manner.

   b. **Advantage**s: Prolonged drug retention and sustained release.

7. **Microneedles:**

   a. **Mechanism**: Microneedles create microchannels in the conjunctival tissue, enhancing drug penetration without causing significant pain or discomfort.

   b. **Advantages**: Minimal invasiveness and enhanced drug delivery.

8. **Contact Lenses:**

a. **Mechanism:** Drug-embedded contact lenses release drugs over an extended period, maintaining therapeutic drug levels on the ocular surface.

b. **Advantages**: Continuous drug delivery and improved patient compliance.

Scleral Barrier

The sclera, the white part of the eye, is another significant barrier to drug permeation in ocular drug delivery systems. Understanding the structure, function, and permeability characteristics of the sclera is crucial for developing effective ocular drug delivery strategies.

Structure of the Sclera

The sclera is a dense, fibrous, and opaque tissue that forms the outer protective layer of the eye. It extends from the cornea at the front of the eye to the optic nerve at the back. The sclera is composed of three layers:

1. **Episclera:**
   a. **Structure**: The outermost layer consisting of loose, vascular connective tissue.
   b. **Function**: Provides a site for attachment of the conjunctiva and facilitates the passage of blood vessels.

2. **Stroma (Scleral Proper):**
   a. **Structure:** The thickest layer, composed of dense collagen fibers arranged in a crisscross pattern, interspersed with elastin fibers.
   b. **Function**: Provides structural support and maintains the shape of the eyeball.

3. **Lamina Fusca:**
   a. **Structure:** The innermost layer, consisting of loosely arranged collagen fibers and fibroblasts, adjacent to the choroid.
   b. **Function:** Connects the sclera to the underlying choroidal tissue.

Functions of the Sclera

1. **Protection**: Acts as a protective barrier against physical injury and pathogens.
2. **Support:** Maintains the shape and integrity of the eyeball.
3. **Attachment**: Provides attachment sites for the extraocular muscles, facilitating eye movements.
4. **Optical**: Contributes to the overall structural integrity and refractive properties of the eye.

Barriers to Drug Delivery

1. **Dense Collagen Matrix:**
   a. **Challenge:** The dense collagenous structure of the scleral stroma acts as a physical barrier to drug penetration, particularly for large and hydrophilic molecules.
   b. **Impact**: Limits the passive diffusion of drugs through the scleral tissue.

2. **Limited Blood Supply:**
   a. **Challenge:** The sclera is relatively avascular, with minimal blood vessels in the episcleral region and none in the stroma.
   b. **Impact:** Reduced blood flow means limited systemic absorption of drugs, but also limits nutrient supply, affecting drug metabolism and clearance.

3. **Variable Thickness:**
   a. **Challenge:** The thickness of the sclera varies from the anterior to the posterior regions, affecting drug diffusion rates. It is thickest at the posterior pole (1 mm) and thinnest at the equator (0.3 mm).
   b. **Impact:** Variable thickness influences the uniformity of drug delivery across different parts of the sclera.

4. **Hydration and Porosity:**
   a. **Challenge:** The sclera has a high water content (about 70%), which influences the permeability of hydrophilic versus lipophilic drugs.

b. **Impact:** Hydrophilic drugs may diffuse more readily through the hydrated matrix, while lipophilic drugs may encounter resistance.

5. **Presence of Proteoglycans:**
   a. **Challenge:** The extracellular matrix contains proteoglycans that can bind and sequester drugs, reducing their availability for diffusion.
   b. **Impact:** Proteoglycans can hinder the penetration of certain drugs, particularly those that bind to these molecules.

Strategies to Overcome the Scleral Barrier

1. **Prodrug Approach:**
   a. **Mechanism:** Prodrugs are designed to enhance lipophilicity or hydrophilicity, improving penetration through the scleral tissue. They are converted to active drugs within the ocular tissues.
   b. **Examples:** Prodrugs of corticosteroids for anti-inflammatory purposes.

2. **Nanoparticles and Microparticles:**
   a. **Mechanism:** Encapsulation of drugs in nanoparticles or microparticles to enhance penetration through the sclera and provide controlled release.
   b. **Types:** PLGA (poly(lactic-co-glycolic acid)) nanoparticles, liposomes, dendrimers.
   c. **Advantages:** Improved bioavailability, sustained release, and reduced systemic side effects.

3. **Collagenase Treatment:**
   a. **Mechanism:** Enzymatic treatment with collagenase to temporarily degrade collagen fibers and enhance drug penetration through the sclera.
   b. **Considerations:** Potential for tissue damage and inflammation; careful control of enzyme activity is required.

4. **Permeation Enhancers:**

   a. **Mechanism**: Use of chemical agents to temporarily disrupt the scleral extracellular matrix and enhance drug permeability.

   b. **Examples:** Surfactants, fatty acids, and chelating agents.

   c. **Considerations**: Risk of toxicity and irritation; optimization of concentration and exposure time is essential.

5. **Electroporation:**

   a. **Mechanism**: Application of short electrical pulses to create temporary pores in the scleral tissue, enhancing drug diffusion.

   b. **Advantages**: Non-invasive and can be precisely controlled; suitable for large and charged molecules.

   c. **Considerations**: Requires specialized equipment and training.

6. **Micro-Needle Arrays:**

   a. **Mechanism:** Use of micro-needle arrays to create microchannels in the sclera, facilitating direct drug delivery to the posterior segment of the eye.

   b. **Advantage**s: Minimally invasive, precise delivery, and reduced systemic exposure.

   c. **Considerations**: Potential for patient discomfort and infection; requires proper sterilization and technique.

7. **Ultrasound and Iontophoresis:**

   a. **Mechanism**: Use of ultrasound waves or electrical currents to enhance drug penetration through the sclera.

   b. **Advantage**s: Non-invasive and can target specific regions.

   c. **Considerations**: Requires specialized equipment and training; potential for tissue damage with improper use.

8. **Hydrogel Carriers:**

a. **Mechanism**: Use of hydrogel-based systems to encapsulate drugs and provide sustained release while enhancing penetration through the hydrated scleral tissue.

b. **Advantages**: Biocompatibility, prolonged drug release, and enhanced drug stability.

c. **Considerations:** Optimization of hydrogel properties for specific drugs and delivery requirements.

Blood-Aqueous Barrier

The blood-aqueous barrier (BAB) is one of the critical barriers encountered in ocular drug delivery systems. It plays a significant role in regulating the passage of substances from the blood circulation into the aqueous humor of the eye. Understanding the BAB is crucial for designing effective ocular drug delivery strategies. Let's delve into it in detail.

Anatomy of the Blood-Aqueous Barrier:

The BAB is a complex system involving both anatomical and physiological components:

1. **Anatomical Components:**

    a. **Non-fenestrated Capillaries**: The blood vessels supplying the anterior segment of the eye, including the ciliary body and iris, have non-fenestrated endothelial cells. These cells are tightly packed, preventing the passage of large molecules.

    b. **Tight Junctions**: Endothelial cells in the blood vessels are connected by tight junctions, which restrict the movement of substances between cells.

2. **Physiological Components:**

    a. **Active Transport Mechanisms**: Transporters present on the endothelial cells regulate the movement of specific molecules across the barrier.

b. **Metabolic Enzymes**: Enzymes within the endothelial cells metabolize certain substances, affecting their availability in the aqueous humor.

c. **Ion Pumps**: Ion pumps maintain the ionic balance necessary for normal eye function.

Function of the Blood-Aqueous Barrier:

The primary function of the BAB is to maintain the composition and homeostasis of the aqueous humor, which is crucial for the health and function of the anterior segment of the eye. It achieves this by:

1. **Preventing Entry of Harmful Substances**: The barrier restricts the passage of potentially harmful substances, such as pathogens and toxins, from the bloodstream into the aqueous humor.

2. **Controlling Nutrient and Waste Exchange**: It regulates the exchange of nutrients, oxygen, and waste products between the blood and the aqueous humor, ensuring proper nourishment and waste removal for the ocular tissues.

3. **Protecting Against Inflammation**: By limiting the entry of immune cells and inflammatory mediators, the barrier helps prevent inflammation and maintain ocular immune privilege.

Implications for Ocular Drug Delivery Systems:

When designing ocular drug delivery systems, understanding the BAB is crucial because it presents a formidable barrier to the delivery of therapeutic agents. Strategies to overcome or bypass the BAB include:

1. **Prodrug Approaches**: Conjugating the drug with a substrate that can cross the barrier and then be enzymatically cleaved to release the active drug within the eye.

2. **Nanotechnology**: Utilizing nanoparticles or liposomes that can penetrate the barrier or actively target specific cells within the eye.

3. **Intravitreal Injection**: Directly injecting the drug into the vitreous humor bypasses the BAB altogether, allowing for higher drug concentrations at the target site.

4. **Periocular Administration**: Delivering the drug through periocular routes, such as subconjunctival or subtenon injections, can provide sustained release and bypass the BAB to some extent.

Vitreous Humor Barrier

The vitreous humor barrier (VHB) is another crucial obstacle in ocular drug delivery systems. It acts as a barrier between the anterior and posterior segments of the eye, impeding the penetration of drugs from the anterior chamber to the retina and vitreous humor. Understanding the VHB is essential for designing effective drug delivery strategies for treating posterior segment ocular diseases. Let's explore it in detail:

Anatomy of the Vitreous Humor Barrier:

The VHB consists of several anatomical and physiological components:

1. **Anatomical Components:**

    a. **Vitreous Humor**: The vitreous humor is a gel-like substance that fills the posterior segment of the eye. It is composed mostly of water, collagen fibrils, and hyaluronic acid.

    b. **Vitreoretinal Interface**: The interface between the vitreous humor and the retina is characterized by structures such as the internal limiting membrane (ILM) and the vitreous cortex.

2. **Physiological Components:**

    a. **Size Exclusion**: The dense collagen fibrils within the vitreous humor create a meshwork that restricts the movement of large molecules.

    b. **Electrostatic Repulsion**: Negative charges on the collagen fibrils repel negatively charged molecules, further limiting their penetration.

c. **Binding Interactions**: Some drugs may bind to components within the vitreous humor, reducing their availability for therapeutic action.

Function of the Vitreous Humor Barrier:

The VHB serves several important functions:

1. **Protection**: It acts as a physical barrier, protecting the delicate structures of the retina from external insults and pathogens.
2. **Maintaining Shape**: The vitreous humor helps maintain the shape of the eye and supports the retina, facilitating proper vision.
3. **Metabolism:** Metabolic processes within the vitreous humor help maintain its composition and contribute to the overall health of the eye.

Implications for Ocular Drug Delivery Systems:

The VHB presents significant challenges for drug delivery to the posterior segment of the eye. Strategies to overcome or bypass the VHB include:

1. **Intravitreal Injection**: Directly injecting drugs into the vitreous humor bypasses the VHB and delivers therapeutics directly to the target site.
2. **Intravitreal Implants**: Biodegradable implants can release drugs slowly over time, maintaining therapeutic levels within the vitreous humor and retina.
3. **Nanoparticle Formulations**: Nanoparticles can be designed to penetrate the VHB and release drugs at the desired site of action.
4. **Enzymatic Degradation**: Enzymes capable of degrading components of the vitreous humor can be used to facilitate drug penetration.

Blood-Retinal Barrier

The blood-retinal barrier (BRB) is a highly specialized structure that regulates the exchange of substances between the systemic circulation and the neural retina. It comprises both anatomical and physiological components that tightly control the passage of molecules into and out of the retina. Understanding the

BRB is crucial for designing effective ocular drug delivery systems targeting retinal diseases. Let's explore the BRB in detail:

Anatomy of the Blood-Retinal Barrier:

1. **Anatomical Components:**
   a. **Endothelial Cells**: The innermost layer of retinal blood vessels is lined by endothelial cells connected by tight junctions, forming the inner blood-retinal barrier (iBRB) in retinal capillaries.
   b. **Retinal Pigment Epithelium (RPE):** The RPE forms the outer blood-retinal barrier (oBRB) between the choriocapillaris and the neural retina. The RPE is connected by tight junctions, creating a physical barrier.

2. **Physiological Components:**
   a. **Tight Junctions**: Tight junctions between endothelial cells and RPE cells restrict the paracellular transport of molecules, maintaining barrier integrity.
   b. **Transporters:** Specialized transport proteins on endothelial and RPE cells regulate the transcellular transport of nutrients, ions, and waste products.
   c. **Metabolic Enzymes**: Enzymes within the BRB cells metabolize certain substances, influencing their availability in the retina.
   d. **Efflux Pumps**: ATP-binding cassette (ABC) transporters actively pump out xenobiotics, protecting the retina from potentially harmful substances.

Function of the Blood-Retinal Barrier:

The BRB serves several critical functions:

1. **Protection**: It protects the neural retina from harmful substances present in the systemic circulation, such as toxins and pathogens.

2. **Homeostasis**: The BRB maintains the microenvironment necessary for retinal function by regulating the transport of nutrients, oxygen, and waste products.

3. **Immunomodulation**: It regulates the entry of immune cells and inflammatory mediators into the retina, helping to maintain immune privilege and prevent inflammation.

Implications for Ocular Drug Delivery Systems:

The BRB presents significant challenges for drug delivery to the retina. Strategies to overcome or bypass the BRB include:

1. **Intravitreal Injection**: Direct injection of drugs into the vitreous humor bypasses the BRB, delivering therapeutics directly to the retina.

2. **Intravitreal Implants**: Slow-release implants can sustain therapeutic drug levels within the vitreous humor and retina over an extended period.

3. **Nanoparticle Formulations**: Nanoparticles can be designed to penetrate the BRB and release drugs at the desired site of action within the retina.

4. **Receptor-Mediated Transport**: Utilizing endogenous transport mechanisms, such as receptor-mediated transcytosis, to facilitate drug delivery across the BRB.

Efflux Transporters

Efflux transporters play a significant role in the barriers encountered by drugs in ocular drug delivery systems. These transporters are membrane proteins that actively pump out drugs and xenobiotics from cells, thereby reducing their intracellular concentration. Understanding the role of efflux transporters is crucial for designing effective drug delivery strategies for ocular diseases. Let's delve into efflux transporters in detail:

Types of Efflux Transporters:

1. **ATP-Binding Cassette (ABC) Transporters:**

    a. **P-glycoprotein (P-gp; ABCB1):** P-gp is one of the most extensively studied efflux transporters. It is expressed in various ocular tissues, including the cornea, iris-ciliary body, and retina. P-gp efflux activity can limit the intraocular penetration of substrates.

b. **Breast Cancer Resistance Protein (BCRP; ABCG2):** BCRP is another ABC transporter expressed in ocular tissues. It plays a role in protecting the eye from xenobiotics and may affect the penetration of drugs into the retina and anterior segment.

2. **Multidrug Resistance-Associated Proteins (MRPs):**

a. **MRP1 (ABCC1) and MRP2 (ABCC2):** These transporters are expressed in the retina and retinal pigment epithelium (RPE). They are involved in the efflux of various substrates, including drugs and metabolites.

Role of Efflux Transporters in Ocular Drug Delivery:

1. **Barrier Function**: Efflux transporters in ocular tissues, such as the cornea, iris-ciliary body, and retina, contribute to the blood-ocular barrier by actively pumping out drugs and xenobiotics, thereby reducing their intraocular concentration.

2. **Drug Resistance**: Overexpression of efflux transporters, particularly P-gp, is associated with multidrug resistance in ocular diseases such as retinoblastoma and ocular tumors. This can limit the efficacy of chemotherapy and targeted therapies.

3. **Pharmacokinetics:** Efflux transporters influence the pharmacokinetics of drugs in the eye by affecting their absorption, distribution, metabolism, and excretion. Understanding the interplay between efflux transporters and drug disposition is essential for optimizing drug delivery.

Strategies to Overcome Efflux Transporters:

1. **Inhibition:** Co-administration of efflux transporter inhibitors can inhibit their activity, thereby increasing the intraocular concentration of co-administered drugs. However, care must be taken to avoid potential drug interactions and toxicity.

2. **Prodrug Design**: Conjugating drugs with transporter substrates can enhance their ocular penetration by exploiting efflux transporter-mediated uptake mechanisms.

3. **Nanoparticle Formulations**: Nanoparticles can be engineered to bypass efflux transporters or deliver drugs to specific ocular tissues while evading efflux-mediated clearance.

4. **Targeted Delivery**: Utilizing ligand-receptor interactions or receptor-mediated transcytosis can facilitate the targeted delivery of drugs to ocular tissues, bypassing efflux transporters.

Strategies to Overcome Barriers

1. **Prodrugs:** Designed to improve lipophilicity and enhance corneal penetration.

2. **Nanoparticles**: Enhance drug stability, prolong retention time, and facilitate penetration through ocular barriers.

3. **Mucoadhesive Polymers**: Increase the residence time of drugs on the ocular surface.

4. **Permeation Enhancers**: Temporarily disrupt tight junctions to enhance drug absorption.

5. **Implantable Devices**: Provide sustained drug release directly to the target site, bypassing some barriers.

6. **In Situ Gels**: Form a gel upon contact with the ocular surface, prolonging drug residence time.

METHODS TO OVERCOME BARRIERS

Overcoming the various barriers to drug delivery in the eye requires innovative strategies to enhance drug bioavailability, prolong residence time, and ensure effective therapeutic outcomes. Here are detailed methods employed to address these challenges:

1. Prodrugs

a. **Definition:** Prodrugs are chemically modified derivatives of active drugs designed to improve their physicochemical properties, such as lipophilicity, which enhances their ability to penetrate ocular barriers.

b. **Mechanism:** Once administered, prodrugs undergo enzymatic conversion in the eye to release the active drug.

c. **Examples:**

i. **Latanoprost**: A prostaglandin analogue used to treat glaucoma; its ester form enhances corneal penetration and is hydrolyzed to the active acid form in the eye.

2. Nanoparticles

a. **Definition:** Nanoparticles are tiny particles (typically less than 100 nm) that can encapsulate drugs, protecting them from degradation and enhancing delivery.

b. **Types:** Lipid-based (liposomes, solid lipid nanoparticles), polymeric (PLGA, chitosan), and inorganic (gold, silica).

c. **Advantages:**

i. Enhanced drug stability

ii. Prolonged residence time

iii. Targeted delivery

iv. Controlled release profiles

d. **Examples:**

i. **Liposomes:** Vesicles that can encapsulate both hydrophilic and hydrophobic drugs, improving corneal penetration and sustained release.

ii. **Chitosan Nanoparticles**: Biodegradable and mucoadhesive, enhancing drug retention on the ocular surface.

3. Mucoadhesive Polymers

a. **Definition**: Polymers that adhere to the mucin layer of the ocular surface, prolonging the residence time of the drug.

b. **Mechanis**m: Interaction with mucins in the tear film, providing sustained release.

c. **Examples:**

    i. **Chitosan**: A naturally occurring polymer with mucoadhesive properties, used to formulate various ocular drug delivery systems.

    ii. **Hyaluronic Acid**: Enhances moisture retention and adhesion to the ocular surface.

4. Permeation Enhancers

a. **Definition:** Chemical agents that temporarily disrupt the tight junctions in epithelial cells, enhancing drug permeation.

b. **Types:** Surfactants, bile salts, and fatty acids.

c. **Examples:**

    i. **Benzalkonium Chloride (BAC):** A surfactant used in eye drops that enhances corneal permeability but must be used cautiously due to potential toxicity.

    ii. **EDTA**: A chelating agent that can enhance drug permeation by disrupting epithelial tight junctions.

5. Implantable Devices

a. **Definition**: Devices implanted in or around the eye that provide sustained and controlled drug release over an extended period.

b. **Types**: Biodegradable and non-biodegradable implants.

c. **Examples:**

    i. **Ozurdex:** A biodegradable implant containing dexamethasone for treating macular edema.

    ii. **Retisert:** A non-biodegradable implant for the sustained release of fluocinolone acetonide in chronic uveitis.

6. In Situ Gels

a. **Definition**: Formulations that undergo a sol-to-gel transition upon instillation into the eye, providing prolonged contact time with the ocular surface.

b. **Mechanism:** Triggered by physiological conditions such as temperature, pH, or ion concentration.

c. **Examples:**

   i. **Thermosensitive Gels**: Poloxamers that gel at body temperature, providing sustained release (e.g., Pilopine HS for glaucoma).

   ii. **pH-Sensitive Gels**: Carbopol-based formulations that gel at the ocular pH.

7. Microneedles

a. **Definition**: Tiny needles that create microchannels in the ocular tissue for drug delivery, minimizing discomfort and enhancing permeability.

b. **Advantages:**

   i. Minimally invasive

   ii. Precise delivery to target tissues

   iii. Reduced risk of complications compared to traditional injections

c. **Examples:**

   i. **Hollow Microneedles**: Allow direct infusion of drugs into the ocular tissues.

   ii. **Solid Microneedles**: Coated with drugs that dissolve upon insertion into the tissue.

8. Contact Lenses

a. **Definition**: Contact lenses designed to release drugs slowly over time, providing sustained delivery to the cornea and conjunctiva.

b. **Types:** Conventional and silicone hydrogel lenses, drug-embedded or coated.

c. **Examples:**

i. **Drug-Loaded Silicone Hydrogel Lenses**: Used for the sustained release of drugs like timolol for glaucoma.

9. Gene Therapy

a. **Definition**: Delivery of genetic material to ocular cells to treat genetic disorders or provide therapeutic proteins.

b. **Mechanism**: Uses viral or non-viral vectors to deliver genes to specific ocular tissues.

c. **Examples:**

i. **Luxturna:** An FDA-approved gene therapy for RPE65 mutation-associated retinal dystrophy.

Multiple-Choice Questions:

1. What is the primary role of the sclera in the eye?

    A) To control the size of the pupil

    B) To maintain the shape of the eyeball

    C) To focus light on the retina

    D) To produce aqueous humor

2. Which of the following is a mechanism of the prodrugs used in ocular drug delivery?

    A) They enhance the ionic balance within the eye

    B) They provide mechanical support to the retina

    C) They undergo enzymatic conversion to release the active drug

    D) They reduce the inflammatory response in the eye

3. What is the purpose of using nanoparticles in ocular drug delivery?

    A) To provide a rigid structure to the eye

    B) To enhance drug stability and prolong retention time

    C) To increase the volume of tear production

    D) To decrease the turnover rate of the tear film

4. Which type of gel forms upon contact with the ocular surface and provides prolonged drug residence time?

    A) Hydrogel

    B) In situ forming gel

    C) Silicone hydrogel

    D) Poloxamers

5. What challenge does the blood-aqueous barrier (BAB) pose for ocular drug delivery?

    A) It allows all substances from the blood to enter the aqueous humor

    B) It restricts the movement of substances from the blood into the aqueous humor

    C) It provides a pathway for drugs to directly reach the retina

    D) It assists in the diffusion of drugs to the anterior chamber

6. Which of the following efflux transporters is known for its role in the eye?

    A) P-glycoprotein (P-gp)

    B) Glucose transporters

    C) Hemoglobin

    D) Myoglobin

7. What is the function of mucoadhesive polymers in ocular drug delivery?

    A) To decrease the viscosity of ocular fluids

    B) To enhance the absorption of drugs through the mucin layer

    C) To reduce drug penetration through the cornea

    D) To act as a barrier against pathogens

8. What effect do permeation enhancers have in ocular drug delivery?

    A) They increase the tear production

    B) They disrupt tight junctions to enhance drug absorption

    C) They act as a structural barrier

    D) They decrease drug stability

9. Which is an example of a biodegradable implant used in ocular drug delivery?

    A) Ozurdex

    B) Retisert

    C) Poloxamers

    D) Silicone hydrogel lenses

10. Which barrier does intravitreal injection primarily bypass?

    A) Blood-aqueous barrier

    B) Corneal barrier

    C) Conjunctival barrier

    D) Vitreous humor barrier

11. What is the main function of the vitreous humor in the eye?

    A) To regulate nutrient and waste exchange

    B) To maintain the shape of the eye and support the retina

    C) To control the entry of immune cells

    D) To produce visual signals to the brain

12. Which type of ocular drug delivery system uses a sol-to-gel transition?

    A) Contact lenses

    B) In situ gels

    C) Implantable devices

    D) Prodrugs

13. What type of nanoparticles are used for encapsulating drugs in ocular drug delivery?

    A) Gold and silica

    B) Iron oxide

    C) Zinc oxide

    D) Magnesium sulfate

14. Which method involves creating microchannels in the ocular tissue for drug delivery?

    delivery?

A) Hydrogels

B) Microneedles

C) Mucoadhesive polymers

D) Liposomes

15. Which drug delivery system is specifically designed to release drugs slowly over time to the cornea?

A) Biodegradable implants

B) Contact lenses

C) In situ gels

D) Hydrogels

16. What is the primary role of the blood-retinal barrier (BRB)?

A) To maintain the shape of the eyeball

B) To regulate the exchange of substances between the systemic circulation and the neural retina

C) To focus light onto the retina

D) To produce aqueous humor

17. What is the main advantage of using gene therapy in ocular drug delivery?

A) It enhances the mechanical strength of the eye

B) It treats genetic disorders by delivering therapeutic proteins

C) It increases the size of the pupil

D) It decreases the production of tears

18. What is the primary challenge posed by the mucin layer in ocoral drug delivery?

A) It increases the turnover rate of the tear film

B) It acts as a barrier to the penetration of hydrophobic drugs

C) It facilitates the spread of infectious agents

D) It reduces the refractive power of the eye

19. Which of the following is a mechanism by which liposomes enhance ocular drug delivery?

A) By increasing tear production

B) By reducing drug stability

C) By encapsulating hydrophilic and lipophilic drugs

D) By acting as a barrier to drug entry

20. What is the role of ATP-binding cassette (ABC) transporters in the eye?

A) To facilitate the absorption of all drugs

B) To pump out xenobiotics and reduce intraocular drug concentration

C) To increase the permeability of the corneal epithelium

D) To decrease the efficacy of enzymatic degradation

Short Answer Questions:

1. What is the primary function of the sclera in the eye?

2. How do prodrugs enhance ocular drug delivery?

3. What role do nanoparticles play in ocular drug delivery systems?

4. Describe the function of in situ forming gels in ocular drug delivery.

5. What challenge does the blood-aqueous barrier present for drug delivery in the eye?

6. Name a common efflux transporter found in ocular tissues and its function.

7. How do mucoadhesive polymers aid in drug delivery to the eye?

8. What effect do permeation enhancers have on ocular drug delivery?

9. What is one example of a biodegradable implant used in ocular drug delivery and its use?

10. Which ocular barrier does intravitreal injection primarily bypass?

11. Explain the main function of the vitreous humor in the eye.

12. What type of ocular drug delivery system uses a sol-to-gel transition?

13. What are the types of nanoparticles used for encapsulating drugs in ocular drug delivery?

14. Which method involves creating microchannels in ocular tissue for drug delivery?

15. Which drug delivery system is specifically designed to release drugs over time to the cornea?

16. Describe the primary role of the blood-retinal barrier.

17. What is the main advantage of using gene therapy in ocular drug delivery?

18. What is the primary challenge posed by the mucin layer in ocular drug delivery?

19. How do liposomes enhance ocular drug delivery?

20. What role do ATP-binding cassette transporters play in the eye?

Long Answer Questions:

1. Explain how the structure and function of the tear film barrier affect ocular drug delivery and the strategies used to overcome these challenges.

2. Describe the structure of the cornea and the barriers it presents to drug permeation in ocular drug delivery systems.

3. Discuss the role of the conjunctival barrier in ocular drug delivery, including its structure, function, and strategies to overcome it.

4. Explain the challenges posed by the scleral barrier in ocular drug delivery and the methods used to enhance drug penetration through this barrier.

5. Describe the anatomy and function of the blood-aqueous barrier and its implications for ocular drug delivery.

6. Explain the structure and function of the vitreous humor barrier and discuss the strategies to overcome this barrier for effective drug delivery to the posterior segment of the eye.

7. Discuss the anatomy and function of the blood-retinal barrier and the challenges it poses for drug delivery to the retina.

8. Describe the role of efflux transporters in ocular drug delivery and the strategies employed to overcome their effects.

9. Discuss the use of nanoparticles in ocular drug delivery, including the types, advantages, and specific applications.

10. Explain the significance of gene therapy in ocular drug delivery and describe an FDA-approved gene therapy product, including its mechanism and therapeutic target.

Answer Key:

1. (B) To maintain the shape of the eyeball
2. (C) They undergo enzymatic conversion to release the active drug
3. (B) To enhance drug stability and prolong retention time
4. (B) In situ forming gel
5. (B) It restricts the movement of substances from the blood into the aqueous humor
6. (A) P-glycoprotein (P-gp)
7. (B) To enhance the absorption of drugs through the mucin layer
8. (B) They disrupt tight junctions to enhance drug absorption
9. (A) Ozurdex
10. (D) Vitreous humor barrier
11. (B) To maintain the shape of the eye and support the retina
12. (B) In situ gels
13. (A) Gold and silica
14. (B) Microneedles
15. (B) Contact lenses
16. (B) To regulate the exchange of substances between the systemic circulation and the neural retina
17. (B) It treats genetic disorders by delivering therapeutic proteins
18. (B) It acts as a barrier to the penetration of hydrophobic drugs

19.(C) By encapsulating hydrophilic and lipophilic drugs

20.(B) To pump out xenobiotics and reduce intraocular drug concentration

CHAPTER – 6

TRANSDERMAL DRUG DELIVERY SYSTEMS

INTROUCTION:

Transdermal Drug Delivery Systems (TDDS) are an advanced method of administering drugs through the skin, offering a non-invasive and controlled release of medication. This method has been increasingly popular due to its ability to bypass the gastrointestinal tract, thereby reducing potential side effects and improving patient compliance. Below is a detailed introduction to TDDS.

Overview of Transdermal Drug Delivery Systems

Definition

Transdermal Drug Delivery Systems are pharmaceutical formulations designed to deliver therapeutic substances through the skin and into the bloodstream. These systems typically come in the form of patches applied to the skin, which release the drug at a controlled rate over an extended period.

History

The concept of transdermal drug delivery has been around for centuries, with early uses involving topical applications of natural substances for therapeutic effects. The modern transdermal patch was first approved by the FDA in 1979 for the delivery of scopolamine to prevent motion sickness.

Advantages of TDDS

1. **Non-Invasive**: TDDS provides a needle-free method of drug administration, reducing the risk of infections and improving patient comfort.

2. **Controlled Release**: Drugs can be delivered at a steady rate over a prolonged period, maintaining consistent therapeutic levels in the bloodstream.

3. **Bypasses First-Pass Metabolism**: The drug avoids degradation by the liver, which can enhance bioavailability and efficacy.

4. **Improved Patient Compliance**: Convenient and easy to use, TDDS can improve adherence to medication regimens, especially for chronic conditions.

5. **Reduced Side Effects**: Lower systemic exposure and targeted delivery can reduce the risk of adverse effects.

Mechanism of Action

Transdermal patches typically consist of several layers:

1. **Backing Layer**: Protects the patch from the external environment.

2. **Drug Reservoir or Matrix**: Contains the active pharmaceutical ingredient (API).

3. **Release Liner**: Protects the drug layer and is removed before application.

4. **Adhesive Layer:** Ensures the patch sticks to the skin.

The drug is delivered through the skin by passive diffusion, driven by the concentration gradient between the drug in the patch and the bloodstream. The stratum corneum, the outermost layer of the skin, acts as the primary barrier to drug penetration. To enhance drug permeation, various techniques can be employed, such as chemical enhancers, iontophoresis, and microneedles.

Types of Transdermal Patches

1. **Reservoir Patches**: Contain a liquid or gel drug reservoir separated from the skin by a semi-permeable membrane. This type allows for a more controlled release rate.

2. **Matrix Patches**: The drug is dispersed in a polymer matrix that controls the release rate directly from the patch.

3. **Adhesive Patches**: The drug is incorporated into the adhesive layer, simplifying the design and often improving skin adhesion.

Commonly Used Drugs in TDDS

1. **Hormones:** Estradiol and testosterone for hormone replacement therapy.

2. **Pain Relievers**: Fentanyl and buprenorphine for chronic pain management.

3. **Nicotine**: For smoking cessation.

4. **Cardiovascular Drugs**: Nitroglycerin for angina.

5. **Motion Sickness**: Scopolamine.

Challenges and Limitations

1. **Skin Barrier**: The stratum corneum is a significant barrier, limiting the types and sizes of molecules that can be effectively delivered.

2. **Skin Irritation**: Prolonged use of patches can cause skin irritation or allergic reactions in some patients.

3. **Drug Formulation**: Developing stable formulations that can release the drug at a consistent rate over time can be complex.

4. **Cost:** TDDS can be more expensive to produce compared to traditional dosage forms.

Future Directions

The field of TDDS is continually evolving, with ongoing research aimed at overcoming current limitations. Innovations include:

1. **Microneedles:** Tiny needles that painlessly penetrate the skin barrier to deliver drugs directly.

2. **Electroporation and Sonophoresis**: Techniques using electric fields or ultrasound to enhance drug permeation.

3. **Nanotechnology**: Nanocarriers can improve the delivery and stability of drugs.

4. **Personalized Medicine**: Tailoring TDDS to individual patient needs for more effective treatment outcomes.

STRUCTURE OF SKIN AND BARRIERS

Understanding the structure of the skin and the barriers it presents is crucial for the effective design and implementation of Transdermal Drug Delivery Systems (TDDS). The skin is a complex organ that acts as a protective barrier while also being a potential route for drug delivery. Here is a detailed look at the skin's structure and the barriers relevant to TDDS.

Structure of the Skin

The skin consists of three main layers: the epidermis, dermis, and hypodermis (subcutaneous layer).

1. Epidermis

The outermost layer of the skin, the epidermis, is primarily composed of keratinocytes and can be subdivided into several layers:

a. **Stratum Corneum**: The outermost layer, composed of dead, flattened keratinocytes (corneocytes) embedded in a lipid matrix. It is the primary barrier to drug permeation, often referred to as the rate-limiting step for transdermal drug delivery.

b. **Stratum Lucidum**: A thin, clear layer found only in thick skin regions such as the palms and soles.

c. **Stratum Granulosum**: Characterized by granule-containing keratinocytes that are in the process of dying and forming a more robust barrier.

d. **Stratum Spinosum**: Composed of several layers of living keratinocytes that provide structural strength and flexibility.

e. **Stratum Basale**: The deepest layer, containing proliferating keratinocytes and melanocytes, which continuously divide and push new cells towards the surface.

2. Dermis

Beneath the epidermis, the dermis provides structural support and nourishment. It is divided into:

a. **Papillary Dermis**: The upper layer, consisting of loose connective tissue and capillaries that nourish the epidermis.

b. **Reticular Dermis**: The deeper, thicker layer composed of dense connective tissue, including collagen and elastin fibers, providing skin with strength and elasticity.

The dermis also contains hair follicles, sebaceous (oil) glands, sweat glands, nerves, and blood vessels, which can play a role in drug delivery.

3. Hypodermis (Subcutaneous Layer)

The hypodermis is the deepest layer, composed mainly of adipose (fat) tissue and connective tissue. It acts as a cushion, insulates the body, and anchors the skin to underlying structures such as muscles and bones.

Barriers in Transdermal Drug Delivery

The primary challenge in TDDS is overcoming the skin's natural barrier properties. The main barriers are:

1. Stratum Corneum

a. **Structure:** The stratum corneum is composed of dead keratinocytes (corneocytes) embedded in a lipid matrix (often described as a "brick and mortar" structure, where corneocytes are the bricks and the lipid matrix is the mortar).

b. **Barrier Function**: This layer acts as the main barrier to drug penetration due to its low permeability. Only small, lipophilic, and uncharged molecules can penetrate it effectively without assistance.

2. Epidermal Lipid Matrix

a. **Composition**: The lipid matrix consists of ceramides, free fatty acids, and cholesterol. These lipids form multiple lamellar (layered) structures that further impede the passage of substances.

b. **Barrier Function**: The tightly packed lipid layers create a highly ordered structure that is difficult for many drugs to traverse.

3. Tight Junctions and Cellular Barriers

a. **Location**: Tight junctions are present in the lower layers of the epidermis.

b. **Barrier Function**: These junctions seal the space between cells, further restricting the paracellular (between cells) pathway for drug molecules.

Methods to Overcome Skin Barriers

To enhance drug delivery through the skin, various strategies can be employed:

1. Chemical Enhancers

a. **Function**: Substances that temporarily disrupt the stratum corneum lipid structure or increase skin permeability.

b. **Examples**: Alcohols, fatty acids, surfactants, and terpenes.

2. Physical Methods

a. **Iontophoresis**: Uses a small electric current to drive charged drug molecules through the skin.

b. **Sonophoresis (Ultrasound):** Utilizes ultrasound waves to enhance drug penetration by disrupting the lipid structure.

c. **Microneedles**: Involves the use of tiny needles that painlessly pierce the stratum corneum, creating microchannels for drug delivery.

3. Formulation Strategies

a. **Lipid-Based Systems**: Such as liposomes and niosomes, which can fuse with the skin lipids to enhance drug delivery.

b. **Nanoparticles**: Provide a means to encapsulate drugs and facilitate their transport through the skin barrier.

PENETRATION ENHANCERS

Penetration enhancers, also known as permeation enhancers, play a crucial role in Transdermal Drug Delivery Systems (TDDS) by facilitating the transport of therapeutic agents through the skin barrier, primarily the stratum corneum. These enhancers can modify the skin's barrier properties temporarily, allowing for increased drug permeation. Here is a detailed examination of penetration enhancers in TDDS.

Types of Penetration Enhancers

Penetration enhancers can be classified into several categories based on their chemical nature and mechanism of action:

1. Chemical Enhancers

Chemical enhancers are compounds that interact with the skin's structure to enhance drug permeability. They work by disrupting the lipid matrix, interacting with keratin, or increasing the solubility of the drug in the skin.

Common Chemical Enhancers:

a. **Alcohols:** Ethanol and isopropanol can disrupt the lipid structure of the stratum corneum and improve drug solubility.

b. **Fatty Acids and Fatty Alcohols**: Oleic acid and lauryl alcohol can fluidize the lipid layers and increase skin permeability.

c. **Surfactants:** Sodium lauryl sulfate and polysorbates can solubilize lipids and enhance drug transport.

d. **Terpenes:** Menthol and limonene can disrupt the lipid structure and enhance the partitioning of drugs into the skin.

e. **Urea and Pyrrolidones**: These can increase skin hydration and alter the keratin structure, facilitating drug penetration.

2. Physical Enhancers

Physical methods enhance drug delivery by physically disrupting the skin barrier or using external energy sources to drive drugs into the skin.

Common Physical Enhancers:

a. **Iontophoresis:** Uses a small electric current to drive charged drug molecules through the skin. It enhances the permeation of ionic and hydrophilic drugs.

b. **Sonophoresis (Ultrasound):** Employs ultrasound waves to disrupt the lipid structure and enhance drug transport. It can be used for both hydrophilic and lipophilic drugs.

c. **Microneedles:** Tiny needles create microchannels in the stratum corneum, allowing drugs to bypass this barrier and penetrate the deeper layers of the skin.

d. **Electroporation:** Uses short, high-voltage pulses to create transient pores in the skin, enhancing drug delivery.

3. Biochemical Enhancers

Biochemical enhancers involve the use of enzymes or other biological agents to modify the skin barrier properties.

Common Biochemical Enhancers:

a. **Enzymes:** Such as lipases and proteases, which can degrade specific components of the stratum corneum, enhancing permeability.

b. **Peptides:** Certain peptides can interact with skin lipids and proteins to increase drug transport.

Mechanisms of Action

Penetration enhancers work through various mechanisms to improve drug delivery through the skin:

1. **Lipid Disruption**: Many chemical enhancers disrupt the ordered lipid structure in the stratum corneum, increasing the fluidity of the lipid matrix and allowing drugs to diffuse more easily.

2. **Protein Interaction**: Some enhancers interact with keratin in the corneocytes, altering the protein structure and increasing drug permeability.

3. **Partitioning Enhancement**: Enhancers can increase the solubility of the drug within the skin layers, improving the partitioning of the drug from the formulation into the skin.

4. **Hydration**: Enhancers that increase skin hydration can swell the stratum corneum, opening up pathways for drug penetration.

5. **Transient Pores**: Physical methods like electroporation create temporary pores in the skin, providing direct pathways for drug molecules.

Evaluation of Penetration Enhancers

The effectiveness of penetration enhancers is evaluated using various in vitro, ex vivo, and in vivo methods:

a. **In Vitro Studies**: Using skin models or artificial membranes to study the impact of enhancers on drug permeability.

b. **Ex Vivo Studies**: Utilizing excised human or animal skin to assess the permeation of drugs with and without enhancers.

c. **In Vivo Studies**: Conducting clinical trials to evaluate the safety and efficacy of enhancers in human subjects.

Safety and Toxicity Considerations

While penetration enhancers can significantly improve drug delivery, their safety and potential for causing skin irritation or toxicity must be carefully evaluated:

a. **Irritation and Sensitization**: Some enhancers can cause skin irritation or allergic reactions, necessitating thorough dermatological testing.

b. **Reversibility:** The effects of enhancers should be reversible, with the skin returning to its normal barrier function after the enhancer is removed.

c. **Concentration**: The concentration of enhancers must be optimized to balance efficacy with safety.

Examples of Transdermal Systems Utilizing Penetration Enhancers

1. **Nicotine Patches**: Often use alcohols and surfactants to enhance nicotine permeation.

2. **Hormone Replacement** Therapy Patches: Utilize fatty acids and terpenes to facilitate the delivery of estradiol and other hormones.

3. **Pain Relief Patches**: Employ chemical enhancers like oleic acid to improve the delivery of analgesics such as fentanyl.

TRANSDERMAL DRUG DELIVERY SYSTEMS

Transdermal Drug Delivery Systems (TDDS) are a sophisticated and innovative method of delivering drugs through the skin for systemic effects. These systems offer numerous advantages over traditional routes of administration, including improved patient compliance, controlled drug release, and avoidance of gastrointestinal and hepatic first-pass metabolism. Here's a detailed exploration of TDDS.

Key Components of TDDS

TDDS typically consist of several key components, each playing a critical role in the effective delivery of drugs through the skin:

1. **Drug Reservoir or Matrix**: Contains the active pharmaceutical ingredient (API).
2. **Polymeric Matrix or Membrane**: Controls the rate at which the drug is released from the system.
3. **Adhesive Layer**: Ensures the patch adheres securely to the skin.
4. **Backing Layer**: Protects the system from the external environment.
5. Release Liner: Removed before application to expose the adhesive layer.

Types of Transdermal Patches

TDDS come in various designs, each tailored to specific therapeutic needs and drug properties:

1. **Reservoir Patches**: Contain a liquid or gel reservoir with the drug, separated from the skin by a rate-controlling membrane.
2. **Matrix Patches**: The drug is dispersed in a polymer matrix that controls the release rate directly from the patch.
3. **Drug-in-Adhesive Patches**: The drug is incorporated into the adhesive layer, simplifying the design and enhancing skin adhesion.
4. **Microreservoir Patches**: Combine aspects of both reservoir and matrix designs, with multiple microreservoirs within the patch.

Mechanism of Drug Delivery

TDDS deliver drugs through the skin via passive diffusion. The drug must pass through several layers of the skin before reaching systemic circulation:

1. **Stratum Corneum**: The outermost layer, which is the primary barrier to drug permeation.
2. **Epidermis:** Provides additional barriers but less restrictive than the stratum corneum.
3. **Dermis:** Contains blood vessels that absorb the drug into the systemic circulation.

The rate of drug delivery is influenced by factors such as the drug's physicochemical properties, the design of the TDDS, and the condition of the skin.

Advantages of TDDS

1. **Non-Invasive:** Provides a needle-free method of drug administration.
2. **Controlled Release**: Maintains consistent therapeutic levels of the drug over an extended period.
3. **Bypasses First-Pass Metabolism**: Enhances bioavailability by avoiding hepatic metabolism.
4. **Improved Patient Compliance**: Simplifies drug administration, especially for chronic conditions.
5. **Reduced Side Effects**: Minimizes systemic exposure and potential gastrointestinal side effects.

Challenges and Limitations

1. **Skin Barrier**: The stratum corneum is a formidable barrier, limiting the types of drugs that can be effectively delivered transdermally.
2. **Skin Irritation**: Prolonged use of patches can cause local skin reactions such as irritation or allergic contact dermatitis.
3. **Limited Drug Types**: Effective transdermal delivery is typically limited to potent, low molecular weight, lipophilic drugs.

4. **Complex Formulation**: Developing stable and effective TDDS formulations can be technically challenging and costly.

Examples of TDDS

Several commercially available transdermal patches demonstrate the diverse applications of this technology:

1. **Nicotine Patches**: Used for smoking cessation, they release nicotine steadily to help reduce withdrawal symptoms.
2. **Hormone Replacement Therapy (HRT) Patches**: Deliver hormones such as estradiol or testosterone for hormone replacement therapy.
3. **Analgesic Patches**: Fentanyl patches provide long-term pain relief for chronic pain conditions.
4. **Hypertension Patches**: Clonidine patches help manage high blood pressure.

Advanced Technologies in TDDS

To enhance the efficiency and applicability of TDDS, several advanced technologies are being explored:

1. **Microneedles**: Tiny needles that penetrate the stratum corneum, allowing for the direct delivery of drugs into the dermis.
2. **Iontophoresis**: Uses electrical currents to enhance the permeation of charged drug molecules.
3. **Sonophoresis**: Utilizes ultrasound waves to disrupt the skin barrier and increase drug permeation.
4. **Nanotechnology**: Nanocarriers such as liposomes, niosomes, and solid lipid nanoparticles can improve the stability and penetration of drugs.

Regulatory and Quality Considerations

The development and approval of TDDS involve rigorous regulatory oversight to ensure their safety, efficacy, and quality. Key considerations include:

1. **Preclinical Studies**: In vitro and in vivo studies to evaluate skin permeation, toxicity, and pharmacokinetics.

2. **Clinical Trials:** Human studies to assess safety, efficacy, and potential side effects.

3. **Manufacturing Standards**: Adherence to Good Manufacturing Practices (GMP) to ensure product consistency and quality.

4. **Post-Marketing Surveillance**: Ongoing monitoring to detect any long-term adverse effects and ensure continued safety.

Future Directions

The future of TDDS is promising, with ongoing research and development aimed at overcoming current limitations and expanding the range of drugs that can be delivered transdermally. Innovations in formulation science, material engineering, and nanotechnology are expected to enhance the efficacy, safety, and patient acceptability of TDDS.

FORMULATION OF TRANSDERMAL DRUG DELIVERY SYSTEMS

Formulating Transdermal Drug Delivery Systems (TDDS) is a complex process that involves the careful selection and combination of components to ensure effective delivery of the drug through the skin. The goal is to design a system that can consistently release the drug at a controlled rate while maintaining stability and patient compliance. Here's a detailed look at the formulation of TDDS.

Key Components of TDDS Formulation

1. **Active Pharmaceutical Ingredient (API):** The drug substance that is intended to be delivered through the skin.

2. **Polymers:** Serve as the matrix or reservoir for the drug and control the release rate.

3. **Penetration Enhancers**: Substances that enhance the permeability of the skin to facilitate drug absorption.

4. **Adhesive**: Ensures the patch adheres to the skin securely for the duration of therapy.

5. **Backing Layer**: Provides structural support and protects the patch from the external environment.

6. **Release Liner**: A removable layer that protects the adhesive and drug layer before application.

Types of TDDS Formulations

1. Reservoir Systems

Structure: These systems contain a liquid or gel reservoir that holds the drug, separated from the skin by a rate-controlling membrane.

Advantages:

a. Precise control over drug release rate.

b. Suitable for drugs that require a consistent release profile.

Challenges:

a. Complex manufacturing process.

b. Risk of dose dumping if the reservoir is damaged.

Example: Nitroglycerin patches for angina.

2. Matrix Systems

Structure: The drug is dispersed in a polymer matrix, which controls the drug release directly from the matrix material.

Advantages:

a. Simplified manufacturing process.

b. Thin and flexible design.

Challenges:

a. Drug release rate can be affected by the properties of the polymer matrix.

Example: Estradiol patches for hormone replacement therapy.

3. Drug-in-Adhesive Systems

Structure: The drug is incorporated directly into the adhesive layer, which also serves to attach the patch to the skin.

Advantages:

a. Simplified design and manufacturing.

b. Good adhesion to the skin.

Challenges:

a. Potential for skin irritation due to the presence of the drug in the adhesive.

Example: Nicotine patches for smoking cessation.

4. Microreservoir Systems

Structure: Combine elements of both reservoir and matrix systems, containing multiple microreservoirs within the patch.

Advantages:

a. Improved control over drug release.

b. Versatile design.

Challenges:

a. Complex manufacturing process.

Example: Fentanyl patches for chronic pain management.

Formulation Process

The formulation of TDDS involves several key steps:

1. Selection of Drug and Excipients

a. **Drug Properties**: The drug should have suitable physicochemical properties for transdermal delivery, including low molecular weight, lipophilicity, and potency.

b. **Excipients:** Polymers, plasticizers, solvents, and penetration enhancers must be selected to optimize drug release and skin permeability.

2. Preparation of the Drug Matrix or Reservoir

a. **Dissolution:** The drug is dissolved or dispersed in the selected polymer matrix or reservoir medium.

b. **Mixing**: Homogeneous mixing ensures uniform distribution of the drug throughout the formulation.

3. Casting or Coating

a. **Reservoir Systems**: The drug reservoir is created by casting the drug-polymer mixture onto a backing layer and covering it with a rate-controlling membrane.

b. **Matrix and Drug-in-Adhesive Systems**: The drug-polymer mixture is cast or coated directly onto a backing layer.

4. Assembly of the Patch

a. **Layering**: Layers, including the backing layer, drug matrix or reservoir, adhesive, and release liner, are assembled.

b. **Cutting:** The assembled patch is cut into the desired size and shape.

5. Packaging

a. **Protection:** The patches are packaged in protective pouches to maintain stability and prevent contamination.

b. **Labeling:** Proper labeling ensures correct usage and storage information for the patient.

Penetration Enhancers

Penetration enhancers play a vital role in TDDS by increasing the permeability of the stratum corneum. They can be classified based on their mechanism of action:

1. **Chemical Enhancers**: Disrupt the lipid structure of the stratum corneum or alter protein conformation to increase drug diffusion.

   a. **Examples:** Ethanol, oleic acid, dimethyl sulfoxide (DMSO).

2. **Physical Enhancers**: Use physical methods to improve drug delivery.

   a. **Examples**: Microneedles, iontophoresis, sonophoresis.

3. **Biochemical Enhancers**: Utilize biological agents to enhance drug permeability.

   a. **Examples**: Enzymes, peptides.

Evaluation and Optimization

Formulating TDDS requires thorough evaluation and optimization to ensure efficacy and safety:

1. **In Vitro Permeation Studies**: Using skin models to evaluate the rate and extent of drug permeation.
2. **Ex Vivo Skin Studies**: Using excised human or animal skin to study drug delivery characteristics.
3. **In Vivo Studies**: Clinical trials to assess pharmacokinetics, efficacy, and safety in humans.
4. **Stability Testing**: Ensuring the patch maintains its integrity and performance over its shelf life.
5. **Skin Irritation Tests**: Assessing potential skin irritation or allergic reactions through dermatological testing.

Regulatory Considerations

Developing TDDS involves adhering to stringent regulatory guidelines to ensure product safety and efficacy:

1. **Good Manufacturing Practices (GMP):** Ensuring consistent quality during manufacturing.
2. **Preclinical and Clinical Testing**: Comprehensive testing to demonstrate safety and therapeutic efficacy.
3. **Regulatory Approvals**: Submitting data to regulatory authorities (e.g., FDA, EMA) for approval before market release.

Future Trends

Advancements in materials science, nanotechnology, and delivery techniques continue to enhance the potential of TDDS:

1. **Nanocarriers**: Utilizing nanoparticles to improve drug stability and delivery efficiency.
2. **Smart Patches**: Incorporating sensors and electronics for real-time monitoring and controlled drug release.
3. **Personalized Medicine**: Tailoring TDDS formulations to individual patient needs based on genetic and physiological factors.

EVALUATION OF TRANSDERMAL DRUG DELIVERY SYSTEMS

Evaluating Transdermal Drug Delivery Systems (TDDS) is a critical step to ensure their efficacy, safety, stability, and patient acceptability. The evaluation process involves a combination of in vitro, ex vivo, and in vivo studies. Here's a detailed look at the evaluation methods and criteria for TDDS.

In Vitro Evaluation

In vitro evaluation is a crucial step in the development of Transdermal Drug Delivery Systems (TDDS) as it allows researchers to study the release and permeation characteristics of the drug without the variability associated with biological systems. This phase of evaluation is essential for understanding how the drug behaves within the delivery system and how it permeates through the skin. Here is a detailed examination of in vitro evaluation methods used in TDDS.

Key Objectives of In Vitro Evaluation

1. **Drug Release Rate**: Determine the rate at which the drug is released from the TDDS.

2. **Permeation Rate**: Assess how effectively the drug permeates through the skin layers.

3. **Stability**: Evaluate the chemical and physical stability of the drug within the TDDS.

4. **Effect of Penetration Enhancers**: Study the impact of penetration enhancers on drug permeation.

5. **Formulation Optimization**: Optimize the formulation parameters to achieve desired drug release and permeation profiles.

In Vitro Drug Release Studies

Purpose

To determine the kinetics of drug release from the transdermal system into a surrounding medium.

Methods

1. **Franz Diffusion Cells**

a. **Setup:** The TDDS is placed in the donor compartment, and a receptor compartment is filled with a suitable buffer or solvent that simulates bodily fluids.

b. **Procedure**: The receptor medium is sampled at various time intervals to measure the concentration of the drug released.

c. **Analysis:** Drug release data are plotted against time to determine the release kinetics.

2. **Rotating Paddle Apparatus (USP Apparatus 5)**

   a. **Setup:** The TDDS is attached to a disk, which is then placed in a dissolution vessel containing a suitable medium.

   b. **Procedure:** The medium is sampled at set intervals while the paddle rotates, providing gentle agitation.

   c. **Analysis:** The concentration of the drug in the medium is measured over time to understand the release profile.

In Vitro Skin Permeation Studies

Purpose

To evaluate the ability of the drug to permeate through the skin and to study the rate of permeation.

Methods

1. **Franz Diffusion Cells**

   a. **Setup:** Human or animal skin is mounted between the donor and receptor compartments of the cell. The TDDS is placed on the stratum corneum side of the skin.

   b. **Procedure**: The receptor compartment is filled with a buffer that simulates interstitial fluid, and samples are taken at regular intervals.

   c. **Analysis**: The amount of drug permeated through the skin is measured, and permeation profiles are generated.

2. **Vertical Diffusion Cells (Side-by-Side Cells)**

a. **Setup:** Similar to Franz cells but with a vertical orientation, allowing for separate control of temperature and stirring on both sides of the skin.

b. **Procedure**: The donor and receptor compartments are filled with appropriate media, and samples are collected from the receptor side over time.

c. **Analysis**: Drug concentration in the receptor medium is measured to assess permeation.

In Vitro Stability Studies

Purpose

To ensure the chemical and physical stability of the drug within the TDDS under various conditions.

Methods

1. **Chemical Stability**

   a. **Procedure**: The TDDS is stored under different environmental conditions (e.g., varying temperatures, humidity levels) and sampled at different time points.

   b. **Analysis:** The drug content is analyzed using techniques such as High-Performance Liquid Chromatography (HPLC) to detect any degradation products.

2. **Physical Stability**

   a. **Procedure**: The physical appearance, adhesiveness, and integrity of the TDDS are monitored over time.

   b. **Analysis:** Parameters such as tensile strength, flexibility, and adhesion properties are assessed to ensure the patch remains functional.

Evaluation of Penetration Enhancers

Purpose

To determine the effectiveness of penetration enhancers in improving drug permeation through the skin.

Methods

1. **Comparative Permeation Studies**

   a. **Setup:** Permeation studies are conducted using TDDS formulations with and without penetration enhancers.

   b. **Procedure**: The permeation profiles are compared to assess the impact of enhancers.

   c. **Analysis**: The enhancement ratio is calculated by comparing the permeation rates with and without the enhancer.

2. **Skin Integrity Testing**

   a. **Setup:** Evaluate the integrity of the skin after exposure to penetration enhancers.

   b. **Procedure:** Histological examination of the skin can be performed to check for any structural changes.

   c. **Analysis:** Microscopic examination reveals any disruption or damage to the skin layers.

Optimization of Formulation Parameters

Purpose

To refine the formulation of the TDDS to achieve the desired drug release and permeation characteristics.

Methods

1. **Experimental Design and Statistical Analysis**

   a. **Setup:** Utilize factorial design or response surface methodology to systematically vary formulation parameters.

   b. **Procedure**: Conduct experiments to study the effect of different variables such as polymer concentration, plasticizer content, and drug load.

c. **Analysis**: Use statistical tools to analyze data and determine the optimal formulation parameters.

Analytical Techniques

1. High-Performance Liquid Chromatography (HPLC)

a. **Purpose:** To quantify the drug content in samples.

b. **Procedure**: Samples are injected into the HPLC system, separated on a chromatographic column, and detected using appropriate detectors.

c. **Analysis**: The concentration of the drug is determined based on peak areas compared to standard curves.

2. Mass Spectrometry (MS)

a. **Purpose**: To identify and quantify the drug and its degradation products.

b. **Procedure**: The sample is ionized, and the mass-to-charge ratio of ions is measured.

c. **Analysis:** Provides detailed information on the molecular structure and concentration of compounds.

3. UV-Visible Spectroscopy

a. **Purpose:** To measure drug concentration in samples.

b. **Procedure**: The absorbance of the sample at specific wavelengths is measured.

c. **Analysis:** The concentration is determined using Beer-Lambert law.

Ex Vivo Evaluation

Ex vivo evaluation of Transdermal Drug Delivery Systems (TDDS) involves studying drug permeation and skin interactions using excised animal or human skin. This method provides a more biologically relevant model than in vitro studies, offering insights into how the drug will interact with actual skin tissue without the complexity of a living organism. Here's a detailed look at the ex vivo evaluation of TDDS.

Key Objectives of Ex Vivo Evaluation

1. **Drug Permeation**: Assess the rate and extent of drug permeation through the skin.

2. **Skin Interaction**: Study the interaction between the TDDS and the skin, including potential irritation or sensitization.

3. **Penetration Enhancers**: Evaluate the effectiveness and safety of penetration enhancers.

4. **Formulation Optimization**: Fine-tune formulation parameters based on permeation and interaction data.

Methods for Ex Vivo Evaluation

1. Preparation of Skin Samples

a. **Source:** Human skin from surgical waste (e.g., abdominal or breast reduction surgeries) or animal skin (e.g., porcine, which closely resembles human skin).

b. **Processing:** Skin is typically excised, cleaned, and stored under appropriate conditions (e.g., frozen) until use. Thickness and integrity of the skin should be consistent across samples.

2. Skin Permeation Studies

Purpose

To evaluate the rate and extent of drug permeation through the skin.

Methods

1. **Franz Diffusion Cells**

   a. **Setup:** The excised skin is mounted between the donor and receptor compartments of the diffusion cell, with the stratum corneum facing the donor compartment.

   b. **Procedure:** The TDDS is applied to the skin in the donor compartment, and the receptor compartment is filled with a suitable buffer or simulated body fluid. The receptor medium is sampled at specific time intervals.

c. **Analysis:** Drug concentration in the receptor medium is measured using analytical techniques like HPLC or UV spectroscopy to generate permeation profiles.

2. **Side-by-Side Diffusion Cells**

   a. **Setup:** Similar to Franz cells but with a vertical orientation. Skin is placed between two half-cells, with the donor and receptor media on either side.

   b. **Procedure**: The TDDS is applied to the skin, and samples are taken from the receptor side over time.

   c. **Analysis**: Drug concentration is measured to assess permeation rates.

Parameters to Assess

1. **Cumulative Amount Permeated**: Total amount of drug that has permeated through the skin over time.

2. **Permeation Rate:** Rate at which the drug permeates the skin, often expressed as flux ($\mu g/cm^2/h$).

3. **Lag Time**: Time required for the drug to start appearing in the receptor compartment, indicating the initial permeation delay.

3. Skin Interaction Studies

Purpose

To study the potential irritation, sensitization, and structural changes in the skin due to TDDS application.

Methods

1. **Skin Irritation Tests**

   a. **Procedure:** The TDDS is applied to the excised skin for a specified duration. Post-application, the skin is visually inspected and histologically examined for signs of irritation, erythema, or edema.

b. **Scoring**: Irritation is typically scored based on a standardized scale.

2. **Sensitization Tests**

   a. **Procedure**: Similar to irritation tests, but focus is on identifying allergic reactions. The skin is examined for delayed hypersensitivity reactions post-application.

   b. **Analysis**: Histopathological examination to identify immune cell infiltration or other markers of sensitization.

3. **Histological Examination**

   a. **Purpose:** To observe any microscopic changes in the skin structure.

   b. **Procedure**: Skin samples are fixed, sectioned, and stained (e.g., H&E staining). They are then examined under a microscope to assess any cellular or structural damage.

4. Evaluation of Penetration Enhancers

Purpose

To determine the effectiveness and safety of penetration enhancers used in TDDS.

Methods

1. **Permeation Studies with Enhancers**

   a. **Procedure:** Conduct skin permeation studies with and without the penetration enhancer in the TDDS formulation.

   b. **Analysis**: Compare the permeation profiles to assess the enhancement effect. Calculate enhancement ratios to quantify the improvement in drug permeation.

2. **Skin Integrity Tests**

   a. **Procedure:** Post-application, the skin is examined for any structural damage caused by the penetration enhancer.

b. **Analysis:** Histological examination and integrity tests (e.g., transepidermal water loss measurements) are used to assess skin barrier function.

Analytical Techniques

1. High-Performance Liquid Chromatography (HPLC)

a. **Purpose:** Quantify drug concentration in receptor media.

b. **Procedure:** Samples from permeation studies are injected into the HPLC system, separated on a chromatographic column, and detected using suitable detectors.

c. **Analysis**: Peak areas are compared to standard curves to determine drug concentration.

2. UV-Visible Spectroscopy

a. **Purpose:** Measure drug concentration in receptor media.

b. **Procedure**: The absorbance of the sample at specific wavelengths is measured.

c. **Analysis:** Concentration is determined using the Beer-Lambert law.

3. Mass Spectrometry (MS)

a. **Purpose**: Identify and quantify drugs and degradation products.

b. **Procedure**: Samples are ionized, and the mass-to-charge ratio of ions is measured.

c. **Analysis:** Provides detailed molecular information.

Data Analysis

1. **Permeation Profiles**: Plot cumulative drug permeated against time to generate permeation curves.

2. **Flux Calculation**: Calculate the steady-state flux to determine the rate of drug permeation.

3. **Enhancement Ratio**: Compare permeation rates with and without enhancers to quantify their effect.

In Vivo Evaluation

In vivo evaluation of Transdermal Drug Delivery Systems (TDDS) involves testing these systems in live animal models and human subjects. This phase is crucial to understand the pharmacokinetics, efficacy, safety, and overall performance of TDDS in a complex biological environment. Here's a detailed look at the in vivo evaluation process for TDDS.

Key Objectives of In Vivo Evaluation

1. **Pharmacokinetics**: Determine the absorption, distribution, metabolism, and excretion (ADME) of the drug.
2. **Efficacy:** Assess the therapeutic effectiveness of the TDDS.
3. **Safety:** Evaluate potential toxicological effects and skin reactions.
4. **Patient Compliance and Acceptability**: Study the ease of use, comfort, and overall patient acceptance.

Animal Studies

Animal studies are typically the first step in in vivo evaluation and are used to gather preliminary data on pharmacokinetics, efficacy, and safety before progressing to human trials.

1. Selection of Animal Model

a. **Common Models**: Rodents (rats, mice), rabbits, and pigs are commonly used due to their skin properties and manageable size.
b. **Relevance to Human Skin**: Porcine skin is often preferred due to its close similarity to human skin in terms of structure and permeability.

2. Pharmacokinetic Studies

Purpose

To understand the drug's absorption, distribution, metabolism, and excretion profiles when delivered transdermally.

Methods

1. **Application of TDDS**

a. **Procedure**: The TDDS is applied to a specific area of the animal's skin.

b. **Sampling:** Blood samples are collected at various time intervals to measure drug concentration.

2. **Analysis**

    a. **Techniques:** Blood samples are analyzed using HPLC, mass spectrometry, or other appropriate analytical methods.

    b. **Parameters Assessed:**

        i. **C_max**: Maximum plasma concentration.

        ii. **T_max**: Time to reach maximum concentration.

        iii. **AUC (Area Under the Curve):** Total drug exposure over time.

        i. **Half-life**: Time taken for the drug concentration to reduce by half.

3. Efficacy Studies

Purpose

To evaluate the therapeutic effectiveness of the TDDS.

Methods

1. **Disease Models**

    a. **Procedure:** Animals are induced with conditions similar to human diseases (e.g., pain, hypertension) to assess the therapeutic impact of the drug delivered via TDDS.

    b. **Outcome Measures**: Disease-specific parameters such as pain relief, blood pressure reduction, or other relevant clinical endpoints.

4. Safety and Toxicological Studies

Purpose

To determine any adverse effects of the TDDS on the skin and systemic toxicity.

Methods

1. **Skin Irritation and Sensitization**

a. **Procedure**: The TDDS is applied, and the skin is monitored for signs of irritation (redness, swelling) and sensitization (allergic reactions).

b. **Assessment:** Visual scoring and histopathological examination of the skin.

2. **Systemic Toxicity**

a. **Procedure**: Blood and organ samples are analyzed to detect any toxic effects.

b. **Assessment**: Clinical chemistry, hematology, and histopathology.

Human Clinical Trials

Clinical trials are conducted in phases to systematically evaluate the TDDS in human subjects.

Phase I: Safety and Pharmacokinetics

Purpose

To assess the safety, tolerability, and pharmacokinetics in healthy volunteers.

Methods

1. **Single and Multiple Dosing**

a. **Procedure:** Single and multiple doses of the TDDS are applied to volunteers.

b. **Sampling:** Blood samples are collected at various time points.

2. **Analysis**

a. **Techniques**: Drug concentration in plasma is measured using HPLC or mass spectrometry.

b. **Parameters Assessed**: Safety (adverse events), C_max, T_max, AUC, half-life.

Phase II: Efficacy and Safety

Purpose

To evaluate the efficacy and safety in patients with the target condition.

Methods

1. **Patient Population**
    a. **Procedure:** The TDDS is applied to patients with the target condition (e.g., chronic pain, hypertension).
    b. **Outcome Measures**: Disease-specific efficacy endpoints, safety assessments.
2. **Analysis**
    a. **Techniques:** Clinical assessments, blood samples for pharmacokinetics, adverse event monitoring.

Phase III: Large-Scale Efficacy and Safety

Purpose

To confirm the efficacy and safety in a larger, more diverse patient population.

Methods

1. **Randomized Controlled Trials (RCTs)**
    a. **Procedure:** Large-scale RCTs comparing the TDDS to placebo or standard treatment.
    b. **Outcome Measures**: Primary efficacy endpoints, secondary endpoints, safety profiles.
2. **Analysis**
    a. **Techniques**: Statistical analysis of clinical outcomes, pharmacokinetics, and safety data.

Phase IV: Post-Marketing Surveillance

Purpose

To monitor long-term safety and effectiveness after the TDDS is marketed.

Methods

1. **Real-World Data Collection**
    a. **Procedure:** Collect data from patients using the TDDS in real-world settings.
    b. **Outcome Measures**: Long-term safety, effectiveness, patient compliance.

2. **Pharmacovigilance**

   a. **Procedure**: Continuous monitoring and reporting of adverse events.

   b. **Analysis**: Identify rare or long-term adverse effects.

Patient Compliance and Acceptability Studies

Purpose

To assess the ease of use, comfort, and overall acceptability of the TDDS among patients.

Methods

1. **Patient Surveys and Feedback**

   a. **Procedure**: Collect qualitative and quantitative data from patients using questionnaires and interviews.

   b. **Outcome Measures**: Ease of application, comfort, wearability, satisfaction.

2. **Wearability Studies**

   a. **Procedure**: Assess the patch's performance during daily activities, including exercise, bathing, and sleeping.

   b. **Outcome Measures**: Adhesion, flexibility, skin irritation.

Analytical Techniques

1. **HPLC and Mass Spectrometry**

   a. **Purpose:** Quantify drug concentration in biological samples.

   b. **Procedure**: Analyze blood, urine, and tissue samples.

   c. **Analysis**: Determine pharmacokinetic parameters and detect metabolites.

2. **Clinical Chemistry and Hematology**

   a. **Purpose**: Assess systemic toxicity and overall health.

   b. **Procedure**: Blood tests for liver and kidney function, blood cell counts.

   c. **Analysis**: Monitor for signs of toxicity.

Data Analysis

1. **Pharmacokinetic Modeling**

   a. **Purpose:** Understand the drug's behavior in the body.

   b. **Procedure:** Use software tools to model and simulate pharmacokinetic data.

   c. **Analysis:** Generate pharmacokinetic parameters and predict drug behavior.

2. **Statistical Analysis**

   a. **Purpose:** Assess efficacy and safety.

   b. **Procedure:** Use statistical methods to analyze clinical trial data.

   c. **Analysis:** Determine significance of results, confidence intervals.

Quality Control and Regulatory Considerations

Quality control (QC) and regulatory considerations are essential aspects of the development and evaluation of Transdermal Drug Delivery Systems (TDDS). Ensuring the quality, safety, and efficacy of TDDS involves rigorous testing and adherence to regulatory guidelines throughout the product's lifecycle. Here's a detailed overview of these critical aspects:

Quality Control in TDDS

Quality control encompasses a range of tests and procedures to ensure that TDDS meet predefined standards of quality, safety, and efficacy. Key QC parameters include the physical and chemical properties of the drug and the delivery system, as well as performance characteristics.

1. Physicochemical Characterization

a. Drug Content Uniformity

1. **Purpose:** Ensure consistent drug dosage in each patch.

2. **Method:** Measure the drug content in multiple samples from a batch using techniques like High-Performance Liquid Chromatography (HPLC).

3. **Acceptance Criteria**: The drug content must fall within a specified range (e.g., ±5% of the label claim).

b. Adhesive Properties

1. **Purpose**: Assess the patch's ability to adhere to the skin without causing irritation or detachment.
2. **Method:** Conduct peel, tack, and shear tests to evaluate adhesion strength and duration.
3. **Acceptance Criteria**: The patch must adhere effectively under specified conditions (e.g., during movement, perspiration).

c. Thickness and Weight Uniformity

1. **Purpose**: Ensure uniformity in patch dimensions and weight.
2. **Method:** Measure the thickness and weight of patches using micrometers and analytical balances.
3. **Acceptance Criteria**: Variations must be within specified limits.

d. Moisture Content

1. **Purpose**: Maintain stability and efficacy by controlling moisture levels.
2. **Method:** Use techniques like Karl Fischer titration or loss on drying.
3. **Acceptance Criteria**: Moisture content must be within specified limits to prevent degradation.

2. In Vitro Performance Testing

a. Drug Release Studies

1. **Purpose**: Assess the rate and extent of drug release from the TDDS.
2. **Method:** Use Franz diffusion cells to measure drug release into a receptor medium over time.
3. **Acceptance Criteria**: Release profiles must match predetermined specifications.

b. Skin Permeation Studies

1. **Purpose:** Evaluate drug permeation through the skin.

2. **Method**: Use excised human or animal skin in diffusion cells to measure permeation rates.

3. **Acceptance Criteria**: Permeation rates must fall within specified limits.

3. Stability Testing

a. Chemical Stability

1. **Purpose**: Ensure the drug remains stable throughout the product's shelf life.

2. **Method**: Store patches under different conditions (e.g., temperature, humidity) and analyze drug content over time using HPLC.

3. **Acceptance Criteria**: The drug should remain within specified potency limits (e.g., 90-110% of label claim).

b. Physical Stability

1. **Purpose:** Maintain the integrity and performance of the TDDS.

2. **Method:** Assess physical attributes like appearance, adhesion, and flexibility under various storage conditions.

3. **Acceptance Criteria**: The physical properties should remain within acceptable limits.

Regulatory Considerations in TDDS

Regulatory agencies like the FDA (Food and Drug Administration) and EMA (European Medicines Agency) provide guidelines for the development, evaluation, and approval of TDDS. Key regulatory considerations include:

1. Good Manufacturing Practices (GMP)

a. **Purpose**: Ensure that TDDS are consistently produced and controlled according to quality standards.

b. **Requirements**: Compliance with GMP involves stringent controls over manufacturing processes, facilities, equipment, and personnel.

c. **Documentation:** Detailed records of production and quality control testing must be maintained.

2. Preclinical and Clinical Testing

a. Preclinical Studies

1. **Purpose:** Assess the safety and efficacy of the TDDS in animal models.
2. **Requirements**: Conduct pharmacokinetic, efficacy, and toxicology studies.
3. **Documentation**: Submit preclinical study reports as part of the Investigational New Drug (IND) application.

b. Clinical Trials

1. **Purpose:** Evaluate the safety and efficacy of the TDDS in humans.
2. **Phases:** Conduct Phase I (safety and pharmacokinetics), Phase II (efficacy and dose-ranging), and Phase III (large-scale efficacy and safety) trials.
3. **Documentation**: Submit clinical trial data as part of the New Drug Application (NDA) or Marketing Authorization Application (MAA).

3. Regulatory Submissions

a. Investigational New Drug (IND) Application

1. **Purpose:** Obtain approval to conduct clinical trials.
2. **Content**: Include preclinical data, manufacturing information, and clinical trial protocols.

b. New Drug Application (NDA) / Marketing Authorization Application (MAA)

1. **Purpose**: Obtain approval to market the TDDS.
2. **Content**: Include clinical trial data, manufacturing details, QC test results, and labeling information.
3. **Review Process**: Regulatory agencies review the application for safety, efficacy, and quality compliance.

4. Post-Marketing Surveillance

a. Pharmacovigilance

1. **Purpose**: Monitor the safety of the TDDS after market approval.

2. **Requirements**: Report adverse events and conduct periodic safety updates.

3. **Documentation**: Maintain detailed records of adverse events and submit safety reports to regulatory agencies.

b. Quality Audits

1. **Purpose:** Ensure ongoing compliance with GMP and regulatory standards.

2. **Requirements**: Conduct regular internal and external audits of manufacturing facilities and processes.

3. **Documentation**: Keep detailed audit reports and corrective action plans.

Patient Compliance and Acceptability

Patient compliance and acceptability are crucial factors in the evaluation of Transdermal Drug Delivery Systems (TDDS). Ensuring that patients are willing and able to use the TDDS as intended is essential for treatment success. Here's a detailed overview of patient compliance and acceptability considerations in the evaluation of TDDS:

Patient Compliance

Patient compliance refers to the extent to which patients adhere to prescribed treatment regimens, including the proper use of medication delivery systems like TDDS. Factors influencing patient compliance with TDDS include:

1. **Ease of Use:** TDDS should be easy to apply and remove, with clear instructions provided to patients.

2. **Comfort:** The patch should be comfortable to wear, with minimal irritation or discomfort experienced by the patient.

3. **Frequency of Application**: Patients may be more compliant with TDDS if it requires less frequent application compared to other dosage forms (e.g., once-daily versus multiple daily doses).

4. **Visibility**: Patients may be more likely to adhere to treatment if the TDDS is discreet and does not draw attention.

5. **Adhesion:** Proper adhesion of the patch to the skin is essential to ensure consistent drug delivery. Poor adhesion may lead to non-compliance if the patch falls off prematurely.

6. **Skin Tolerance**: The TDDS should be well-tolerated by the skin, with minimal irritation or sensitization experienced by the patient.

7. **Patient Education**: Providing thorough instructions and education about the TDDS, including how to apply, remove, and dispose of the patch, can improve patient compliance.

Acceptability

Patient acceptability refers to the overall satisfaction and willingness of patients to use a particular medication delivery system. Factors influencing patient acceptability of TDDS include:

1. **Effectiveness**: Patients are more likely to accept TDDS if they perceive it to be effective in managing their condition.

2. **Convenience**: TDDS offers the convenience of non-invasive drug delivery, which may be preferable to other dosage forms like injections or oral medications.

3. **Flexibility**: Some TDDS may offer flexibility in dosing or application sites, allowing patients to tailor treatment to their individual needs.

4. **Minimal Side Effects**: Patients are more likely to accept TDDS if it has minimal side effects and is well-tolerated.

5. **Aesthetics:** The appearance of the TDDS, including size, shape, and color, may impact patient acceptability. Discreet patches that can be worn under clothing may be more acceptable to patients.

6. **Psychological Factors**: Patient attitudes, beliefs, and perceptions about TDDS, including trust in the technology and confidence in its ability to deliver medication effectively, can influence acceptability.

7. **Cost:** The cost of TDDS and insurance coverage may impact patient acceptability, particularly for long-term treatments.

Methods for Evaluation

To assess patient compliance and acceptability of TDDS, various methods can be employed:

1. **Patient Surveys and Interviews**: Gather feedback from patients using questionnaires or interviews to assess their experiences, preferences, and challenges with TDDS.

2. **Usability Testing**: Conduct usability testing to evaluate the ease of use and understandability of TDDS instructions and packaging.

3. **Wearability Studies**: Assess the performance of TDDS during daily activities, including adhesion, comfort, and wear time.

4. **Adverse Event Monitoring**: Monitor and document any adverse events related to TDDS use, including skin reactions, to understand their impact on patient compliance and acceptability.

5. **Focus Groups**: Engage patients in focus group discussions to explore their attitudes, beliefs, and concerns about TDDS and identify opportunities for improvement.

6. **Clinical Trials**: Include patient-reported outcomes and satisfaction measures in clinical trials to assess the impact of TDDS on compliance and acceptability.

Multiple Choice Questions (MCQs):

1. What is the primary function of Transdermal Drug Delivery Systems (TDDS)?

   A) To administer drugs orally

   B) To administer drugs through the skin

   C) To administer drugs intravenously

   D) To administer drugs via inhalation

2. Which year was the modern transdermal patch first approved by the FDA?

A) 1985

B) 1979

C) 1990

D) 2000

3. What does the stratum corneum function as in TDDS?

   A) An enhancer for drug delivery

   B) The primary barrier to drug penetration

   C) A source of nutrients for the skin

   D) The innermost layer of the skin

4. Which type of TDDS patch contains a liquid or gel drug reservoir separated from the skin by a semi-permanent membrane?

   A) Matrix Patches

   B) Drug-in-Adhesive Patches

   C) Reservoir Patches

   D) Microreservoir Patches

5. What are penetration enhancers used for in TDDS?

   A) To decrease the drug's efficacy

   B) To enhance the transport of drugs through the skin barrier

   C) To change the color of the patch

   D) To make the patch waterproof

6. Which method uses electric currents to enhance the permeation of charged drug molecules through the skin?

   A) Iontophoresis

   B) Sonophoresis

   C) Microneedles

   D) Electroporation

7. What is the key advantage of using TDDS in terms of patient compliance?

   A) Quick absorption

B) Controlled drug release

C) Non-invasive

D) All of the above

8. What type of molecules are typically difficult to deliver through TDDS due to the properties of the stratum corneum?

    A) Large, hydrophilic molecules

    B) Small, lipophilic molecules

    C) Gaseous molecules

    D) Inorganic compounds

9. What is the primary physical barrier that TDDS must overcome for effective drug delivery?

    A) Dermis

    B) Epidermis

    C) Hypodermis

    D) Stratum corneum

10. Which regulatory body oversees the approval and regulation of TDDS in the United States?

    A) FDA

    B) CDC

    C) WHO

    D) NIH

11. In what form is the drug typically held within a matrix patch?

    A) Liquid

    B) Gel

    C) Dispersed in a polymer matrix

    D) Encapsulated in a microbead

12. Which of the following is NOT a common drug used in TDDS?

    A) Fentanyl

    B) Nicotine

C) Insulin

D) Estradiol

13. What type of patch design incorporates the drug into the adhesive layer?

A) Reservoir patch

B) Matrix patch

C) Drug-in-adhesive patch

D) Microreservoir patch

14. What testing method is used to evaluate the chemical stability of a TDDS?

A) Peel testing

B) Franz diffusion cells

C) High-performance liquid chromatography (HPLC)

D) pH testing

15. What is a major challenge in the development of TDDS formulations?

A) Cost-effectiveness

B) Skin irritation

C) Flavoring

D) Color stability

16. What does the future direction of TDDS research focus on?

A) Reducing the size of the patches

B) Enhancing drug absorption through the skin

C) Developing oral versions of the patches

D) Removing all drug types from patches

17. Which technology involves using ultrasound waves to enhance drug delivery through the skin?

A) Iontophoresis

B) Sonophoresis

C) Microneedling

D) Phototherapy

18. Which component of the skin is the TDDS designed to bypass to improve drug bioavailability?

A) Hair follicles

B) Gastrointestinal tract

C) Blood-brain barrier

D) Liver

19. How does the drug typically pass through the skin in a TDDS?

A) Active transport

B) Passive diffusion

C) Facilitated diffusion

D) Endocytosis

20. Which of the following is NOT a method used to overcome skin barriers in TDDS? A) Chemical enhancers

B) Physical methods

C) Increasing the molecular weight of the drug

D) Formulation strategies

Short Answer Type Questions (Subjective)

1. What is the primary function of Transdermal Drug Delivery Systems (TDDS)?

2. What are the advantages of using TDDS over traditional drug delivery methods?

3. Describe the typical structure of a transdermal patch.

4. What role does the stratum corneum play in TDDS?

5. List three types of drugs commonly delivered through TDDS.

6. What are the main barriers that TDDS must overcome to effectively deliver drugs?

7. Explain the concept of "first-pass metabolism" and how TDDS bypasses it.

8. Name two physical methods used to enhance the permeation of drugs in TDDS.

9. What is the significance of the drug reservoir in a TDDS?

10. How do matrix patches differ from reservoir patches in their drug delivery mechanism?

11. What challenges are associated with the development of TDDS?

12. What future directions are being explored to improve the effectiveness of TDDS?

13. Describe the role of penetration enhancers in TDDS.

14. What are some safety and toxicity considerations for penetration enhancers in TDDS?

15. How can TDDS improve patient compliance compared to other drug delivery methods?

16. What types of testing are used to evaluate the stability of TDDS?

17. How do microneedles enhance drug delivery in TDDS?

18. Describe the regulatory considerations involved in the development of TDDS.

19. Explain how patient acceptability influences the success of TDDS.

20. What are the key components involved in the formulation of a TDDS?

Long Answer Type Questions (Subjective)

1. Discuss the historical development of Transdermal Drug Delivery Systems and their evolution from early uses to modern technologies.

2. Explain in detail the mechanism by which drugs are delivered through the skin using TDDS.

3. Describe the various types of transderal patches and their specific uses in medical treatment.

4. Analyze the impact of the skin's structure on the effectiveness of drug delivery through TDDS.

5. Evaluate the methods used to overcome the skin barriers in TDDS, including both chemical and physical enhancers.

6. Discuss the role of nanotechnology in enhancing the delivery and stability of drugs in TDDS.

7. Explain the process of formulating a TDDS, including the selection of components and the assembly of the patch.

8. Analyze the challenges and limitations faced in the development of TDDS and propose potential solutions.

9. Discuss the regulatory pathway for TDDS, including preclinical and clinical testing requirements.

10. Evaluate the significance of patient compliance and acceptability in the development and marketing of TDDS, including methods to assess and improve these factors.

Answer Key:

1. (B) To administer drugs through the skin
2. (B) 1979
3. (B) The primary barrier to drug penetration
4. (C) Reservoir Patches
5. (B) To enhance the transport of drugs through the skin barrier
6. (A) Iontophoresis
7. (D) All of the above
8. (A) Large, hydrophilic molecules
9. (D) Stratum corneum
10. (A) FDA
11. (C) Dispersed in a polymer matrix
12. (C) Insulin
13. (C) Drug-in-adhesive patch
14. (C) High-performance liquid chromatography (HPLC)

15.(B) Skin irritation

16.(B) Enhancing drug absorption through the skin

17.(B) Sonophoresis

18.(D) Liver

19.(B) Passive diffusion

20.(C) Increasing the molecular weight of the drug

CHAPTER – 7

PROTEIN AND PEPTIDE DELIVERY

INTRODUCTION:

Protein and peptide delivery is a crucial area in pharmaceutical and biomedical research due to the therapeutic potential of these biomolecules. Proteins and peptides can serve as drugs to treat a wide range of diseases, including diabetes, cancer, and infectious diseases. However, their delivery poses significant challenges due to their complex structure and sensitivity to environmental conditions.

Proteins and Peptides: An Overview

Proteins are large, complex molecules made up of one or more long chains of amino acids. They perform a variety of functions in the body, including catalyzing metabolic reactions (enzymes), replicating DNA, responding to stimuli (receptors), and transporting molecules (hemoglobin).

Peptides are shorter chains of amino acids, typically comprising 2 to 50 amino acids. They are simpler in structure compared to proteins and can function as hormones, neurotransmitters, or antibiotics.

Therapeutic Applications

Diabetes: Insulin, a peptide hormone, is a well-known example used to manage blood sugar levels.

Cancer: Monoclonal antibodies and therapeutic proteins such as trastuzumab are used to target specific cancer cells.

Infectious Diseases: Proteins and peptides can act as vaccines or antiviral agents.

Challenges in Protein and Peptide Delivery

1. **Stability**: Proteins and peptides can be easily denatured or degraded by enzymes in the body.

2. **Size and Charge**: Their large size and charge can prevent them from crossing cellular membranes.

3. **Immunogenicity**: They can provoke immune responses, which can reduce their efficacy or cause adverse effects.

4. **Short Half-life**: They often have short half-lives in the bloodstream, requiring frequent administration.

Delivery Strategies

Several strategies have been developed to overcome these challenges:

1. **Parenteral Delivery:**
   a. **Intravenous (IV):** Direct injection into the bloodstream.
   b. **Subcutaneous (SC):** Injection into the tissue layer between the skin and muscle.
   c. **Intramuscular (IM):** Injection into muscle tissue.
   d. *Advantages*: Immediate and controlled delivery.
   e. *Disadvantages*: Invasiveness, patient discomfort, and the need for medical professionals.

2. **Oral Delivery:**
   a. Development of oral formulations that protect proteins and peptides from degradation in the gastrointestinal tract and facilitate their absorption.
   b. **Techniques**: Enteric coatings, enzyme inhibitors, absorption enhancers.
   c. *Advantages*: Convenience and patient compliance.
   d. *Disadvantages*: Poor bioavailability and stability.

3. **Transdermal Delivery:**
   a. Use of patches or gels that allow proteins and peptides to be absorbed through the skin.
   b. **Techniques:** Microneedles, iontophoresis, and chemical enhancers.

c. *Advantages*: Non-invasive and sustained release.

d. *Disadvantages*: Limited to small peptides and skin irritation.

4. Pulmonary Delivery:

a. Inhalation of aerosolized proteins or peptides for absorption through the lung epithelium.

b. **Techniques**: Dry powder inhalers, nebulizers.

c. *Advantages*: Rapid absorption and non-invasiveness.

d. *Disadvantages*: Formulation challenges and variability in dose delivery.

5. Nanotechnology-Based Delivery:

a. Use of nanoparticles, liposomes, and other nanocarriers to protect and deliver proteins and peptides.

b. *Advantages*: Enhanced stability, targeted delivery, and controlled release.

c. *Disadvantages*: Complexity in formulation and potential toxicity.

Innovations and Future Directions

1. **PEGylation**: Attachment of polyethylene glycol (PEG) chains to proteins and peptides to increase their stability and half-life.

2. **Fusion Proteins**: Combining therapeutic proteins with other proteins to enhance their stability and activity.

3. **Smart Delivery Systems**: Development of systems that release proteins and peptides in response to specific physiological conditions (e.g., pH-sensitive or temperature-sensitive systems).

4. **Gene Therapy**: Delivering genes that encode therapeutic proteins directly into patients' cells.

BARRIERS FOR PROTEIN DELIVERY

Protein and peptide delivery faces several significant barriers, which can be broadly categorized into physiological, biochemical, and physical challenges.

Understanding these barriers is crucial for developing effective delivery systems.

Physiological Barriers

1. **Gastrointestinal (GI) Tract:**

    a. **Enzymatic Degradation**: Proteins and peptides are susceptible to proteolytic enzymes such as pepsin, trypsin, and chymotrypsin, which can degrade them into inactive fragments.

    b. **Acidic Environment**: The acidic pH of the stomach can denature proteins and peptides, leading to loss of activity.

    c. **Mucosal Barrier**: The mucus layer lining the GI tract can trap and degrade proteins and peptides, preventing their absorption.

    d. **Epithelial Barrier:** Tight junctions between epithelial cells restrict the passage of large molecules like proteins and peptides.

2. **Blood-Brain Barrier (BBB):**

    a. **Selective Permeability**: The BBB restricts the passage of most proteins and peptides due to its highly selective permeability, limiting the delivery of therapeutics to the brain.

    b. **Efflux Transporters**: Proteins like P-glycoprotein actively pump many drugs and peptides out of the brain, reducing their effectiveness.

3. **Renal Clearance:**

    a. **Glomerular Filtration**: Proteins and peptides can be rapidly filtered out of the bloodstream by the kidneys, leading to a short half-life and necessitating frequent dosing.

Biochemical Barriers

1. **Immune Response:**

    a. **Immunogenicity**: Proteins and peptides can be recognized as foreign by the immune system, leading to the production of antibodies that neutralize their activity or cause adverse immune reactions.

2. **Protein Aggregation:**

   a. **Stability Issues**: Proteins can aggregate under physiological conditions, leading to reduced efficacy and potential immunogenicity.

3. **Post-Translational Modifications:**

   a. **Variability:** Post-translational modifications such as glycosylation can affect the stability, activity, and immunogenicity of protein therapeutics.

Physical Barriers

1. **Molecular Size and Charge:**

   a. **Permeability:** The large size and hydrophilicity of proteins and peptides hinder their ability to diffuse across cellular membranes.

2. **Structural Integrity:**

   a. **Denaturation**: Proteins and peptides can lose their three-dimensional structure when exposed to physical stresses (e.g., temperature changes, agitation), leading to loss of function.

Overcoming Barriers

To address these challenges, various strategies have been developed:

1. **Chemical Modifications:**

   a. **PEGylation:** Attaching polyethylene glycol (PEG) chains to proteins and peptides can enhance their stability and half-life by reducing renal clearance and proteolytic degradation.

   b. **Cyclization:** Cyclizing peptides can enhance their stability against enzymatic degradation and improve their ability to cross cellular membranes.

2. **Formulation Strategies:**

a. **Encapsulation**: Encapsulating proteins and peptides in nanoparticles, liposomes, or other carriers can protect them from degradation and enhance their absorption.

b. **Enteric Coatings**: Using coatings that protect proteins and peptides from the acidic environment of the stomach and release them in the more neutral pH of the intestine.

3. **Delivery Systems:**

a. **Injectable Systems**: Intravenous, subcutaneous, and intramuscular injections bypass many physiological barriers, providing direct access to the bloodstream.

b. **Inhalable Systems**: Pulmonary delivery can bypass the GI tract and avoid enzymatic degradation, offering a non-invasive alternative for systemic delivery.

c. **Transdermal Patches**: Patches or microneedle arrays can deliver proteins and peptides through the skin, bypassing the GI tract and first-pass metabolism.

4. **Targeted Delivery:**

a. **Ligand-Targeted Carriers**: Using ligands that specifically bind to receptors on target cells can enhance the specificity and efficacy of protein and peptide delivery.

b. **Responsive Systems**: Developing carriers that release their payload in response to specific physiological conditions (e.g., pH, temperature) can improve the targeted delivery of proteins and peptides.

Conclusion

The delivery of proteins and peptides is hindered by numerous barriers that reduce their efficacy and stability. Addressing these barriers requires a multifaceted approach, combining chemical modifications, innovative formulations, and advanced delivery systems to enhance the stability, bioavailability, and therapeutic effectiveness of protein and peptide-based drugs. Advances in biotechnology and materials science continue to drive progress in this field, offering new solutions to overcome these challenges and improve patient outcomes.

FORMULATION OF DELIVERY SYSTEMS OF PROTEINS AND OTHER MACROMOLECULES

Formulating delivery systems for proteins and other macromolecules is a complex and multi-disciplinary task, essential for ensuring their stability, bioavailability, and therapeutic efficacy. Here is a detailed exploration of various formulation strategies and technologies used in the delivery of these biomolecules:

1. Encapsulation Techniques

Nanoparticles:

i. **Polymeric Nanoparticles**: Made from biodegradable polymers like PLGA (poly(lactic-co-glycolic acid)), these nanoparticles protect proteins from degradation and enhance their stability. They can be engineered for controlled release and targeted delivery.

ii. **Lipid Nanoparticles**: These include solid lipid nanoparticles (SLNs) and nanostructured lipid carriers (NLCs). They offer high loading capacity, biocompatibility, and the ability to protect encapsulated proteins from enzymatic degradation.

Liposomes:

i. **Structure**: Composed of phospholipid bilayers, liposomes can encapsulate both hydrophilic and hydrophobic molecules.

ii. **Advantages**: They improve the solubility, stability, and bioavailability of encapsulated proteins. Liposomes can be functionalized with targeting ligands to enhance specificity.

iii. **Applications:** Widely used in cancer therapy and vaccine delivery.

Microspheres:

i. **Composition**: Typically made from biodegradable polymers like PLGA.

ii. **Advantages:** Suitable for sustained and controlled release of proteins. They protect the encapsulated protein from environmental degradation.

iii. **Applications:** Used for long-term drug delivery, such as in the case of hormone therapies.

2. Chemical Modifications

PEGylation:

i. **Process:** Covalent attachment of polyethylene glycol (PEG) chains to proteins.

ii. **Benefits**: Increases molecular size, reduces renal clearance, enhances stability, and decreases immunogenicity. PEGylation extends the half-life of proteins in the bloodstream.

iii. **Application**s: Used in various FDA-approved drugs like PEG-interferon and PEG-asparaginase.

Cyclization:

i. **Process**: Creating cyclic peptides by linking the N- and C-termini of the peptide chain.

ii. **Benefits**: Increases resistance to proteolytic degradation and improves cell permeability.

iii. **Applications**: Used in developing peptide-based drugs with enhanced stability and bioactivity.

3. Physical Methods

Freeze-Drying (Lyophilization):

i. **Process**: Involves freezing the protein solution and then removing water by sublimation under low pressure.

ii. **Benefits:** Enhances the stability and shelf-life of proteins by keeping them in a dry state. Ideal for formulating stable protein pharmaceuticals.

iii. **Applications**: Commonly used for vaccines, therapeutic proteins, and enzyme preparations.

Spray-Drying:

i. **Process:** Converts protein solutions into dry powders by spraying the solution into a hot drying medium.

ii. **Benefits:** Produces fine, uniform particles suitable for inhalation or oral delivery. Enhances protein stability and bioavailability.

iii. **Applications:** Used in pulmonary delivery systems and for oral vaccines.

4. Targeted Delivery Systems

Antibody-Drug Conjugates (ADCs):

i. **Structure**: Combines an antibody specific to cancer cells with a cytotoxic drug.

ii. **Benefits**: Provides targeted delivery of the drug to cancer cells, minimizing systemic toxicity.

iii. **Applications:** Used in oncology for the treatment of various cancers.

Ligand-Targeted Delivery:

i. **Process:** Functionalizing nanoparticles or other carriers with ligands (e.g., peptides, antibodies) that bind to specific receptors on target cells.

ii. **Benefits:** Enhances the specificity and efficacy of protein and peptide therapeutics.

iii. **Applications:** Used in targeted cancer therapies and personalized medicine.

5. Advanced Delivery Systems

Hydrogels:

i. **Structure**: Hydrophilic polymer networks that can hold a large amount of water.

ii. **Benefits**: Provide a moist environment for protein stability, and can be engineered for controlled and sustained release.

iii. **Applications**: Used in wound healing, tissue engineering, and sustained drug delivery.

Microneedles:

i. **Design:** Arrays of tiny needles that can painlessly penetrate the skin to deliver drugs directly into the systemic circulation.

ii. **Benefits**: Non-invasive, improves patient compliance, and can be used for self-administration.

iii. **Applications**: Used for vaccine delivery, insulin administration, and other protein-based therapies.

BioMEMS (Biological Microelectromechanical Systems):

i. **Technology**: Miniaturized devices combining mechanical and electrical components for precise drug delivery.

ii. **Benefits**: Allows for controlled, on-demand release of therapeutic proteins and peptides.

iii. **Applications**: Used in advanced drug delivery systems for chronic disease management.

EVALUATION OF DELIVERY SYSTEMS OF PROTEINS AND OTHER MACROMOLECULES

Evaluating delivery systems for proteins and other macromolecules is crucial to ensuring their effectiveness, safety, and reliability. This evaluation involves a comprehensive set of criteria and methodologies that assess various aspects such as stability, bioavailability, pharmacokinetics, and therapeutic efficacy. Here's a detailed exploration of the evaluation process:

Stability Studies

Stability studies are a crucial part of evaluating delivery systems for proteins and other macromolecules. These studies ensure that the therapeutic efficacy and safety of the proteins and peptides are maintained throughout their shelf life and during their delivery to the target site. Here's a detailed look at the different aspects and methodologies involved in stability studies:

1. Physicochemical Stability

1.1. Chemical Stability

a. **Objective**: Assess the degradation and chemical modifications of proteins and peptides over time.

b. **Methods:**

   i. **High-Performance Liquid Chromatography (HPLC):** Separates and quantifies protein degradation products and modifications.

   ii. **Mass Spectrometry (MS):** Identifies molecular changes, such as oxidation, deamidation, and glycation.

   iii. **Fourier Transform Infrared Spectroscopy (FTIR):** Analyzes changes in the protein's secondary structure.

1.2. Physical Stability

a. **Objective:** Evaluate changes in the physical state of proteins, such as aggregation, precipitation, and denaturation.

b. **Methods:**

   i. **Differential Scanning Calorimetry (DSC):** Measures thermal transitions, providing information on protein stability and denaturation temperatures.

   ii. **Dynamic Light Scattering (DLS):** Assesses particle size distribution and aggregation.

   iii. **UV-Visible Spectroscopy**: Detects changes in absorbance that indicate aggregation or denaturation.

   iv. **Circular Dichroism (CD):** Analyzes secondary and tertiary structure changes.

2. Biological Stability

2.1. Enzymatic Degradation

a. **Objective:** Determine the resistance of proteins and peptides to proteolytic enzymes.

b. **Methods:**

i. **In vitro Enzyme Assays**: Incubate proteins with enzymes like trypsin, chymotrypsin, and pepsin, followed by analysis with HPLC or SDS-PAGE to detect degradation products.

ii. **Mass Spectrometry (MS):** Identifies specific cleavage sites and degradation patterns.

2.2. In Vivo Stability

a. **Objective**: Assess the stability of proteins and peptides in biological environments.

b. **Methods:**

i. **Animal Models**: Administer proteins and peptides to animals, followed by blood sampling and analysis to determine stability.

ii. **Biological Fluids**: Incubate proteins in plasma, serum, or other relevant biological fluids and analyze using HPLC, MS, or immunoassays to measure degradation.

3. Formulation Stability

3.1. Excipients and Additives

a. **Objective:** Evaluate the impact of excipients and additives on protein stability.

b. **Methods:**

i. **Compatibility Studies**: Mix proteins with various excipients and analyze stability using techniques like HPLC and DSC.

ii. **Forced Degradation Studies**: Subject formulations to stress conditions (e.g., high temperature, pH extremes) to identify potential degradation pathways and stabilizing excipients.

4. Environmental Stability

4.1. Temperature Stability

a. **Objective**: Assess stability under different temperature conditions.

b. **Methods:**

i. **Accelerated Stability Studies**: Store proteins at elevated temperatures (e.g., 40°C) and analyze at regular intervals to predict shelf life.

ii. **Real-Time Stability Studies**: Store proteins at recommended storage temperatures (e.g., 2-8°C) and analyze over an extended period.

4.2. pH Stability

a. **Objective**: Evaluate the impact of pH on protein stability.

b. **Methods**:

i. **Buffer Studies**: Incubate proteins in buffers of varying pH and analyze stability using techniques like HPLC and DLS.

4.3. Light Stability

a. **Objective**: Determine the sensitivity of proteins to light exposure.

b. **Methods**:

i. **Photostability Testing**: Expose proteins to light and analyze for degradation products using HPLC and UV-Visible spectroscopy.

5. Mechanical Stability

5.1. Agitation and Shear Stress

a. **Objective:** Assess the impact of mechanical stress on protein stability.

b. **Methods**:

i. **Agitation Studies**: Subject proteins to shaking or stirring and analyze for aggregation and denaturation.

ii. **Shear Stress Testing**: Pass proteins through syringes or pumps and analyze using DLS and SEC (size-exclusion chromatography).

6. Packaging Stability

6.1. Container-Closure Systems

a. **Objective**: Evaluate the interaction between proteins and packaging materials.

b. **Methods**:

i.   **Leachables and Extractables Studies**: Analyze potential contaminants from packaging materials using techniques like LC-MS.

ii. **Container Closure Integrity Testing**: Ensure that packaging maintains sterility and stability of the protein formulation.

Bioavailability and Pharmacokinetics

Bioavailability and pharmacokinetics (PK) are critical parameters in evaluating the efficacy and safety of delivery systems for proteins and other macromolecules. These parameters help determine the fate of the delivered drug in the body, including its absorption, distribution, metabolism, and excretion (ADME). A thorough understanding of these factors is essential for developing effective and reliable therapeutic delivery systems.

1. Bioavailability

Bioavailability refers to the proportion of an administered drug that reaches the systemic circulation in an active form. For proteins and peptides, achieving high bioavailability can be challenging due to their size, susceptibility to enzymatic degradation, and difficulty crossing biological membranes.

1.1. In Vitro Bioavailability Studies

a. **Objective**: Predict the absorption and release profile of the protein or peptide.

b. **Methods:**

i.   **Cell Culture Models**: Use epithelial cell lines like Caco-2 to simulate intestinal absorption.

ii. **Transwell Assays**: Measure transport across cell monolayers to mimic absorption barriers.

iii. **Release Kinetics Studies**: Use dissolution apparatus to study the release profile of encapsulated proteins from delivery systems.

1.2. In Vivo Bioavailability Studies

a. **Objective**: Evaluate the extent and rate at which the active drug reaches systemic circulation.

b. **Methods:**

    i. **Animal Models**: Administer the delivery system to animals (e.g., mice, rats) and measure plasma drug concentrations over time.

    ii. **Blood Sampling and Analysis**: Use techniques like HPLC, LC-MS/MS, or ELISA to quantify drug levels in the blood.

    iii. **Bioavailability Calculations**: Determine absolute and relative bioavailability by comparing plasma levels with those achieved by intravenous administration.

2. Pharmacokinetics (PK)

Pharmacokinetics involves studying the ADME processes to understand the drug's behavior in the body over time. Key PK parameters include the half-life, volume of distribution, clearance, and area under the curve (AUC).

2.1. Absorption

a. **Objective**: Determine how the drug is absorbed from the site of administration into the bloodstream.

b. **Methods:**

    i. **Oral Administration Studies**: Measure plasma concentrations after oral delivery to evaluate gastrointestinal absorption.

    ii. **Parenteral Administration Studies**: Assess absorption kinetics for subcutaneous, intramuscular, or transdermal delivery systems.

2.2. Distribution

a. **Objective**: Assess how the drug distributes throughout the body's tissues and organs.

b. **Methods:**

    i. **Biodistribution Studies**: Use radiolabeled or fluorescently labeled proteins to track distribution in animal models.

    ii.   **Imaging Techniques**: Employ PET, MRI, or fluorescence imaging to visualize drug distribution in vivo.

    iii. **Volume of Distribution (Vd):** Calculate Vd to understand the extent of drug distribution.

2.3. Metabolism

a. **Objective:** Study the biochemical modifications the drug undergoes in the body, primarily in the liver.

b. **Methods:**

    i.   **In Vitro Metabolism Studies**: Use liver microsomes or hepatocytes to study metabolic pathways.

    ii. **In Vivo Metabolism Studies**: Analyze metabolites in plasma, urine, and other biological samples using LC-MS/MS.

    iii. **Metabolite Identification**: Identify and quantify major metabolites to understand the metabolic fate of the drug.

2.4. Excretion

a. **Objective**: Determine how the drug and its metabolites are eliminated from the body.

b. **Methods:**

    i.   **Urinary and Fecal Excretion Studies**: Measure drug levels in urine and feces to calculate renal and biliary excretion.

    ii. **Clearance (CL):** Calculate total body clearance to understand the efficiency of drug elimination.

3. Pharmacokinetic Modeling

3.1. Compartmental Models

a. **Objective:** Simplify the complex processes of drug distribution and elimination into compartments for analysis.

b. **Methods:**

    i.   **One-Compartment Model**: Assumes the body acts as a single homogeneous compartment.

ii. **Two-Compartment Model**: Considers central (blood) and peripheral (tissue) compartments for more accurate modeling.

iii. **Non-Compartmental Analysis**: Uses statistical moments to analyze PK data without assuming specific compartmental behavior.

3.2. Advanced PK Modeling

a. **Objective:** Use sophisticated mathematical models to predict drug behavior and optimize delivery systems.

b. **Methods:**

i. **Physiologically-Based Pharmacokinetic (PBPK) Models**: Incorporate physiological parameters and biological processes to simulate drug kinetics.

ii. **Population PK Modeling:** Analyze PK data from diverse populations to understand variability and predict dosing regimens.

4. Evaluating Delivery Systems

4.1. Enhancing Absorption

a. **Objective:** Improve the bioavailability of proteins and peptides by enhancing absorption.

b. **Strategies:**

i. **Use of Absorption Enhancers**: Incorporate permeation enhancers like bile salts or fatty acids.

ii. **Nanocarrier**s: Employ nanoparticles, liposomes, or micelles to protect the drug and facilitate absorption.

iii. **Mucoadhesive Formulations**: Develop formulations that adhere to mucosal surfaces, prolonging residence time and enhancing absorption.

4.2. Controlled Release

a. **Objective**: Achieve sustained or controlled release of the drug to maintain therapeutic levels over time.

b. Strategies:

    i.   **Polymeric Systems**: Use biodegradable polymers (e.g., PLGA) to create matrices for controlled release.

    ii.   **Hydrogel**s: Develop hydrogels that swell and release the drug in a controlled manner.

    iii.   **Microspheres and Nanoparticles**: Formulate microspheres or nanoparticles for delayed or sustained release.

4.3. Targeted Delivery

a. **Objective**: Direct the drug to specific tissues or cells to enhance therapeutic efficacy and reduce side effects.

b. **Strategies**:

    i.   **Ligand-Targeted Systems**: Attach targeting ligands (e.g., antibodies, peptides) to delivery carriers.

    ii.   **Active Targeting**: Use magnetic or ultrasound-responsive systems to direct the drug to the target site.

    iii.   **Passive Targeting**: Exploit the enhanced permeability and retention (EPR) effect in tumor tissues for cancer therapies.

Safety and Toxicity

Evaluating the safety and toxicity of delivery systems for proteins and other macromolecules is paramount to ensure that these systems are not only effective but also safe for clinical use. This evaluation encompasses a variety of tests and methodologies designed to assess potential adverse effects, immunogenicity, biocompatibility, and overall safety of the delivery system. Here's a detailed look at these aspects:

1. Immunogenicity

Immunogenicity refers to the ability of a substance to provoke an immune response. Proteins and peptides, by nature, can be immunogenic, which may lead to unwanted immune reactions.

1.1. In Vitro Immunogenicity Studies

a. **Objective**: Assess the potential of the protein or peptide to induce an immune response.

b. **Methods:**

    i. **Enzyme-Linked Immunosorbent Assay (ELISA):** Detects specific antibodies generated against the protein or peptide.

    ii. **T-Cell Proliferation Assays**: Measures the proliferation of T-cells in response to the antigen using flow cytometry or radioactive labeling.

    iii. **Cytokine Release Assays**: Quantifies cytokine levels (e.g., IL-2, IFN-γ) released by immune cells upon exposure to the protein.

1.2. In Vivo Immunogenicity Studies

a. **Objective**: Evaluate immune responses in animal models.

b. **Methods:**

    i. **Animal Models**: Administer the protein or peptide to animals (e.g., mice, rats) and monitor for antibody production and T-cell responses.

    ii. **Histopathology**: Examine tissues for signs of inflammation or immune cell infiltration.

2. Acute and Chronic Toxicity

2.1. Acute Toxicity Studies

a. **Objective:** Assess the immediate toxic effects of the delivery system following a single dose.

b. **Methods:**

    i. **LD50 Determination**: Identify the lethal dose for 50% of the test population.

    ii. **Clinical Observations**: Monitor animals for signs of toxicity, such as changes in behavior, body weight, and organ function.

    iii. **Blood Chemistry and Hematology**: Measure blood parameters to detect organ damage or systemic effects.

2.2. Chronic Toxicity Studies

a. **Objective**: Evaluate the long-term toxic effects of repeated or continuous administration.

b. **Methods:**

   i. **Subchronic and Chronic Exposure**: Administer the delivery system over weeks to months and monitor for cumulative toxicity.

   ii. **Organ Weights and Histopathology**: Measure organ weights and perform histological examinations to detect pathological changes.

   iii. **Biomarker Analysis**: Assess biomarkers of organ damage (e.g., liver enzymes, renal function markers) in blood or urine.

3. Biocompatibility

Biocompatibility refers to the ability of the delivery system to interact with biological systems without eliciting harmful effects.

3.1. In Vitro Biocompatibility Studies

a. **Objective:** Evaluate the compatibility of the delivery system with cells and tissues.

b. **Methods**:

   i. **Cytotoxicity Assays**: Use assays like MTT, XTT, or LDH release to measure cell viability in the presence of the delivery system.

   ii. **Hemolysis Assays**: Assess the potential of the delivery system to cause red blood cell lysis.

3.2. In Vivo Biocompatibility Studies

a. **Objective**: Confirm the biocompatibility of the delivery system in animal models.

b. **Methods:**

   i. **Implantation Studies**: Implant the delivery system in animals and monitor for local tissue reactions and inflammation.

   ii. **Histological Analysis**: Examine tissues surrounding the implant for signs of inflammation, fibrosis, or necrosis.

4. Genotoxicity and Carcinogenicity

4.1. Genotoxicity Studies

a. **Objective**: Assess the potential of the delivery system to cause genetic mutations or chromosomal damage.

b. **Methods:**

    i. **Ames Test**: Uses bacteria to detect mutations induced by the test substance.

    ii. **Micronucleus Assay**: Detects chromosomal damage in cultured cells or animal bone marrow.

    iii. **Comet Assay**: Measures DNA strand breaks in individual cells.

4.2. Carcinogenicity Studies

a. **Objective**: Determine if the delivery system has the potential to cause cancer over long-term exposure.

b. **Methods:**

    i. **Long-Term Animal Studies**: Administer the delivery system to animals over their lifespan and monitor for tumor development.

    ii. **Histopathological Examination**: Examine tissues for preneoplastic and neoplastic lesions.

5. Local Tolerance

5.1. Local Irritation Studies

a. **Objective**: Evaluate the potential of the delivery system to cause local irritation at the site of administration.

b. **Methods:**

    i. **Skin Irritation Tests**: Apply the delivery system to animal skin and observe for erythema, edema, and other signs of irritation.

    ii. **Mucosal Irritation Tests**: Administer the delivery system to mucosal surfaces (e.g., eyes, nasal cavity) and monitor for irritation.

5.2. Sensitization Studies

a. **Objective**: Assess the potential of the delivery system to cause allergic reactions upon repeated exposure.

b. **Methods**:

   i. **Guinea Pig Maximization Test**: Induce and challenge animals with the delivery system to detect sensitization.

   ii. **Local Lymph Node Assay (LLNA):** Measure lymphocyte proliferation in response to the delivery system in mice.

6. Regulatory Toxicology

6.1. Compliance with Guidelines

a. **Objective**: Ensure that safety and toxicity studies comply with regulatory guidelines (e.g., FDA, EMA).

b. **Methods:**

   i. **Good Laboratory Practice (GLP):** Conduct studies in compliance with GLP standards to ensure data quality and integrity.

   ii. **Regulatory Submissions**: Prepare comprehensive safety and toxicity data for regulatory review and approval.

6.2. Preclinical Safety Assessment

a. **Objective:** Perform a thorough preclinical safety evaluation before initiating clinical trials.

b. **Methods:**

   i. **Integrated Toxicology Studies**: Combine various toxicity assessments (acute, chronic, genotoxicity) to provide a comprehensive safety profile.

   ii. **Safety Pharmacology**: Evaluate the effects of the delivery system on major organ systems (e.g., cardiovascular, respiratory, CNS).

Efficacy and Functional Evaluation

Evaluating the efficacy and functional performance of delivery systems for proteins and other macromolecules is critical to ensure that these systems achieve the desired therapeutic outcomes. This involves assessing the biological activity, therapeutic efficacy, and functional properties of the delivered proteins or peptides. Here's a detailed look at the methodologies and considerations involved in this evaluation:

1. Biological Activity

1.1. In Vitro Activity Assays

a. **Objective:** Measure the biological activity of the protein or peptide after delivery to ensure it remains functional.

b. **Methods:**

 i. **Enzyme Assays**: Assess enzymatic activity using specific substrates and measure the product formation.

 ii. **Binding Assays**: Evaluate the binding affinity of the protein to its target using techniques such as ELISA, surface plasmon resonance (SPR), or biolayer interferometry (BLI).

 iii. **Cell-Based Assays**: Test the biological activity in relevant cell lines by measuring parameters like cell proliferation, apoptosis, signal transduction, or reporter gene expression.

1.2. In Vivo Activity Assays

a. **Objective:** Confirm the biological activity of the delivered protein or peptide in animal models.

b. **Methods:**

 i. **Pharmacodynamic (PD) Studies**: Monitor biomarkers or physiological responses indicative of the protein's activity in vivo.

 ii. **Functional Assays**: Assess the functional outcomes such as enzyme activity, hormone release, or receptor activation in animal models.

2. Therapeutic Efficacy

2.1. Disease Models

a. **Objective**: Evaluate the therapeutic efficacy of the delivery system in relevant disease models.

b. **Methods:**

    i. **Animal Models of Disease**: Use disease-specific animal models to assess therapeutic outcomes, such as tumor regression in cancer models, blood glucose control in diabetic models, or reduction of inflammation in arthritis models.

    ii. **Clinical Endpoints**: Measure relevant clinical endpoints such as survival rates, tumor size, blood glucose levels, or inflammatory markers.

2.2. Comparative Efficacy Studies

a. **Objective:** Compare the efficacy of the new delivery system with existing treatments.

b. **Methods:**

    i. **Benchmarking:** Compare the therapeutic outcomes of the new delivery system with those of standard treatments or previously developed delivery systems.

    ii. **Dose-Response Studies**: Evaluate the efficacy across different doses to determine the optimal therapeutic dose.

3. Functional Properties

3.1. Targeting Efficiency

a. **Objective:** Assess the ability of the delivery system to target specific tissues or cells.

b. **Methods:**

    i. **Biodistribution Studies**: Use imaging techniques (e.g., PET, MRI, fluorescence imaging) to visualize and quantify the distribution of the protein in vivo.

    ii. **Cell Uptake Studies**: Evaluate the uptake of the protein by target cells using flow cytometry or confocal microscopy.

3.2. Controlled Release

a. **Objective:** Determine the ability of the delivery system to provide sustained or controlled release of the protein or peptide.

b. **Methods**:

   i. **In Vitro Release Studies**: Measure the release profile of the protein from the delivery system over time using dissolution or diffusion assays.

   ii. **In Vivo Release Studies**: Assess the release kinetics in animal models by measuring plasma or tissue concentrations of the protein over time.

4. Pharmacokinetics and Pharmacodynamics (PK/PD) Relationship

4.1. PK/PD Modeling

a. **Objective:** Understand the relationship between the pharmacokinetics (PK) and pharmacodynamics (PD) of the delivered protein.

b. **Methods:**

   i. **PK Studies**: Measure the concentration of the protein in plasma or tissues over time to determine PK parameters (e.g., half-life, clearance, volume of distribution).

   ii. **PD Studies**: Monitor the biological effects or clinical endpoints over time to establish the PD profile.

   iii. **PK/PD Modeling**: Develop mathematical models to describe and predict the relationship between drug concentration and therapeutic effect.

5. Therapeutic Index

5.1. Safety and Efficacy Balance

a. **Objective:** Determine the therapeutic index, which is the ratio of the toxic dose to the effective dose, to ensure a safe and effective treatment.

b. **Methods:**

i. **Dose Escalation Studies**: Identify the minimum effective dose (MED) and the maximum tolerated dose (MTD) in animal models.

ii. **Therapeutic Window**: Calculate the therapeutic window by comparing the MED and MTD to ensure the delivery system provides an adequate safety margin.

6. Patient-Centric Considerations

6.1. Administration Route and Convenience

a. **Objective:** Evaluate the suitability of the delivery system for the intended route of administration and patient compliance.

b. **Methods:**

i. **Formulation Studies**: Develop formulations suitable for various routes of administration (e.g., oral, injectable, transdermal).

ii. **Patient Compliance Studies**: Assess factors such as ease of use, dosing frequency, and patient comfort through surveys or clinical studies.

6.2. Personalized Medicine

a. **Objective**: Tailor the delivery system to individual patient needs for personalized therapy.

b. **Methods:**

i. **Biomarker Studies**: Identify biomarkers that predict patient response to the therapy.

ii. **Genetic Studies**: Evaluate genetic factors that influence drug metabolism and response to optimize dosing and treatment regimens.

Targeting and Specificity

Targeting and specificity are critical aspects in the evaluation of delivery systems for proteins and other macromolecules. Effective targeting ensures that the therapeutic agent reaches the desired site of action, thereby enhancing efficacy and minimizing side effects. Here's a detailed overview of the methodologies and considerations for evaluating targeting and specificity:

1. Targeting Mechanisms

1.1. Passive Targeting

a. **Objective:** Utilize natural physiological processes to direct the delivery system to specific sites.

b. **Methods:**

    i. **Enhanced Permeability and Retention (EPR) Effect**: Leverage the leaky vasculature of tumors and inflamed tissues to accumulate nanoparticles or macromolecules.

    ii. **Size and Surface Properties**: Optimize the size and surface characteristics of nanoparticles to enhance circulation time and target accumulation.

1.2. Active Targeting

a. **Objective:** Employ specific interactions between the delivery system and target cells or tissues.

b. **Methods:**

    i. **Ligand-Conjugated Delivery Systems**: Attach ligands such as antibodies, peptides, or small molecules that specifically bind to receptors on target cells.

    ii. **Receptor-Mediated Endocytosis**: Utilize ligands that trigger receptor-mediated uptake by target cells.

2. Evaluation of Targeting Efficiency

2.1. In Vitro Studies

a. **Objective:** Assess the binding and uptake of the delivery system by target cells.

b. **Methods:**

    i. **Binding Assays**: Use radiolabeled or fluorescently labeled ligands to measure binding affinity and kinetics to target receptors.

ii. **Cell Uptake Studies**: Measure the internalization of the delivery system in target cells using flow cytometry, confocal microscopy, or fluorescence microscopy.

iii. **Competition Assays**: Confirm specificity by competing the targeting ligand with free ligand or blocking antibodies.

2.2. In Vivo Studies

a. **Objective**: Evaluate the biodistribution and accumulation of the delivery system in target tissues.

b. **Methods:**

i. **Imaging Techniques**: Use non-invasive imaging methods such as PET, MRI, or fluorescence imaging to track the delivery system in live animals.

ii. **Biodistribution Studies**: Quantify the accumulation of the delivery system in various tissues using techniques like gamma counting, HPLC, or mass spectrometry.

iii. **Histological Analysis**: Examine tissue sections for localization of the delivery system using immunohistochemistry or fluorescence microscopy.

3. Specificity and Off-Target Effects

3.1. In Vitro Specificity Testing

a. **Objective**: Confirm that the delivery system specifically targets the intended cells or tissues without affecting non-target cells.

b. **Methods:**

i. **Co-Culture Systems**: Use co-cultures of target and non-target cells to assess selective uptake and cytotoxicity.

ii. **Selectivity Index**: Calculate the ratio of uptake or effect in target cells to that in non-target cells.

3.2. In Vivo Specificity Testing

a. **Objective**: Ensure the delivery system selectively accumulates in target tissues in vivo.

b. **Methods:**

    i. **Off-Target Biodistribution**: Measure the distribution of the delivery system in off-target organs and compare with target tissues.

    ii. **Functional Consequences**: Monitor for adverse effects in non-target tissues through histopathological analysis and biomarker studies.

4. Functional Validation of Targeting

4.1. Target Engagement

a. **Objective**: Demonstrate that the delivery system effectively engages with the target receptor or biomolecule.

b. **Methods:**

    i. **Receptor Occupancy Studies**: Measure the extent of receptor binding by the delivered protein using labeled ligands or antibodies.

    ii. **Functional Assays**: Assess downstream signaling or biological effects indicative of target engagement.

4.2. Therapeutic Efficacy

a. **Objective:** Confirm that targeted delivery translates to enhanced therapeutic outcomes.

b. **Methods:**

    i. **Efficacy Studies in Disease Models**: Compare therapeutic outcomes (e.g., tumor regression, inflammation reduction) between targeted and non-targeted delivery systems.

    ii. **Dose-Response Relationships**: Evaluate whether targeting allows for reduced dosing while maintaining or enhancing efficacy.

5. Advanced Targeting Strategies

5.1. Multi-Functional Delivery Systems

a. **Objective:** Develop systems that combine targeting with other functionalities such as imaging, controlled release, or combined therapy.

b. **Methods:**

    i. **Theranostic Systems**: Create systems that provide both therapeutic and diagnostic capabilities, allowing for real-time monitoring of delivery and treatment.

    ii. **Stimuli-Responsive Systems**: Design systems that respond to specific triggers (e.g., pH, temperature, enzymes) present in target tissues to enhance specificity.

5.2. Personalized Targeting Approaches

a. **Objective**: Tailor delivery systems to individual patient profiles for personalized therapy.

b. **Methods**:

    i. **Biomarker Identification**: Identify patient-specific biomarkers or genetic profiles that guide the selection of targeting ligands.

    ii. **Adaptive Targeting**: Develop delivery systems that can be easily modified or adapted based on individual patient needs and responses.

6. Regulatory and Translational Considerations

6.1. Regulatory Compliance

a. **Objective**: Ensure that targeting strategies comply with regulatory standards for safety and efficacy.

b. **Methods:**

    i. **GLP Studies**: Conduct preclinical studies in compliance with Good Laboratory Practice (GLP) to ensure reliability and reproducibility.

    ii. **Regulatory Submissions**: Prepare comprehensive data packages for regulatory review, including targeting and specificity studies.

6.2. Clinical Translation

a. **Objective:** Facilitate the translation of targeted delivery systems from preclinical studies to clinical applications.

b. **Methods:**

    i. **Clinical Trial Design**: Design clinical trials that specifically evaluate the targeting efficiency and therapeutic benefits of the delivery system.

    ii. **Patient Selection**: Use biomarkers and diagnostic tools to select appropriate patients for targeted therapies.

Regulatory and Quality Control

Regulatory and quality control aspects play a crucial role in the evaluation of delivery systems for proteins and other macromolecules in the context of protein and peptide delivery. These systems are often intricate and must adhere to strict standards to ensure efficacy, safety, and consistency. Here's a detailed breakdown of regulatory and quality control considerations:

1. **Regulatory Framework**: Compliance with regulatory guidelines is paramount for any delivery system intended for human use. Depending on the country or region, regulatory bodies like the FDA (Food and Drug Administration) in the United States or the EMA (European Medicines Agency) in Europe oversee the approval and monitoring of drug delivery systems. These agencies provide guidelines and regulations that manufacturers must follow to ensure the safety and efficacy of their products.

2. **Quality Control Standards**: Quality control encompasses measures taken throughout the manufacturing process to ensure that products meet predefined specifications. This includes raw material testing, in-process monitoring, and final product analysis. Quality control standards may include parameters such as particle size distribution, drug loading

efficiency, stability under various conditions, and release kinetics of the encapsulated molecules.

3. **Characterization of Delivery Systems**: Comprehensive characterization of the delivery system is essential to understand its properties and performance. This includes physicochemical characterization (particle size, surface charge, morphology), structural analysis (using techniques like microscopy, spectroscopy), and functional assays (drug release kinetics, stability under physiological conditions).

4. **Biological Evaluation**: Assessment of the biological response to the delivery system is crucial for determining its safety and efficacy. This may involve in vitro studies using cell culture models to evaluate cytotoxicity, cell uptake, and intracellular trafficking of the delivered molecules. In vivo studies, such as pharmacokinetic and pharmacodynamic evaluations in animal models, provide valuable insights into the system's behavior in a physiological environment.

5. **Stability Studies**: Stability testing is conducted to assess the shelf-life of the delivery system under various storage conditions (temperature, humidity, light exposure). Accelerated stability studies can help predict the long-term stability of the product and guide storage recommendations.

6. **Sterility and Endotoxin Testing**: For delivery systems intended for parenteral administration, ensuring sterility and absence of endotoxins is critical. Sterility testing confirms the absence of viable microorganisms, while endotoxin testing verifies the absence of bacterial endotoxins, which can cause severe adverse reactions.

7. **Validation Studies**: Validation studies are conducted to demonstrate the consistency and reproducibility of the manufacturing process and analytical methods. This includes validation of manufacturing processes, analytical methods used for quality control, and cleaning procedures to prevent cross-contamination.

8. **Documentation and Reporting**: Comprehensive documentation of all aspects of the development, manufacturing, and testing processes is essential for regulatory submissions. This includes detailed reports of formulation development, manufacturing procedures, analytical methods, validation studies, and quality control test results.

9. **Compliance with Good Manufacturing Practices (GMP):** GMP guidelines provide a framework for ensuring that pharmaceutical products are consistently produced and controlled according to quality standards. Compliance with GMP regulations is mandatory for obtaining regulatory approval and ensuring product quality and safety.

Multiple-Choice Questions (MCQs)

1. What is a primary function of proteins in the body?

   A) Energy storage

   B) Catalyzing metabolic reactions

   C) Hormone regulation

   D) Nutrient transport

2. Which peptide hormone is used to manage diabetes?

   A) Glucagon

   B) Dopamine

   C) Insulin

   D) Serotonin

3. What is a major challenge in protein and peptide delivery?

   A) High energy consumption

   B) Immunogenicity

   C) Cost of production

   D) Refrigeration requirements

4. Which is NOT a method of parenteral delivery?

   A) Oral ingestion

B) Intravenous injection

C) Subcutaneous injection

D) Intramuscular injection

5. What is an advantage of oral delivery of proteins and peptides?

    A) High bioavailability

    B) Patient compliance

    C) Rapid absorption

    D) High stability

6. Which technique is used in pulmonary delivery?

    A) Nebulizers

    B) Patches

    C) Gels

    D) Tablets

7. What does PEGylation do to proteins and peptides?

    A) Reduces their size

    B) Increases their immunogenicity

    C) Increases their half-life

    D) Decreases their effectiveness

8. Which barrier does the gastrointestinal (GI) tract pose to protein and peptide delivery? A) Enzymatic degradation

    B) Increased absorption

    C) Alkaline pH

    D) Low temperatures

9. What is the purpose of encapsulation in protein delivery?

    A) To decrease the molecule size

    B) To enhance stability and absorption

    C) To increase the reaction rate

    D) To reduce the cost of production

10. What role does PEGylation play in the formulation of protein therapies?

A) It decreases the protein's molecular weight.

B) It enhances the therapeutic activity of proteins.

C) It reduces immunogenicity and increases half-life.

D) It functions as a preservative.

11. What is a primary use of liposomes in drug delivery?

A) To decrease drug solubility

B) To target specific organs

C) To increase drug volatility

D) To simplify drug synthesis

12. Which method is NOT used for stability testing of proteins?

A) High-Performance Liquid Chromatography (HPLC)

B) Mass Spectrometry (MS)

C) Crystallization

D) Differential Scanning Calorimetry (DSC)

13. What is the main objective of in vitro bioavailability studies?

A) To observe drug effects on human subjects

B) To predict absorption and release profiles

C) To evaluate color and texture

D) To test packaging materials

14. Which parameter is NOT directly assessed in pharmacokinetics?

A) Metabolism

B) Color stability

C) Absorption

D) Excretion

15. What is a significant benefit of antibody-drig conjugates (ADCs)?

A) They are cheaper to produce than traditional drugs.

B) They provide targeted delivery to cancer cells.

C) They can be administered orally.

D) They increase the risk of systemic toxicity.

16. What is tested in genotoxicity studies?

   A) Biological half-life

   B) Genetic mutations or chromosomal damage

   C) Immunogenicity

   D) Protein aggregation

17. Which is a main focus of regulatory toxicology?

   A) Designing drug formulas

   B) Ensuring safety studies comply with guidelines

   C) Marketing pharmaceuticals

   D) Developing stronger medications

18. How do biocompatibility studies assess a delivery system?

   A) By determining cost-effectiveness

   B) By observing patient psychological response

   C) By evaluating interaction with biological systems

   D) By testing drug flavor

19. Which is NOT a method of targeted delivery?

   A) Using ligands that bind to specific receptors

   B) Employing non-specific diffusion

   C) Magnetic or ultrasound-responsive systems

   D) Antibody-mediated targeting

20. What is the main advantage of using pharmacokinetic/pharmacodynamic (PK/PD) modeling?

   A) To predict financial costs

   B) To determine drug distribution and therapeutic effect

   C) To assess the drug's taste

   D) To design drug packaging

Short Answer Type Questions (Subjective)

1. What are the primary functions of proteins in the body?

2. Describe the role of peptides in medical treatments.

3. List three challenges associated with protein and peptide delivery.

4. Explain the concept of parenteral delivery and list its types.

5. What are the advantages and disadvantages of oral delivery for proteins and peptides?

6. How does transdermal delivery work for protein and peptide therapies?

7. Define what PEGylation is and its purpose in protein therapy.

8. What are enzymatic degradation and its implications in protein delivery?

9. Describe the significance of nanoparticle encapsulation in protein delivery.

10. What role do chemical modifications like cyclization play in peptide stability?

11. How do stability studies impact the development of protein and peptide delivery systems?

12. What is meant by bioavailability in the context of protein and peptide drugs?

13. Discuss the importance of pharmacokinetics in the evaluation of protein therapies.

14. What are antibody-drug conjugates and how are they used in cancer treatment?

15. Describe the potential toxic effects evaluated in safety studies for protein delivery systems.

16. How do genotoxicity studies contribute to the safety assessment of protein therapies?

17. What is the significance of biocompatibility testing in the development of new drug delivery systems?

18. Explain the concept of targeted delivery in protein and peptide therapies.

19. Discuss the importance of regulatory compliance in the development of drug delivery systems.

20. How does patient-centric considerations influence the design and evaluation of protein delivery systems?

Long Answer Type Questions (Subjective)

1. Discuss the various physiological barriers that protein and peptide delivery systems must overcome and the strategies used to address these barriers.

2. Explain the process and importance of stability testing in the development of protein and peptide delivery systems, focusing on both physicochemical and biological stability.

3. Describe the methodologies used to assess the bioavailability and pharmacokinetics of protein and peptide drugs and their implications for therapeutic efficacy.

4. Evaluate the role of nanotechnology in enhancing the delivery and efficacy of protein and peptide therapeutics, including specific examples such as nanoparticles and liposomes.

5. Analyze the challenges and advancements in pulmonary delivery of proteins and peptides, including the types of devices used and the formulation considerations.

6. Discuss the role and mechanisms of advanced delivery systems such as hydrogels and microneedles in the context of controlled and sustained release of proteins.

7. Describe the development and function of targeted delivery systems, focusing on the use of ligand-targeted carriers and responsive systems for disease-specific treatment.

8. Explain the regulatory and quality control measures necessary for the approval and production of protein and peptide delivery systems, including GMP practices.

9. Analyze the impact of immunogenicity on the safety and efficacy of protein therapies and the methods used to evaluate and mitigate this risk.

10. Discuss the implications of pharmacokinetic/pharmacodynamic (PK/PD) modeling in optimizing the delivery and dosing of protein and peptide drugs.

Answer Key

1. (B) Catalyzing metabolic reactions
2. (C) Insulin
3. (B) Immunogenicity
4. (A) Oral ingestion
5. (B) Patient compliance
6. (A) Nebulizers
7. (C) Increases their half-life
8. (A) Enzymatic degradation
9. (B) To enhance stability and absorption
10. (C) It reduces immunogenicity and increases half-life.
11. (B) To target specific organs
12. (C) Crystallization
13. (B) To predict absorption and release profiles
14. (B) Color stability
15. (B) They provide targeted delivery to cancer cells.
16. (B) Genetic mutations or chromosomal damage
17. (B) Ensuring safety studies comply with guidelines
18. (C) By evaluating interaction with biological systems
19. (B) Employing non-specific diffusion
20. (B) To determine drug distribution and therapeutic effect

CHAPTER – 8

VACCINE DELIVERY SYSTEMS

INTRODUCTION:

Vaccine delivery systems are essential for administering vaccines effectively and safely. These systems encompass a range of methods and technologies designed to deliver antigens (the active component of vaccines) to the immune system. Here's a detailed overview of vaccine delivery systems:

1. Traditional Delivery Methods

a. Intramuscular Injection

i. **Method:** Injection into the muscle tissue, typically in the upper arm (deltoid muscle) or thigh.

ii. **Advantages**: Well-established, efficient in inducing systemic immune response.

iii. **Disadvantages**: Requires trained personnel, needles can cause discomfort, risk of needle-stick injuries and infections.

b. Subcutaneous Injection

i. **Method:** Injection into the layer of fat under the skin.

ii. **Advantages:** Easier administration compared to intramuscular, suitable for vaccines like MMR (measles, mumps, and rubella).

iii. **Disadvantages**: Similar to intramuscular, with a slightly slower absorption rate.

c. Intradermal Injection

i. **Method:** Injection into the dermal layer of the skin.

ii. **Advantages**: Uses a lower dose of vaccine, potentially enhancing immune response due to the high concentration of immune cells in the dermis.

iii. **Disadvantages**: Requires precise administration, which can be challenging.

2. Novel Delivery Methods

a. Oral Vaccines

i. **Method**: Administration through the mouth.

ii. **Examples:** Polio vaccine (Sabin), rotavirus vaccine.

iii. **Advantages:** Non-invasive, easy to administer, induces mucosal immunity.

iv. **Disadvantages**: Stability issues in the gastrointestinal tract, requires robust formulation to survive stomach acid and digestive enzymes.

b. Nasal Sprays

i. **Method:** Administration through the nasal mucosa.

ii. **Examples**: Influenza vaccine (FluMist).

iii. **Advantages:** Non-invasive, induces mucosal immunity in the respiratory tract.

iv. **Disadvantages:** Potential discomfort, limited to vaccines effective via this route.

c. Microneedle Patches

i. **Method:** A patch with tiny needles that painlessly penetrate the outer skin layer to deliver the vaccine.

ii. **Advantages:** Minimally invasive, easy to apply, potentially self-administered, reduces needle-stick injuries.

iii. **Disadvantages:** Still under development for widespread use, production costs.

d. Liposomal and Nanoparticle Systems

i. **Method**: Encapsulating the vaccine in lipid-based or polymer-based particles.

ii. **Advantages**: Enhances stability, targeted delivery, and controlled release of antigens, potential to induce strong immune responses.

iii. **Disadvantages:** Complex manufacturing processes, regulatory hurdles.

e. Viral Vectors

i. **Method**: Using modified viruses to deliver genetic material encoding the antigen.

ii. **Examples**: Adenovirus-based COVID-19 vaccines (e.g., AstraZeneca, Johnson & Johnson).

iii. **Advantages:** Strong immune response, versatility in design.

iv. **Disadvantages:** Pre-existing immunity to the viral vector can reduce efficacy, complex manufacturing.

3. Adjuvants and Formulation Enhancements

Adjuvants are substances added to vaccines to enhance the body's immune response to the provided antigen. They can be used with various delivery systems to improve effectiveness.

a. Alum (Aluminum Salts)

i. **Role**: Enhances antigen uptake by immune cells.

ii. **Common Use:** Widely used in traditional vaccines.

b. MF59 (Oil-in-Water Emulsion)

i. **Role**: Stimulates a strong immune response.

ii. **Common Use:** Influenza vaccines.

c. AS01 (Liposome-based)

i. **Role**: Strong adjuvant used in newer vaccines.

ii. **Common Use:** Malaria vaccine (RTS,S).

4. Technological Innovations

a. mRNA Vaccines

i. **Method**: Uses messenger RNA to instruct cells to produce the antigen.

ii. **Examples**: COVID-19 vaccines (Pfizer-BioNTech, Moderna).

iii. **Advantages:** Rapid development, highly effective, adaptable to new pathogens.

iv. **Disadvantages:** Requires cold storage, new technology with ongoing studies on long-term effects.

b. DNA Vaccines

i. **Method**: Uses plasmid DNA to instruct cells to produce the antigen.

ii. **Advantage**s: Stable, easy to produce, induces both B and T cell responses.

iii. **Disadvantages**: Requires electroporation (electric pulses) for efficient delivery into cells, currently limited to veterinary use.

5. Challenges and Future Directions

i. **Cold Chain Requirements**: Many vaccines require stringent temperature control during storage and transport, posing logistical challenges, especially in low-resource settings.

ii. **Needle-free Technologies**: Efforts are ongoing to develop more needle-free methods to reduce discomfort, increase compliance, and minimize waste and risk.

iii. **Universal Vaccines**: Research is underway to develop vaccines that provide broad protection against multiple strains or types of a pathogen, such as universal influenza vaccines.

iv. **Personalized Vaccination**: Advances in genomics and biotechnology could lead to personalized vaccines tailored to an individual's genetic makeup or immune status.

VACCINES

Vaccine delivery systems are crucial in administering vaccines effectively. These systems include a variety of methods designed to deliver antigens to the immune system, stimulating an immune response to protect against diseases. Below is a detailed look at different types of vaccines used within various vaccine delivery systems:

1. Live Attenuated Vaccines

a. **Description**: Contain live pathogens that have been weakened so they cannot cause disease in healthy individuals.

b. **Examples:**

   i. Measles, Mumps, Rubella (MMR) vaccine

   ii. Varicella (chickenpox) vaccine

   iii. Oral polio vaccine (OPV)

   iv. Yellow fever vaccine

c. **Delivery Methods**:

   i. **Intramuscular Injection**: MMR, varicella

   ii. **Oral:** OPV

   iii. **Subcutaneous Injection**: Yellow fever

d. **Advantage**s: Strong and long-lasting immune response, often with a single dose.

e. **Disadvantages**: Not suitable for immunocompromised individuals, requires careful storage.

2. Inactivated (Killed) Vaccines

a. **Description**: Contain pathogens that have been killed or inactivated so they cannot cause disease.

b. **Examples**:

   i. Inactivated polio vaccine (IPV)

   ii. Hepatitis A vaccine

   iii. Rabies vaccine

c. **Delivery Methods:**

   i. **Intramuscular Injection**: IPV, hepatitis A, rabies

d. **Advantage**s: Safer for immunocompromised individuals, stable.

e. **Disadvantages**: May require multiple doses to achieve full immunity.

3. Subunit, Recombinant, Polysaccharide, and Conjugate Vaccines

a. **Description:** Contain specific pieces of the pathogen (like protein, sugar, or capsid) to elicit an immune response.

b. **Examples**:

    i.   Human Papillomavirus (HPV) vaccine

    ii.   Hepatitis B vaccine

    iii.   Pneumococcal conjugate vaccine (PCV)

    iv.   Meningococcal conjugate vaccine

c. **Delivery Methods**:

    i.   **Intramuscular Injection**: HPV, hepatitis B, PCV, meningococcal

d. **Advantage**s: Targeted immune response, safe for immunocompromised individuals.

e. **Disadvantages**: May require adjuvants to enhance the immune response, potentially multiple doses.

4. Toxoid Vaccines

a. **Description:** Contain inactivated toxins produced by the pathogen.

b. **Examples**:

    i.   Diphtheria vaccine

    ii.   Tetanus vaccine

c. **Delivery Methods:**

    i.   Intramuscular Injection: Diphtheria, tetanus (often combined in DTaP with acellular pertussis)

d. **Advantages**: Safe, stable, and effective.

e. **Disadvantages**: Requires booster shots for long-lasting immunity.

5. mRNA Vaccines

a. **Description**: Use messenger RNA to instruct cells to produce a protein that elicits an immune response.

b. **Examples:**

    i.   COVID-19 vaccines (Pfizer-BioNTech, Moderna)

c. **Delivery Methods:**

    i.   **Intramuscular Injection**: COVID-19 mRNA vaccines

d. **Advantages**: Rapid development, highly effective, adaptable to new pathogens.

e. **Disadvantages:** Requires cold storage, relatively new technology.

6. Viral Vector Vaccines

a. **Description:** Use a modified virus (not the pathogen) to deliver genetic material encoding an antigen.

b. **Examples:**

   i.   COVID-19 vaccines (AstraZeneca, Johnson & Johnson)

c. **Delivery Methods**:

   i.   **Intramuscular Injection**: COVID-19 viral vector vaccines

d. **Advantage**s: Strong immune response, can be used for multiple types of pathogens.

e. **Disadvantages:** Pre-existing immunity to the vector can reduce efficacy, complex production.

7. DNA Vaccines

a. **Description:** Use plasmid DNA to instruct cells to produce the antigen.

b. **Examples**:

   i.   Zika virus DNA vaccine (in development)

c. **Delivery Methods**:

   i.   Intramuscular Injection (with electroporation for enhanced delivery)

d. **Advantages**: Stable, easy to produce, elicits both B and T cell responses.

e. **Disadvantages**: Requires electroporation, still under research for human use.

8. Combination Vaccines

a. **Description:** Combine multiple vaccines into one shot to protect against different diseases.

b. **Examples:**

   i.   DTaP (diphtheria, tetanus, acellular pertussis)

ii.   MMR (measles, mumps, rubella)

c. **Delivery Methods**:

i.   **Intramuscular Injection**: DTaP, MMR

d. **Advantages**: Reduces the number of shots required, improving compliance.

e. **Disadvantages:** Complex formulation, risk of interactions between components.

9. Adjuvants in Vaccines

Adjuvants are substances added to vaccines to enhance the body's immune response to the antigen. Different adjuvants are used depending on the type of vaccine and the desired immune response.

a. Alum (Aluminum Salts)

i.   **Role:** Enhances antigen uptake by immune cells.

ii.   **Common Use**: Hepatitis B, DTaP.

b. MF59 (Oil-in-Water Emulsion)

i.   **Role:** Stimulates a strong immune response.

ii.   **Common Use**: Influenza vaccines.

c. AS01 (Liposome-based)

i.   **Role:** Strong adjuvant used in newer vaccines.

ii.   **Common Use**: Malaria vaccine (RTS,S).

10. Future Directions in Vaccine Delivery

i.   **Needle-Free Delivery**: Technologies like microneedle patches and jet injectors aim to eliminate needles, making vaccination less painful and more accessible.

ii.   **Universal Vaccines**: Research is ongoing to develop vaccines that provide broad protection against multiple strains or types of a pathogen, such as universal influenza vaccines.

iii. **Personalized Vaccines**: Advances in genomics could lead to personalized vaccines tailored to an individual's genetic makeup or immune status.

iv. **Therapeutic Vaccines**: Designed to treat existing diseases rather than prevent them, including vaccines for cancer and chronic infections like HIV.

UPTAKE OF ANTIGENS

The uptake of antigens in vaccine delivery systems is a crucial step in initiating a robust immune response. This process involves the recognition, processing, and presentation of antigens to the immune system, primarily by antigen-presenting cells (APCs) such as dendritic cells, macrophages, and B cells. Here's a detailed look at how different vaccine delivery systems facilitate the uptake of antigens:

1. Traditional Delivery Methods

Traditional delivery methods for vaccines primarily involve intramuscular (IM), subcutaneous (SC), and intradermal (ID) injections. Each method introduces the antigen into the body in different ways, influencing how the immune system takes up and processes the antigen to generate an immune response. Here's a detailed look at the uptake of antigens in these traditional vaccine delivery systems:

1. Intramuscular Injection (IM)

Mechanism

a. **Administration**: The vaccine is injected directly into the muscle tissue, typically in the deltoid (upper arm) or gluteal (buttock) muscle.

b. **Antigen Uptake**:

   i. **Muscle Cells:** Limited role in antigen processing, primarily providing a depot for the antigen.

ii.   **Local Immune Cells**: Antigen-presenting cells (APCs) such as dendritic cells and macrophages in the muscle tissue capture the antigen.

iii.   **Lymphatic System**: APCs migrate to the draining lymph nodes via the lymphatic system, where they present the processed antigen to T cells and B cells.

Immune Response

a.   **Initial Response**: Localized inflammation and recruitment of immune cells to the injection site.

b.   **Activation**: Dendritic cells present the antigen to T cells in the lymph nodes, initiating the adaptive immune response.

c.   **Antibody Production**: Activated B cells differentiate into plasma cells and produce antibodies specific to the antigen.

Advantages

a.   **Established Method**: Widely used and understood, with a proven track record of efficacy.

b.   **Strong Immune Response**: Capable of inducing robust systemic immunity.

Challenges

a.   **Pain and Discomfort**: Potential for pain and local side effects at the injection site.

b.   **Need for Healthcare Professionals**: Requires trained personnel for administration.

2. Subcutaneous Injection (SC)

Mechanism

a.   **Administration**: The vaccine is injected into the subcutaneous tissue, which lies between the skin and muscle, typically in the upper arm or thigh.

b.   **Antigen Uptake:**

i. **Subcutaneous Tissue**: Rich in blood vessels and lymphatics, facilitating antigen uptake.

ii. **APCs:** Dendritic cells and macrophages in the subcutaneous tissue capture and process the antigen.

iii. **Lymphatic System**: APCs migrate to the draining lymph nodes where they present the antigen to T cells and B cells.

Immune Response

a. **Initial Response**: Localized inflammation and recruitment of immune cells to the injection site.

b. **Activation:** Antigen presentation in the lymph nodes leads to T cell and B cell activation.

c. **Antibody Production**: B cells produce antibodies specific to the antigen.

Advantages

a. **Less Painful**: Generally less painful than intramuscular injections.

b. **Good Immune Response**: Effective in inducing both humoral and cellular immunity.

Challenges

a. **Absorption Variability**: Slower and potentially more variable absorption compared to IM injections.

b. **Need for Healthcare Professionals**: Requires trained personnel for administration.

3. Intradermal Injection (ID)

Mechanism

a. **Administration:** The vaccine is injected into the dermal layer of the skin, usually on the forearm.

b. **Antigen Uptake:**

i. **Dermal Layer**: Rich in dendritic cells, particularly Langerhans cells, which are highly effective in capturing and processing antigens.

ii. **Local Immune Cells**: Dendritic cells and other APCs in the dermal layer uptake the antigen and migrate to the lymph nodes.

iii. **Lymphatic System**: Antigen presentation occurs in the lymph nodes, initiating the adaptive immune response.

Immune Response

a. **Initial Response:** Strong local immune activation due to the high density of APCs in the dermal layer.

b. **Activation**: Efficient antigen presentation to T cells in the lymph nodes.

c. **Antibody Production**: Robust activation of B cells and production of specific antibodies.

Advantages

a. **Efficient Antigen Uptake**: High concentration of dendritic cells in the dermal layer leads to efficient antigen processing.

b. **Strong Immune Response**: Potentially stronger immune responses due to direct engagement of local immune cells.

Challenges

a. **Technical Difficulty**: Requires precise administration technique to ensure the vaccine is delivered into the dermal layer.

b. **Potential for Local Reactions**: Higher risk of local skin reactions and inflammation.

Comparative Summary

a. Intramuscular Injection (IM)

i. **Strengths**: Strong systemic immunity, well-established method.

ii. **Weaknesses:** Pain and discomfort, requires healthcare professionals.

b. Subcutaneous Injection (SC)

i. **Strengths**: Less painful, effective immune response.

ii. **Weaknesses**: Variable absorption, requires healthcare professionals.

c. **Intradermal Injection (ID)**

    i. **Strengths**: Efficient antigen uptake, strong immune response.

    ii. **Weaknesses**: Technically challenging, potential for local skin reactions.

Factors Influencing Antigen Uptake and Immune Response

a. **Adjuvants:** Substances added to vaccines to enhance the immune response by increasing the uptake and presentation of antigens by APCs.

    i. **Examples:** Alum (aluminum salts), MF59 (oil-in-water emulsion), AS03 (squalene-based adjuvant).

b. **Vaccine Formulation**: The physical form of the vaccine (liquid, lyophilized, nanoparticle-based) can affect antigen stability and uptake.

    i. **Liquid Formulations**: Common and easy to administer but may require refrigeration.

    ii. **Lyophilized Formulations**: More stable and suitable for areas with limited cold chain infrastructure but require reconstitution before use.

    iii. **Nanoparticle-based Vaccines**: Enhanced stability and targeted delivery but require advanced manufacturing techniques.

c. **Administration Technique:** Proper technique is crucial for ensuring the vaccine is delivered to the intended tissue and for optimizing antigen uptake and immune response.

    i. **Training and Standardization**: Healthcare providers need adequate training to standardize administration techniques and ensure consistent vaccine delivery.

2. Novel Delivery Methods

Novel vaccine delivery methods are designed to improve the efficiency of antigen uptake, enhance immune responses, and address limitations associated with traditional delivery methods. These innovative approaches include mucosal delivery, transdermal delivery, nanoparticle-based systems, viral vectors, and DNA/RNA vaccines. Here's a detailed look at these novel delivery systems and their mechanisms of antigen uptake:

1. Mucosal Delivery

Mechanism

   a. **Administration Routes:** Nasal, oral, and sublingual.

   b. **Antigen Uptake**:

      i. **M Cells**: Specialized cells in the mucosal epithelium that transport antigens to underlying immune cells.

      ii. **Dendritic Cells**: Capture antigens at mucosal surfaces and migrate to regional lymph nodes.

      iii. **Mucosa-Associated Lymphoid Tissue (MALT)**: Sites like Peyer's patches and tonsils where antigens are presented to immune cells.

Immune Response

   a. **Local Immunity:** Induces IgA production, which protects mucosal surfaces.

   b. **Systemic Immunity**: Generates systemic antibodies and T cell responses.

Examples

   a. **Oral Polio Vaccine**: Induces both mucosal and systemic immunity.

   b. **Nasal FluMist**: Live attenuated influenza vaccine administered via the nasal route.

Advantages

   a. Non-invasive and easy to administer.

   b. Induces both local and systemic immunity.

Challenges

   a. Antigen stability and degradation in the gastrointestinal tract.

   b. Variability in absorption and immune response.

2. Transdermal Delivery

Mechanism

a. **Microneedle Patches**: Arrays of tiny needles that painlessly penetrate the skin to deliver antigens.

b. **Needle-Free Jet Injectors**: Use high-pressure streams to deliver vaccines through the skin.

c. **Topical Applications**: Use chemical enhancers or physical methods (e.g., electroporation) to increase skin permeability.

Antigen Uptake

a. **Skin Immune Cells**: High density of dendritic cells, particularly Langerhans cells, in the dermal layer capture and process antigens.

b. **Lymphatic System**: Antigen-presenting cells migrate to lymph nodes to present antigens to T cells.

Immune Response

a. Strong local immune activation due to high density of APCs in the skin.

b. Induces robust systemic immune responses.

Examples

a. **Influenza Microneedle Patch**: Under development for seasonal influenza vaccination.

b. **DNA Vaccines with Electroporation**: Enhanced uptake of DNA vaccines using brief electrical pulses.

Advantages

a. Minimally invasive and pain-free.

b. Potential for self-administration and reduced medical waste.

Challenges

a. Manufacturing consistency and scalability.

b. Ensuring adequate dose delivery and stability.

3. Nanoparticle-Based Systems

Mechanism

a. **Nanoparticles:** Can encapsulate antigens, protecting them from degradation and enhancing delivery to immune cells.

b. **Types**: Liposomes, polymeric nanoparticles, and virus-like particles (VLPs).

Antigen Uptake

a. **Enhanced Uptake**: Nanoparticles facilitate endocytosis by dendritic cells and macrophages.

b. **Controlled Release**: Nanoparticles can be engineered to release antigens in a controlled manner, enhancing immune activation.

Immune Response

a. Prolonged antigen presentation and enhanced activation of T cells.

b. Can be designed to target specific tissues or cells.

Examples

a. **Lipid Nanoparticles in mRNA Vaccines**: Used in COVID-19 mRNA vaccines (Pfizer-BioNTech and Moderna).

Advantages

a. Enhanced stability and targeted delivery.

b. Potential for single-dose vaccines due to controlled release.

Challenges

a. Complex manufacturing and regulatory approval processes.

4. Viral Vectors

Mechanism

a. **Recombinant Viruses**: Use of harmless viruses engineered to express vaccine antigens.

b. **Types**: Adenoviruses, lentiviruses, and vesicular stomatitis virus (VSV).

Antigen Uptake

a. **Infection and Transduction**: Viral vectors infect host cells and deliver genetic material encoding the antigen.

b. **Antigen Production**: Host cells produce the antigen, which is then processed and presented by APCs.

Immune Response

a. Strong cellular and humoral responses due to natural viral infection processes.

b. Long-lasting immunity.

Examples

a. **Adenovirus Vectors**: Used in COVID-19 vaccines (Johnson & Johnson and AstraZeneca).

Advantages

a. High immunogenicity and ability to induce both T cell and antibody responses.

b. Potential for rapid development and production.

Challenges

a. Pre-existing immunity to the vector can reduce efficacy.

b. Potential for vector-induced side effects.

5. DNA and RNA Vaccines

Mechanism

a. **DNA Vaccines**: Plasmid DNA encoding the antigen is delivered into host cells.

b. **RNA Vaccines**: mRNA encoding the antigen is delivered into host cells.

Antigen Uptake

a. **Transcription and Translation**: Host cells produce the antigen from the delivered genetic material.

b. **Antigen Presentation**: Newly synthesized antigens are processed and presented by APCs.

Immune Response

a. Induces strong T cell and antibody responses.

b. Can be designed to target specific pathogens quickly.

Examples

a. **mRNA Vaccines**: Pfizer-BioNTech and Moderna COVID-19 vaccines.

b. **DNA Vaccines**: Zydus Cadila's ZyCoV-D for COVID-19.

Advantages

a. Rapid and flexible design and production.

b. No need for live virus handling.

Challenges

a. Stability and delivery of genetic material.

b. Ensuring efficient uptake and expression in host cells.

Comparative Summary

a. Mucosal Delivery:

   i. **Strengths:** Non-invasive, induces local and systemic immunity.

   ii. **Weaknesses:** Antigen stability, absorption variability.

b. Transdermal Delivery:

   i. **Strengths:** Minimally invasive, potential for self-administration.

   ii. **Weaknesses:** Manufacturing and dose consistency challenges.

c. Nanoparticle-Based Systems:

   i. **Strengths**: Enhanced stability, targeted delivery.

   ii. **Weaknesses**: Complex manufacturing and approval processes.

d. Viral Vectors:

   i. **Strengths**: High immunogenicity, strong cellular and humoral responses.

   ii. **Weaknesses**: Pre-existing immunity, potential side effects.

e. DNA and RNA Vaccines:

   i. **Strengths**: Rapid development, strong immune responses.

   ii. **Weaknesses:** Stability, delivery challenges.

Factors Influencing Antigen Uptake and Immune Response

a. **Adjuvants:** Enhance immune responses by stimulating APCs and improving antigen presentation.

i. **Examples**: Alum, saponin-based adjuvants.

b. **Formulation Enhancements**: Improve stability and targeted delivery.

i. **Examples**: Encapsulation in liposomes or nanoparticles.

c. **Administration Technique**: Proper technique ensures optimal antigen delivery and immune response.

d. **Targeting Specific Cells/Tissues**: Designing vaccines to target specific cells or tissues can enhance antigen uptake and immune response.

3. Adjuvants and Formulation Enhancements

Adjuvants and formulation enhancements play a crucial role in improving the uptake of antigens in vaccine delivery systems. They are designed to enhance the immune response, ensure antigen stability, and improve the overall efficacy of vaccines. Here's a detailed look at how adjuvants and formulation enhancements contribute to antigen uptake and immune response:

1. Adjuvants

Adjuvants are substances added to vaccines to enhance the body's immune response to the provided antigen. They can work through various mechanisms, including improving antigen uptake by antigen-presenting cells (APCs), stimulating local inflammation, and enhancing the presentation of antigens to the immune system.

Mechanisms of Action

a. **Depot Effect**: Adjuvants can create a depot at the injection site, slowly releasing the antigen over time, prolonging the exposure to the immune system.

b. **Inflammation Induction**: Some adjuvants induce a mild inflammatory response, recruiting immune cells to the site of injection and enhancing antigen uptake.

c. **APC Activation**: Adjuvants can directly activate dendritic cells and macrophages, improving antigen processing and presentation.

d. **Pattern Recognition Receptors (PRRs):** Adjuvants can engage PRRs such as Toll-like receptors (TLRs) on immune cells, enhancing their activation and the subsequent immune response.

Examples of Adjuvants

a. **Alum (Aluminum Salts)**

   i. **Mechanism:** Creates a depot effect and stimulates the local immune response by inducing inflammation.

   ii. **Uses:** Widely used in vaccines for diphtheria, tetanus, and hepatitis B.

   iii. **Advantages**: Well-established safety profile and effective in inducing antibody responses.

   iv. **Challenges:** Limited ability to induce strong cellular (T-cell) responses.

b. **MF59 (Oil-in-Water Emulsion)**

   i. **Mechanism:** Enhances the recruitment of immune cells to the injection site and promotes uptake by dendritic cells.

   ii. **Uses:** Used in some influenza vaccines.

   iii. **Advantages**: Enhances both antibody and cellular immune responses.

   iv. **Challenges:** More complex manufacturing process compared to alum.

c. **AS03 (Squalene-Based Adjuvant)**

   i. **Mechanism:** Similar to MF59, it promotes immune cell recruitment and antigen uptake.

   ii. **Uses**: Used in H1N1 influenza vaccines.

   iii. **Advantage**s: Strong immunogenicity, capable of dose sparing (lower antigen dose required).

   iv. **Challenges**: Potential for local reactogenicity (inflammation at the injection site).

d. CpG Oligodeoxynucleotides

    i. **Mechanism**: Mimic bacterial DNA, activating TLR9 and enhancing APC activation and antigen presentation.

    ii. **Uses**: Experimental use in various vaccines, including cancer vaccines.

    iii. **Advantages:** Strongly stimulates cellular immune responses.

    iv. **Challenges**: Requires careful formulation to ensure stability and efficacy.

e. Matrix-M (Nanoparticle Adjuvant)

    i. **Mechanism:** Composed of saponin and cholesterol, it enhances both humoral and cellular immune responses by promoting antigen uptake and presentation.

    ii. **Uses**: Used in Novavax's COVID-19 vaccine.

    iii. **Advantages:** Potent immunogenicity and versatile for various antigens.

    iv. **Challenges**: Newer adjuvant with less historical safety data compared to alum.

2. Formulation Enhancements

Formulation enhancements are designed to improve the stability, delivery, and uptake of antigens. These enhancements can involve physical, chemical, and biological methods to optimize the vaccine formulation.

Types of Formulation Enhancements

a. Nanoparticles and Liposomes

    i. **Mechanism:** Encapsulate antigens, protecting them from degradation and enhancing delivery to APCs.

    ii. **Advantages:** Improve antigen stability and controlled release, enhance uptake by dendritic cells.

    iii. **Examples**: Lipid nanoparticles used in mRNA vaccines (e.g., Pfizer-BioNTech and Moderna COVID-19 vaccines).

b. Virus-Like Particles (VLPs)

    i.   **Mechanism**: Mimic the structure of viruses without containing viral genetic material, effectively presenting antigens to the immune system.

    ii.   **Advantages:** Highly immunogenic, safe as they lack infectious components.

    iii.   **Examples:** HPV vaccines (Gardasil and Cervarix).

c. Emulsions and Micelles

    i.   **Mechanism**: Stabilize antigens and enhance their delivery to immune cells.

    ii.   **Advantages:** Enhance antigen presentation and immune response.

    iii.   **Examples:** MF59 and AS03 adjuvants.

d. Polymeric Delivery Systems

    i.   **Mechanism:** Use biodegradable polymers to encapsulate antigens, providing sustained release and protection.

    ii.   **Advantages:** Enhance stability, control release, and target delivery to specific tissues or cells.

    iii.   **Examples:** PLGA (poly(lactic-co-glycolic acid)) nanoparticles for various experimental vaccines.

e. Hydrogels

    i.   **Mechanism**: Gel-like materials that can encapsulate antigens and release them in a controlled manner.

    ii.   **Advantages**: Biocompatible and can provide sustained antigen release.

    iii.   **Examples**: Used in experimental cancer vaccines.

f. Chemical Enhancers

    i.   **Mechanism**: Improve the permeability of biological barriers (e.g., skin, mucosal membranes) to enhance antigen uptake.

    ii.   **Advantages**: Facilitate non-invasive delivery methods.

iii.   **Examples:** Chemical permeation enhancers in transdermal patches.

Comparative Summary

a. **Alum (Aluminum Salts)**

   i.   **Strengths**: Proven safety, effective for antibody responses.

   ii.   **Weaknesses:** Limited T-cell response, potential for local inflammation.

b. **MF59 (Oil-in-Water Emulsion)**

   i.   **Strengths**: Enhances both antibody and cellular responses.

   ii.   **Weaknesses:** More complex manufacturing.

c. **AS03 (Squalene-Based Adjuvant)**

   i.   **Strengths:** Strong immunogenicity, dose-sparing.

   ii.   **Weaknesses**: Potential for local reactogenicity.

d. **CpG Oligodeoxynucleotides**

   i.   **Strengths:** Strong T-cell activation.

   ii.   **Weaknesses**: Stability and formulation challenges.

e. **Matrix-M (Nanoparticle Adjuvant)**

   i.   **Strengths:** Potent, versatile.

   ii.   **Weaknesses**: Newer, less historical data.

f. **Nanoparticles and Liposomes**

   i.   **Strengths**: Protect antigens, enhance delivery.

   ii.   **Weaknesses**: Complex formulation and manufacturing.

g. **Virus-Like Particles (VLPs)**

   i.   **Strengths:** Highly immunogenic, safe.

   ii.   **Weaknesses:** Limited to certain pathogens.

h. **Polymeric Delivery Systems**

   i.   **Strengths:** Controlled release, targeted delivery.

   ii.   **Weaknesses:** Complex formulation.

i. **Hydrogels**

   i.   **Strengths:** Biocompatible, sustained release.

ii. **Weaknesses**: Potential for variable release rates.

j. Chemical Enhancers

i. **Strengths:** Facilitate non-invasive delivery.

ii. **Weaknesses**: Potential for irritation or toxicity.

Factors Influencing Effectiveness

a. **Antigen Stability**: Ensuring the antigen remains stable and intact throughout the delivery process.

b. **Targeting**: Enhancing the delivery of antigens to specific cells or tissues to improve uptake and immune response.

c. **Adjuvant-Antigen Interaction**: Optimizing the interaction between adjuvants and antigens to maximize immune stimulation.

d. **Safety and Tolerability**: Balancing the enhancement of immune responses with the risk of adverse effects.

4. Technological Innovations

Technological innovations in vaccine delivery systems aim to improve the efficiency and effectiveness of antigen uptake, enhancing both the immune response and overall vaccine efficacy. These innovations include novel delivery platforms, advanced formulation techniques, and cutting-edge technologies that optimize antigen presentation and immune system activation. Here is a detailed exploration of these technological innovations:

1. Microneedle Arrays

Mechanism

a. **Design**: Arrays of tiny needles, typically less than a millimeter in length, that painlessly penetrate the skin.

b. **Delivery:** Directly deliver antigens to the epidermis and dermis layers of the skin, which are rich in immune cells.

Antigen Uptake

a. **Dendritic Cells and Langerhans Cells**: High density of these cells in the skin facilitates efficient antigen capture and processing.

b. **Local Inflammation**: Mild local inflammation enhances the recruitment of immune cells to the site.

Immune Response

a. **Robust Activation**: Strong local immune activation due to direct engagement with skin immune cells.

b. **Systemic Immunity**: Leads to both local and systemic immune responses.

Examples

a. **Influenza Microneedle Patch**: Under development for seasonal influenza vaccination.

b. **Polio Vaccine Microneedle Patch**: Shows promise in preclinical studies.

Advantages

a. Minimally invasive and painless.

b. Potential for self-administration and reduced medical waste.

Challenges

a. Ensuring consistent dose delivery and stability.

b. Scaling up manufacturing processes.

2. Nanoparticle-Based Delivery Systems

Mechanism

a. **Design:** Nanoparticles can encapsulate antigens, protecting them from degradation and facilitating targeted delivery.

b. **Types**: Lipid nanoparticles, polymeric nanoparticles, virus-like particles (VLPs), and inorganic nanoparticles.

Antigen Uptake

a. **Enhanced Endocytosis**: Nanoparticles facilitate efficient uptake by dendritic cells and macrophages.

b. **Controlled Release**: Engineered to release antigens in a controlled manner, enhancing immune activation over time.

Immune Response

a. **Prolonged Antigen Presentation**: Extended presence of antigens leads to prolonged immune stimulation.

b. **Targeted Activation**: Can be designed to target specific immune cells or tissues.

Examples

a. **Lipid Nanoparticles in mRNA Vaccines**: Used in Pfizer-BioNTech and Moderna COVID-19 vaccines.

b. **Polymeric Nanoparticles**: Used in experimental cancer vaccines.

Advantages

a. Enhanced stability and targeted delivery.

b. Potential for single-dose vaccines due to controlled release.

Challenges

a. Complex manufacturing and regulatory hurdles.

b. Potential for toxicity and side effects.

3. Viral Vector Vaccines

Mechanism

a. **Design**: Use of genetically engineered viruses to deliver genes encoding the vaccine antigen.

b. **Types**: Adenoviruses, lentiviruses, and vesicular stomatitis virus (VSV).

Antigen Uptake

a. **Infection and Transduction**: Viral vectors infect host cells, delivering genetic material that encodes the antigen.

b. **Antigen Production**: Host cells produce the antigen, which is then processed and presented by APCs.

Immune Response

a. **Natural Infection Mimicry**: Strong immune responses due to the mimicry of natural viral infections.

b. **Both Humoral and Cellular Responses**: Induces robust antibody and T-cell responses.

Examples

a. **Adenovirus Vectors:** Used in Johnson & Johnson and AstraZeneca COVID-19 vaccines.

b. **VSV-Based Vectors**: Used in the Ebola vaccine (Ervebo).

Advantages

a. High immunogenicity and ability to induce both T-cell and antibody responses.

b. Potential for rapid development and production.

Challenges

a. Pre-existing immunity to the viral vector can reduce efficacy.

b. Potential for vector-induced side effects.

4. DNA and RNA Vaccines

Mechanism

a. **Design:** Use of plasmid DNA or mRNA to encode the vaccine antigen.

b. **Delivery:** Delivered into host cells where the genetic material is transcribed and translated into the antigen.

Antigen Uptake

a. **Transcription and Translation**: Host cells produce the antigen from the delivered genetic material.

b. **Antigen Presentation**: Newly synthesized antigens are processed and presented by APCs.

Immune Response

a. **Strong T-Cell and Antibody Responses**: Induces robust immune responses similar to natural infection.

b. **Rapid Response**: Quick to design and produce in response to emerging pathogens.

Examples

a. **mRNA Vaccines**: Pfizer-BioNTech and Moderna COVID-19 vaccines.

b. **DNA Vaccines**: Zydus Cadila's ZyCoV-D for COVID-19.

Advantages

    a. Rapid and flexible design and production.

    b. No need for live virus handling.

Challenges

    a. Stability and delivery of genetic material.

    b. Ensuring efficient uptake and expression in host cells.

5. Adjuvant Innovations

Mechanism

    a. **Design:** New adjuvants are being developed to more effectively stimulate the immune system.

    b. **Types**: Synthetic peptides, saponins, and toll-like receptor (TLR) agonists.

Antigen Uptake

    a. **Enhanced APC Activation**: New adjuvants can more effectively activate dendritic cells and macrophages, improving antigen presentation.

    b. **Depot Formation**: Some adjuvants create a depot effect, releasing antigens slowly over time.

Immune Response

    a. **Improved Immunogenicity**: Enhanced activation of both innate and adaptive immune responses.

    b. **Targeted Activation**: Some adjuvants can be designed to target specific components of the immune system.

Examples

    a. **TLR Agonists**: Enhance innate immune responses by activating pattern recognition receptors.

    b. **Matrix-M (Saponin-Based)**: Used in Novavax's COVID-19 vaccine.

Advantages

    a. Enhanced immune response with lower antigen doses.

    b. Potential for broader protection against diverse pathogens.

Challenges

a. Potential for increased reactogenicity.

b. Regulatory and safety considerations.

6. Smart Delivery Systems

Mechanism

a. **Design:** Smart delivery systems can respond to specific physiological triggers to release the vaccine antigen.

b. **Types:** pH-sensitive, temperature-sensitive, and enzyme-responsive systems.

Antigen Uptake

a. **Triggered Release**: Antigens are released in response to specific conditions, ensuring optimal uptake and immune activation.

b. **Targeted Delivery**: Designed to release antigens at specific sites within the body.

Immune Response

a. **Enhanced Precision**: Ensures that antigens are delivered to the right place at the right time.

b. **Reduced Side Effects**: Minimizes off-target effects and potential toxicity.

Examples

a. **pH-Sensitive Liposomes**: Release contents in response to the acidic environment of endosomes.

b. **Enzyme-Responsive Nanoparticles**: Release antigens in response to specific enzymes present in target tissues.

Advantages

a. Increased specificity and reduced side effects.

b. Potential for single-dose vaccines with controlled release.

Challenges

a. Complex design and manufacturing.

b. Ensuring stability and functionality of the delivery system.

Comparative Summary

a. Microneedle Arrays

i. **Strengths:** Minimally invasive, easy to use.

ii. **Weaknesses:** Consistency and manufacturing challenges.

b. Nanoparticle-Based Systems

i. **Strengths:** Enhanced stability and targeted delivery.

ii. **Weaknesses:** Complex manufacturing, potential toxicity.

c. Viral Vector Vaccines

i. **Strengths:** High immunogenicity, robust responses.

ii. **Weaknesses:** Pre-existing immunity, side effects.

d. DNA and RNA Vaccines

i. **Strengths:** Rapid design and production, strong responses.

ii. **Weaknesses:** Stability and delivery challenges.

e. Adjuvant Innovations

i. **Strengths:** Enhanced immune responses, dose-sparing.

ii. **Weaknesses:** Potential for reactogenicity, regulatory hurdles.

f. Smart Delivery Systems

i. **Strengths:** Precision and reduced side effects.

ii. **Weaknesses:** Complexity and stability issues.

Factors Influencing Effectiveness

a. **Stability**: Ensuring the antigen remains stable and effective throughout the delivery process.

b. **Targeting**: Enhancing the delivery of antigens to specific cells or tissues to improve uptake and immune response.

c. **Adjuvant Compatibility**: Ensuring that adjuvants and antigens work synergistically to maximize immune stimulation.

d. **Safety and Tolerability**: Balancing enhanced immune responses with the risk of adverse effects.

5. Challenges and Future Directions

The uptake of antigens in vaccine delivery systems is a critical aspect of vaccine development and administration. It refers to the process by which the immune system recognizes and internalizes the antigens present in vaccines, triggering an immune response that leads to immunity against the target pathogen. However, despite the significant progress made in vaccine technology, there are still challenges and opportunities for improvement in this area. Let's delve into some of the challenges and future directions:

1. **Enhancing Antigen Presentation**: One challenge is ensuring efficient uptake and presentation of antigens by antigen-presenting cells (APCs) such as dendritic cells. Improving vaccine formulations to better target APCs can enhance antigen presentation and subsequent immune response. This could involve the use of adjuvants, nanoparticles, or delivery systems designed to target specific APC populations.

2. **Overcoming Antigen Degradation**: Antigens in vaccines can be susceptible to degradation, particularly when delivered orally or through mucosal routes. Strategies to stabilize antigens and protect them from degradation, such as encapsulation in nanoparticles or liposomes, could improve vaccine efficacy.

3. **Addressing Immune Tolerance**: Some antigens may induce immune tolerance rather than immunity, particularly in the context of autoimmunity or chronic infections. Overcoming immune tolerance barriers through the use of immunomodulatory agents or delivery systems that promote immune activation could be beneficial.

4. **Improving Mucosal Delivery**: Mucosal surfaces represent a major entry point for pathogens, making mucosal vaccination an attractive strategy. However, achieving efficient antigen uptake and immune response at mucosal sites presents challenges due to the presence of mucus barriers and limited immune surveillance. Future directions may include the

development of novel mucosal adjuvants and delivery systems designed to penetrate mucosal barriers and target immune cells.

5. **Personalized Vaccine Delivery**: Personalized vaccine approaches tailored to individual immune profiles could improve antigen uptake and immune response. This could involve the use of biomarkers or genetic information to customize vaccine formulations or delivery strategies for optimal efficacy.

6. **Combination Vaccine Strategies**: Combining multiple antigens or using antigen cocktails in vaccines can broaden immune responses and enhance protection against multiple pathogens. Future research could focus on optimizing antigen combinations and delivery systems to maximize efficacy while minimizing potential adverse effects.

7. **Incorporating Novel Technologies**: Advances in nanotechnology, synthetic biology, and bioinformatics offer exciting opportunities for improving antigen uptake in vaccine delivery systems. For example, the use of self-assembling nanoparticles or synthetic biology-based platforms for antigen production and delivery could revolutionize vaccine development.

8. **Enhancing Vaccine Stability and Shelf Life**: Improving vaccine stability and shelf life is crucial, especially for vaccines targeting resource-limited settings or requiring cold chain storage. Novel formulation approaches, such as lyophilization or dry powder formulations, could improve vaccine stability and facilitate distribution in challenging environments.

SINGLE SHOT VACCINES

Single-shot vaccines, also known as single-dose vaccines, are designed to provide immunity with just one dose, unlike many traditional vaccines that require multiple doses or boosters to achieve and maintain effective immunity. The development of single-shot vaccines aims to simplify vaccination schedules, improve patient compliance, and enhance immunization coverage, especially in regions with limited healthcare access. Here's a detailed look at single-shot vaccines in various vaccine delivery systems:

1. Traditional Delivery Methods

a. Intramuscular Injection

1. Examples:

    a. Johnson & Johnson's Janssen COVID-19 vaccine.

    b. Yellow fever vaccine.

2. Mechanism:

    a. The antigen is delivered directly into the muscle tissue, where it is taken up by muscle cells and local immune cells.

    b. Dendritic cells and macrophages process the antigen and present it to T cells in the lymph nodes.

3. Advantages:

    a. Established method with proven efficacy.

    b. Generates a strong and long-lasting immune response.

4. Challenges:

    a. Requires trained healthcare professionals for administration.

    b. Potential for local side effects and discomfort at the injection site.

2. Novel Delivery Methods

a. Oral Vaccines

1. Examples:

    a. Vaxchora (cholera vaccine).

    b. Rotarix (rotavirus vaccine).

2. Mechanism:

    a. Antigens are delivered via the oral route and taken up by the gut-associated lymphoid tissue (GALT).

    b. M cells in the Peyer's patches capture and transport antigens to underlying immune cells.

3. Advantages:

   a. Non-invasive and easy to administer.

   b. Induces both mucosal and systemic immunity.

4. Challenges:

   a. Stability of the vaccine in the gastrointestinal tract.

   b. Variable absorption and efficacy based on individual gut microbiota and health status.

b. Nasal Sprays

1. Examples:

   a. FluMist (live attenuated influenza vaccine).

2. Mechanism:

   a. Antigens are delivered to the nasal mucosa, where they are taken up by mucosal dendritic cells.

   b. These cells process and present the antigens to T cells in the local lymphoid tissue.

3. Advantages:

   a. Non-invasive and needle-free.

   b. Induces strong mucosal immunity in the respiratory tract.

4. Challenges:

   a. Limited to certain types of vaccines effective via this route.

   b. Potential discomfort or irritation in the nasal passages.

c. Microneedle Patches

1. Examples:

   a. Still in development, with some promising candidates for influenza and COVID-19.

2. Mechanism:

   a. Microneedles penetrate the outer skin layer to deliver the antigen to the dermis.

b. Dendritic cells and Langerhans cells in the skin capture the antigen and present it to the immune system.

3. **Advantages:**

a. Minimally invasive and potentially self-administered.

b. Reduces needle-stick injuries and medical waste.

4. **Challenges:**

a. Technological and manufacturing hurdles.

b. Ensuring consistent and adequate dosing.

3. Advanced Delivery Systems

a. Liposomal and Nanoparticle Systems

1. **Examples:**

a. Some COVID-19 vaccines (e.g., Pfizer-BioNTech and Moderna) use lipid nanoparticles to deliver mRNA.

2. **Mechanism:**

a. Antigens are encapsulated in nanoparticles, which protect the antigen and facilitate its uptake by dendritic cells and macrophages.

b. Enhanced delivery to lymph nodes and prolonged antigen release.

3. **Advantages:**

a. Increased stability and targeted delivery.

b. Potential for a strong and sustained immune response with a single dose.

4. **Challenges:**

a. Complex manufacturing and higher production costs.

b. Regulatory hurdles and safety evaluations.

b. Viral Vectors

1. **Examples:**

a. Johnson & Johnson's Janssen COVID-19 vaccine.

b. Ebola vaccine (Ervebo).

2. Mechanism:

    a. Modified viruses are used to deliver genetic material encoding the antigen to host cells.

    b. Host cells produce the antigen, which is then processed and presented by the immune system.

3. Advantages:

    a. Induces strong cellular and humoral immunity.

    b. Versatile platform for various pathogens.

4. Challenges:

    a. Pre-existing immunity to the viral vector can reduce efficacy.

    b. Potential for vector-related side effects.

4. Adjuvants and Formulation Enhancements

a. Alum (Aluminum Salts)

1. Mechanism:

    a. Creates a depot effect for slow antigen release and enhances uptake by antigen-presenting cells (APCs).

2. **Use:** Widely used in single-dose vaccines like hepatitis A and B.

3. Advantages:

    a. Enhances the immune response to the antigen.

4. Challenges:

    a. Potential for local inflammation and side effects.

b. MF59 (Oil-in-Water Emulsion)

1. Mechanism:

    a. Enhances the recruitment and activation of APCs, facilitating better antigen uptake.

2. **Use:** Influenza vaccines (e.g., Fluad).

3. Advantages:

    a. Promotes strong and broad immune responses.

4. Challenges:

a. Limited to specific vaccines and populations.

5. Technological Innovations

a. mRNA Vaccines

1. Examples:

a. Pfizer-BioNTech and Moderna COVID-19 vaccines.

2. Mechanism:

a. mRNA is delivered to host cells to produce the target antigen.

b. Host cells present the antigen to the immune system, eliciting a robust response.

3. Advantages:

a. Rapid development and high efficacy.

b. Adaptable to emerging pathogens.

4. Challenges:

a. Requires cold storage and distribution.

b. Relatively new technology with ongoing studies on long-term effects.

b. DNA Vaccines

1. Examples:

a. Inovio's INO-4800 (COVID-19 vaccine candidate).

2. Mechanism:

a. Plasmid DNA is delivered to host cells to produce the target antigen.

b. Antigen presentation stimulates both B and T cell responses.

3. Advantages:

a. Stable and easy to produce.

b. Induces strong immune responses.

4. Challenges:

a. Requires electroporation for efficient delivery.

b. Still under development for human use.

6. Challenges and Future Directions

  a. **Cold Chain Requirements**: Ensuring stability and efficacy of vaccines without extensive refrigeration, particularly for mRNA vaccines.

  b. **Needle-Free Technologies**: Developing more user-friendly delivery methods like microneedle patches and oral vaccines to increase coverage and compliance.

  c. **Adjuvant Development**: Creating new adjuvants to boost immune responses, particularly for single-dose formulations.

  d. **Universal Vaccines**: Researching vaccines that provide broad protection against multiple strains or types of a pathogen to simplify immunization schedules.

  e. **Therapeutic Vaccines**: Developing vaccines that not only prevent but also treat existing diseases, such as therapeutic cancer vaccines.

MUCOSAL DELIVERY OF VACCINES

Mucosal delivery of vaccines is an innovative approach that targets the mucosal surfaces of the body, such as the respiratory, gastrointestinal, and genitourinary tracts. These surfaces are the primary entry points for many pathogens, making mucosal immunization a strategic method to induce both local and systemic immunity. Here's a detailed look at mucosal vaccine delivery systems:

1. Overview of Mucosal Immunity

a. Mucosal Surfaces

  i. **Respiratory Tract**: Includes the nasal passages, throat, and lungs.

  ii. **Gastrointestinal Tract**: Includes the mouth, stomach, intestines, and associated lymphoid tissues.

  iii. **Genitourinary Tract**: Includes the urinary and genital tracts.

b. Mucosal Immune System

  i. **M Cells**: Specialized cells that transport antigens from the mucosal surface to underlying immune cells.

ii. **Dendritic Cells:** Capture and present antigens to T cells, initiating an immune response.

iii. **IgA Antibodies**: Predominant antibodies in mucosal areas that neutralize pathogens.

iv. **Mucosa-Associated Lymphoid Tissue (MALT):** Includes Peyer's patches in the gut, tonsils, and other lymphoid tissues.

2. Delivery Methods for Mucosal Vaccines

a. Oral Vaccines

    i. **Mechanism:**

        a. Antigens are delivered via the oral route and taken up by M cells in the Peyer's patches of the intestines.

        b. Antigens are processed by dendritic cells and macrophages in the gut-associated lymphoid tissue (GALT).

    ii. **Examples:**

        a. Vaxchora (cholera vaccine).

        b. Rotarix (rotavirus vaccine).

    iii. **Advantages:**

        a. Non-invasive and easy to administer.

        b. Induces both mucosal and systemic immunity.

    iv. **Challenges:**

        a. Antigen stability in the gastrointestinal tract.

        b. Variable absorption and efficacy based on individual gut health.

b. Nasal Sprays

    i. **Mechanism:**

        a. Antigens are delivered to the nasal mucosa, where they are taken up by mucosal dendritic cells.

        b. Antigens are processed and presented to T cells in the local lymphoid tissue.

ii. **Examples:**

    a. FluMist (live attenuated influenza vaccine).

iii. **Advantages:**

    a. Non-invasive and needle-free.

    b. Induces strong mucosal immunity in the respiratory tract.

iv. **Challenges:**

    a. Limited to certain types of vaccines.

    b. Potential discomfort or irritation in the nasal passages.

c. Sublingual Delivery

i. **Mechanism:**

    a. Antigens are delivered under the tongue, where they are absorbed by the mucosa and transported to the local lymphoid tissue.

    b. Dendritic cells capture the antigen and present it to T cells.

ii. **Examples:**

    a. Experimental vaccines for various pathogens.

iii. **Advantages:**

    a. Non-invasive and easy to administer.

    b. Avoids degradation in the gastrointestinal tract.

iv. **Challenges:**

    a. Ensuring efficient uptake and sufficient immune response.

3. Technological Advances in Mucosal Vaccines

a. Adjuvants for Mucosal Vaccines

i. **Role**: Enhance the immune response by stimulating local immune cells.

ii. **Examples:**

    a. Cholera toxin B subunit (CTB).

    b. Heat-labile enterotoxin (LT) from E. coli.

iii. **Advantages:**

a. Improved antigen uptake and presentation.

b. Enhanced local and systemic immunity.

iv. Challenges:

a. Ensuring safety and minimizing side effects.

b. Nanoparticles and Microparticles

i. Mechanism:

a. Antigens are encapsulated in nanoparticles or microparticles for better stability and targeted delivery.

b. Particles are designed to be taken up efficiently by mucosal dendritic cells and M cells.

ii. Examples:

a. Experimental formulations for various pathogens.

iii. Advantages:

a. Enhanced stability and controlled release of antigens.

b. Targeted delivery to specific mucosal tissues.

iv. Challenges:

a. Complex manufacturing and regulatory approval processes.

4. Specific Mucosal Vaccine Systems

a. Live Attenuated Vaccines

i. Mechanism:

a. Contain weakened pathogens that replicate in the mucosal tissues, inducing a natural immune response.

ii. Examples:

a. Oral polio vaccine (OPV).

b. FluMist (influenza vaccine).

iii. Advantages:

a. Strong and long-lasting immune response.

b. Mimics natural infection.

iv. Challenges:

        a. Not suitable for immunocompromised individuals.

        b. Requires careful storage and handling.

b. Inactivated and Subunit Vaccines

    i.   Mechanism:

        a. Contain killed pathogens or purified antigenic components.

        b. Often combined with adjuvants to enhance immune response.

    ii.   Examples:

        a. Inactivated rotavirus vaccines (under development).

    iii.   Advantages:

        a. Safer for immunocompromised individuals.

        b. Stable and easy to produce.

    iv.   Challenges:

        a. May require multiple doses or boosters.

        b. Less immunogenic than live vaccines.

5. Applications and Future Directions

a. Targeted Mucosal Immunity

   i. **Respiratory Pathogens**: Vaccines delivered via nasal sprays for influenza, COVID-19, and other respiratory infections.

   ii. **Enteric Pathogens**: Oral vaccines for diseases like cholera, typhoid, and rotavirus.

b. Combination Vaccines

   i. Developing vaccines that target multiple pathogens through a single mucosal delivery route to simplify immunization schedules and improve coverage.

c. Personalized Vaccines

   i. Tailoring mucosal vaccines to individual genetic and microbiome profiles to enhance efficacy and reduce adverse effects.

6. Challenges and Considerations

a. **Stability and Storage**: Ensuring mucosal vaccines remain stable under varying storage conditions, particularly for oral and nasal formulations.

b. **Dosage and Administration**: Determining optimal dosages and administration protocols to achieve desired immunity without significant side effects.

c. **Regulatory Approval**: Navigating the complex regulatory landscape to gain approval for new mucosal vaccine technologies and adjuvants.

d. **Public Acceptance**: Educating the public and healthcare providers on the benefits and safety of mucosal vaccines to increase acceptance and uptake.

TRANSDERMAL DELIVERY OF VACCINES

Transdermal delivery of vaccines involves administering vaccines through the skin using various technologies that penetrate the outer skin barrier. This method has several advantages, including being needle-free, reducing the risk of needle-stick injuries, improving patient compliance, and potentially inducing stronger immune responses due to the rich network of immune cells in the skin. Here's a detailed look at transdermal vaccine delivery systems:

1. Overview of Transdermal Vaccine Delivery

a. Skin Structure

i. **Epidermis**: The outermost layer, which includes the stratum corneum, a barrier to pathogen entry.

ii. **Dermis:** Contains a network of blood vessels, lymphatics, and immune cells like dendritic cells and Langerhans cells.

iii. **Subcutaneous Layer**: Composed of fat and connective tissue, housing larger blood vessels and nerves.

b. Immune Cells in the Skin

i. **Dendritic Cells**: Capture and present antigens to T cells, initiating an immune response.

ii.   **Langerhans Cells**: A type of dendritic cell located in the epidermis, involved in antigen capture.

iii.   **Keratinocytes**: Can produce cytokines and act as a barrier to infections.

2. Transdermal Delivery Technologies

a. Microneedle Patches

   i.   Mechanism:

   a. Patches containing arrays of tiny needles that penetrate the outer skin layers to deliver the vaccine directly into the epidermis and dermis.

   b. Can be coated with vaccine or contain dissolvable needles that release the vaccine upon insertion.

   ii.   Examples:

   a. Influenza vaccine patches.

   b. Experimental COVID-19 vaccine patches.

   iii.   Advantages:

   a. Minimally invasive and pain-free.

   b. Potential for self-administration.

   c. Reduces medical waste.

   iv.   Challenges:

   a. Manufacturing consistency and scalability.

   b. Ensuring adequate dose delivery and stability.

b. Needle-Free Injection Systems

   i.   Mechanism:

   a. Use high-pressure jets to deliver liquid vaccines through the skin without needles.

   ii.   Examples:

   a. Biojector (used for various vaccines).

   iii.   Advantages:

   a. Needle-free and less painful.

b. Rapid administration.

iv. Challenges:

a. Device cost and maintenance.

b. Training required for proper use.

c. Topical Application with Skin Permeabilizers

i. Mechanism:

a. Use of chemical enhancers or physical methods (e.g., ultrasound, iontophoresis) to increase skin permeability and facilitate antigen uptake.

ii. Examples:

a. Experimental formulations for various antigens.

iii. Advantages:

a. Non-invasive.

b. Can be combined with other technologies for enhanced delivery.

iv. Challenges:

a. Ensuring consistent and sufficient antigen delivery.

b. Potential for skin irritation.

d. Electroporation

i. Mechanism:

a. Brief electrical pulses create temporary pores in the skin cells, allowing vaccines to enter.

ii. Examples:

a. DNA vaccines for various infectious diseases.

iii. Advantages:

a. Enhances uptake of large molecules like DNA.

b. Can induce strong immune responses.

iv. Challenges:

a. Requires specialized equipment.

b. Potential discomfort during application.

3. Advantages of Transdermal Vaccine Delivery

i. **Enhanced Immune Response**: The skin contains a high density of immune cells, leading to strong local and systemic immune responses.

ii. **Patient Compliance**: Needle-free methods reduce pain and fear associated with injections, improving compliance, especially in children.

iii. **Reduced Risk:** Lower risk of needle-stick injuries and associated infections.

iv. **Ease of Administration**: Potential for self-administration or administration by non-healthcare professionals.

4. Specific Transdermal Vaccine Systems

a. Live Attenuated Vaccines

i. **Mechanism:**

a. Live but weakened pathogens that replicate in the skin, inducing a natural immune response.

ii. **Examples:**

a. Experimental microneedle patches for measles and rubella.

iii. **Advantages:**

a. Strong and long-lasting immunity.

b. Mimics natural infection.

iv. **Challenges:**

a. Safety concerns for immunocompromised individuals.

b. Stability and storage requirements.

b. Inactivated and Subunit Vaccines

i. **Mechanism:**

a. Contain killed pathogens or purified antigens, often combined with adjuvants to enhance immune response.

ii. **Examples:**

a. Influenza vaccine patches.

iii. **Advantages:**

    a. Safe for immunocompromised individuals.

    b. Stable and easy to produce.

iv. **Challenges:**

    a. May require adjuvants to boost immunogenicity.

    b. Potential need for multiple doses.

5. Adjuvants and Formulation Enhancements

a. Adjuvants

i. **Role:** Enhance the immune response to antigens delivered transdermally.

ii. **Examples:**

    a. Alum (aluminum salts).

    b. QS-21 (saponin-based adjuvant).

iii. **Advantages:**

    a. Improved antigen uptake and presentation.

    b. Enhanced local and systemic immunity.

iv. **Challenges:**

    a. Ensuring safety and minimizing side effects.

    b. Compatibility with transdermal delivery systems.

b. Formulation Enhancements

i. **Role:** Improve stability, uptake, and release of antigens.

ii. **Examples:**

    a. Liposomes and nanoparticles for encapsulation.

    b. Stabilizers and preservatives.

iii. **Advantages:**

    a. Prolonged antigen release.

    b. Enhanced stability and targeted delivery.

iv. **Challenges:**

    a. Manufacturing complexity.

b. Regulatory approval and safety evaluations.

6. Applications and Future Directions

a. Infectious Diseases

    i. Examples:

        a. Influenza, COVID-19, measles, and rubella.

    ii. **Research Focus**: Developing effective transdermal vaccines for a wide range of infectious diseases to improve immunization coverage and response.

b. Therapeutic Vaccines

    i. Examples:

        a. Cancer vaccines targeting tumor antigens.

        b. Therapeutic vaccines for chronic diseases.

    ii. **Research Focus**: Utilizing transdermal delivery to induce targeted immune responses against cancer cells and other chronic disease targets.

7. Challenges and Considerations

i. **Dose Consistency**: Ensuring each application delivers a consistent and effective dose.

ii. **Skin Barrier Variability**: Accounting for differences in skin thickness and integrity among individuals.

iii. **Manufacturing and Scalability**: Developing cost-effective and scalable manufacturing processes for transdermal delivery systems.

iv. **Regulatory Approval**: Navigating the regulatory landscape to gain approval for new transdermal vaccine technologies and formulations.

v. **Public Acceptance**: Educating the public and healthcare providers on the benefits and safety of transdermal vaccines to increase acceptance and uptake.

Multiple Choice Questions (MCQs)

1. Which muscle is typically used for intramuscular injections of vaccines?

    A) Biceps

    B) Deltoid

    C) Gluteal

    D) Triceps

2. What is a disadvantage of subcutaneous injections compared to intramuscular injections?

    A) Faster absorption

    B) Requires less trained personnel

    C) Slower absorption rate

    D) Less effective in inducing immune responses

3. What type of immune cells are highly concentrated in the dermis and enhance the immune response for intradermal injections?

    A) Plasma cells

    B) B cells

    C) Dendritic cells

    D) Macrophages

4. Which method uses a patch with tiny needles for vaccine delivery

    A) Intramuscular injection

    B) Microneedle patches

    C) Nasal sprays

    D) Liposomal systems

5. What is an example of a vaccine that uses a viral vector for delivery?

    A) MMR vaccine

    B) Influenza vaccine

    C) AstraZeneca COVID-19 vaccine

    D) Hepatitis B vaccine

6. What role do adjuvants play in vaccine delivery?

A) Decrease the antigen stability

B) Increase the cost of vaccine production

C) Reduce the immune response to the vaccine

D) Enhance the body's immune response to the antigen

7. Which adjuvant is commonly used in traditional vaccines to enhance antigen uptake? A) AS01

B) MF59

C) Alum

D) CpG Oligodeoxynucleotides

8. Which technology is involved in mRNA vaccines to instruct cells to produce the antigen?

A) Liposomal encapsulation B) Messenger RNA C) Plasmid DNA D) Adjuvant substances

9. What is a major challenge in the widespread use of nasal spray vaccines?

A) High cost

B) Limited to certain types of vaccines

C) Involves painful procedures

D) Requires multiple doses

10. Which type of vaccine contains live pathogens that have been weakened?

A) Subunit vaccines

B) Inactivated vaccines

C) Toxoid vaccines

D) Live attenuated vaccines

11. What is the main advantage of using DNA vaccines?

A) No cold chain requirements

B) High stability and easy production

C) Immediate immune response

D) No need for adjuvants

12. Why are mRNA vaccines required to be stored at cold temperatures?

A) To enhance their effectiveness

B) To prevent the mRNA from degrading

C) To activate the mRNA

D) To preserve the lipid nanoparticles

13. Which method of vaccine delivery is noted for its ability to induce a strong mucosal immunity?

A) Subcutaneous injection

B) Oral vaccines

C) Intradermal injection

D) Intramuscular injection

14. What challenge do microneedle patches face in vaccine delivery?

A) High pain upon application

B) Still under development for widespread use

C) Immediate degradation of vaccine

D) Activation of too strong an immune response

15. What is the main benefit of using viral vectors in vaccines?

A) Low cost of production

B) Versatility and strong immune response

C) No risk of viral infection

D) Simple manufacturing process

16. How do lipid nanoparticles benefit mRNA vaccines?

A) By reducing the dose of mRNA needed

B) By stabilizing the mRNA and facilitating delivery into cells

C) By acting as an adjuvant

D) By allowing oral administration of the vaccine

17. Which is not a typical feature of nanoparticle-based vaccine delivery systems?

A) Controlled release of antigens

B) Targeted delivery to specific tissues

C) High stability and immune evasion

D) Requirement for booster doses

18. What is the primary function of adjuvants like MF59 in vaccines?

    A) To decrease vaccine production time

    B) To stabilize the active ingredient

    C) To recruit and activate immune cells at the injection site

    D) To serve as a preservative

19. Which of the following is a potential future direction for vaccine delivery?

    A) Reducing vaccine efficacy

    B) Developing universal vaccines

    C) Phasing out adjuvants

    D) Limiting vaccine accessibility

20. What major advantage does transdermal delivery offer over traditional injection methods?

    A) Faster systemic circulation of the antigen

    B) Reduced risk of needle-stick injuries and infections

    C) Higher stability of vaccines

    D) More rapid development of vaccine formulations

Short Answer Type Questions

1. What are the main methods of traditional vaccine delivery?

2. Describe the advantages of intramuscular injections for vaccines.

3. What are the challenges associated with subcutaneous vaccine injections?

4. How does intradermal injection enhance the immune response?

5. What are the advantages of using oral vaccines?

6. Why are nasal sprays considered effective for inducing mucosal immunity?

7. Discuss the potential benefits of microneedle patches in vaccine delivery.

8. What are the disadvantages of using liposomal and nanoparticle systems for vaccine delivery?

9. How do viral vectors work in vaccine delivery?

10. What is the role of adjuvants in enhancing vaccine efficacy?

11. Describe the function of alum as an adjuvant in vaccines.

12. How do mRNA vaccines work?

13. What are the main challenges faced by DNA vaccines?

14. Why is cold chain management critical for some vaccines?

15. What are the future directions in vaccine delivery technology?

16. Explain how adjuvants improve the immune response to vaccines.

17. What is the significance of nanoparticle-based systems in vaccine delivery?

18. How do microneedle arrays facilitate transdermal vaccine delivery?

19. What are the potential advantages of using viral vector vaccines?

20. Describe the role of DNA and RNA vaccines in modern immunization strategies.

Long Answer Type Questions

1. Discuss the various traditional methods of vaccine delivery and their impact on the immune response. Include comparisons of their advantages and disadvantages.

2. Explain how novel delivery methods like nasal sprays and oral vaccines are changing the landscape of immunization, especially in terms of mucosal immunity.

3. Analyze the role of technological innovations like microneedle patches and nanoparticle systems in enhancing vaccine efficacy and safety.

4. Describe the mechanism and advantages of mRNA vaccines, particularly focusing on their use in responding to the COVID-19 pandemic.

5. Explore the challenges associated with developing universal vaccines and how current research is addressing these challenges.

6. Explain the significance of adjuvants in vaccine formulations, with a focus on newer adjuvants like MF59 and AS01, and their roles in immune response modulation.

7. Discuss the potential of transdermal vaccine delivery systems, including their benefits over traditional injection methods and the technological challenges they face.

8. Evaluate the future potential of DNA vaccines and the hurdles that must be overcome before they can become widely used in human medicine.

9. Describe how personalized vaccine strategies could be developed and the role genomics might play in tailoring vaccinations to individual immune profiles.

Answer Key

1. B) Deltoid
2. C) Slower absorption rate
3. C) Dendritic cells
4. B) Microneedle patches
5. C) AstraZeneca COVID-19 vaccine
6. D) Enhance the body's immune response to the antigen
7. C) Alum
8. B) Messenger RNA
9. B) Limited to certain types of vaccines
10. D) Live attenuated vaccines
11. B) High stability and easy production
12. B) To prevent the mRNA from degrading
13. B) Oral vaccines
14. B) Still under development for widespread use

15.B) Versatility and strong immune response

16.B) By stabilizing the mRNA and facilitating delivery into cells

17.D) Requirement for booster doses

18.C) To recruit and activate immune cells at the injection site

19.B) Developing universal vaccines

20.B) Reduced risk of needle-stick injuries and infections